BECKETT
WRITING
BECKETT

Also by H. Porter Abbott:

Diary Fiction: Writing as Action

The Fiction of Samuel Beckett: Form and Effect

BECKETT
WRITING
BECKETT

THE AUTHOR IN THE AUTOGRAPH

H. PORTER ABBOTT

CORNELL UNIVERSITY PRESS

ITHACA AND LONDON

First published 1996 by Cornell University Press.

Printed in the United States of America

⊗ The paper in this book meets the minimum requirements of the American National Standard for Information Sciences—Permanence of Paper for Printed Library Materials, ANSI Z39.48-1984.

Library of Congress Cataloging-in-Publication Data

Abbott, H. Porter.
  Beckett writing Beckett : the author in the autograph / H. Porter Abbott.
    p. cm.
  Includes bibliographical references (p.   ) and index.
  ISBN 0-8014-3246-4 (alk. paper)
  1. Beckett, Samuel, 1906–1989—Criticism and interpretation. 2. Autobiography in literature. 3. Self in literature. I. Title.
PR6003.E282Z53 1996
848'.91409—dc20   95-39559

In memory of
Barbara Trueblood Abbott

Contents

Preface

> All these Murphys, Molloys and Malones do not fool me. They have
> made me waste my time, suffer for nothing, speak of them when, in
> order to stop speaking, I should have spoken of me and of me alone.
> —*The Unnamable*

So who wants to speak of whom, then? Do we dare say, This is
Beckett, and he wants to speak of Beckett? Such a statement fairly
bristles with insuperable problems. So well have we been schooled,
for so long and in so many ways, that hardly can we imagine saying
these ten modest words without feeling overwhelmed in advance by
semantic misery. Still, though I would not commit to precisely these
words, it is nonetheless the case that Beckett always pulls us back
to the question of who speaks. And though there is, assuredly, no
unimpeachable answer to this question, this book is dedicated to the
proposition that the sustained originality of Beckett's work can be
best understood as self-writing or, as I much prefer to call it, autographical action.

My argument is intended to contribute to two subjects: to Beckett
studies and to the study of that broad terrain of self-writing which
goes by the name of autobiography. There has been hardly any work
yoking these two subjects, and where such work does exist, it usually
aims at identifying traces, that is, it has been a historical enterprise,
aligning fictional texts with the personal history that went into them.
This has been the case most notably in Deirdre Bair's *Samuel Beckett:
A Biography,* though from the early 1960s books and articles on
Beckett have built up a web of connections between the work and
the life. Such readings can, at a stroke, put a whole new light on a
work, as for example when Hugh Kenner surmised that the aborted
meeting with Godot came out of Beckett's work in the Resistance.

The price we pay for this kind of autobiographical approach can be sadness as we see art shrinking into the epiphenomenal residue of a single life's contingencies. As I hope will become quickly clear in the following pages, the autographical reading that I am proposing is diametrically opposed to such an approach. It responds to writing not as a mode of recovery or reconstruction or even fictionalizing of the past but as a mode of action taken in the moment of writing.

The term "autobiography," with its middle syllable "bio," is literally self-life-writing. It carries with it the strong connotation of a life story, written by the one who lived that life. Autobiography in the sense of a memoir or life story is something Beckett had few illusions about, and the inadequacy of life stories is a theme that recurs throughout his oeuvre. So a better term than "autobiography" is "self-writing" and, better still, "autography," which avoids not only the implications of historical narrative in "bio" but also the semantic baggage of "self," a term as problematical for Beckett as the term "story." Preferable to all these is the coinage "autographical action," for it concentrates attention on the text, both as "self"-writing and as immediate action taking place as it is written.

In Beckett's case, an autographical reading puts his artistic originality well into the foreground. Beckett's inexhaustible capacity to "make strange" was a key element in a project that began to take shape early in his writing career but that was consolidated in the 1950s. The chapters that follow—each of them a different take on the subject—draw largely from this later work. But Beckett may well have been thinking of writing as a life project as early as the 1920s. Doubtless, he was encouraged to think this way by the examples of the two modernist writers, Marcel Proust and James Joyce, within whose combined shadows he first began to write seriously. From the perspective of my project here, what stayed with him most was an attitude of extraordinary intimacy with his art, as if "being in the text," to use Paul Jay's evocative phrase, were somehow possible.

At the age of twenty-six, in his monograph on Proust, Beckett describes the author as inhabiting his work like a "pure subject," foliating in his "vegetable" composition in the same way as Vinteuil grew his music from the inside. The next year (1932), in *Dream of Fair to Middling Women*, his first novel, Beckett (the puckish ephebe?) describes his own textual being as a kind of vermin. He is a "skymole" tunneling in "its firmament in genesis"; he is an "insistent, invisible rat, fidgeting behind the astral incoherence of the art surface." The metaphor was to stay with him. In the late sixties, he told Alec Reid, "It would be impossible for me to talk about my writing because I am constantly working in the dark, . . . it would be like an insect leaving his cocoon." At the same time, he told Charles Juliet that as an author he was like "a mole in a molehill." The composite figure is powerfully suggestive. A small, burrowing creature, Beckett within his work is at once elusive, busy, threatening, purposive, blind, trapped, buried alive.

The seed for this book was a plenary lecture given at the International Beckett Conference at the University of Stirling, Scotland, in 1986. So my thanks go first to the organizers of that conference, Lance St. John Butler and Robin Davis, for giving me a large captive audience on which to test my ideas. That lecture, many times revised, is Chapter 1. I am also grateful for words of encouragement which have come my way since then. Those whose words stand out in memory, though they may have long forgotten what they said, are Enoch Brater, Ruby Cohn, Marjorie Perloff, and Garrett Stewart. The Interdisciplinary Humanities Center and the Academic Senate of the University of California, Santa Barbara, provided welcome support during the period in which this book came together. And once again I have enjoyed the friendly and efficient assistance of the editorial staff at Cornell University Press. My research assistant, Peter Lengyel, did double duty, turning up interesting leads and providing friendly intellectual resistance. Finally, special thanks to three close friends: Jon Pearce, who read every single word and led me to change more than a few; David Gordon, who reads my arguments with empathetic understanding tempered by common sense; and Anita Abbott, who is always my first reader.

A version of Chapter 1 appeared as "Narratricide: Samuel Beckett as Autographer" in *Romance Studies*, no. 11 (Winter 1987); a version of Chapter 2 appeared as "Late Modernism: Samuel Beckett and the Art of the Oeuvre" in *Around the Absurd: Essays on Modern and Postmodern Drama*, ed. Enoch Brater and Ruby Cohn (Ann Arbor:

University of Michigan Press), copyright © by the University of Michigan 1990; a version of Chapter 5 appeared as "Beginning Again: The Post-Narrative Art of *Texts for Nothing* and *How It Is*" in *The Cambridge Companion to Beckett*, ed. John Pilling, © Cambridge University Press 1994, reprinted with the permission of Cambridge University Press; a version of Chapter 6 appeared as "Tyranny and Theatricality: The Example of Samuel Beckett" in *Theatre Journal* 40 (March 1988), reprinted by permission of the Johns Hopkins University Press; a version of Chapter 8 appeared as "Consorting with Spirits: The Arcane Craft of Beckett's Later Drama" in *The Theatrical Gamut: Notes for a Post-Beckettian Stage*, ed. Enoch Brater (Ann Arbor: University of Michigan Press), copyright © by the University of Michigan 1995. Parts of Chapter 9 have been revised from "Reading as Theatre: Understanding Defamiliarization in Beckett's Art" in *Modern Drama* 34 (March 1991).

The author and publisher are grateful to Grove/Atlantic, Inc. for permission to quote from the following works by Samuel Beckett: *Collected Shorter Plays*, copyright © 1984 by Samuel Beckett; *Endgame*, copyright © 1954 by Grove Press; *Waiting for Godot*, copyright © 1954 by Grove Press. Acknowledgment is also given to Faber and Faber, Ltd. for permission to quote from these works.

The author and publisher are grateful to Grove/Atlantic, Inc. for permission to quote from these additional works by Samuel Beckett: *Company*, copyright © 1980 by Samuel Beckett; *How It Is*, copyright © 1964 by Grove Press; *Stories and Texts for Nothing*, copyright © 1967 by Samuel Beckett; *Three Novels: Molloy, Malone Dies, The Unnamable*, copyright © 1955, 1956, 1958 by Grove Press. Acknowledgment is also given to the Samuel Beckett Estate and to The Calder Educational Trust, London, for permission to quote from these works and from Samuel Beckett, *The Collected Shorter Prose*, copyright © 1984 by Samuel Beckett.

The author and publisher are grateful, finally, to the Samuel Beckett Estate for permission to quote from the "*Ohio Impromptu* Holograph."

H. PORTER ABBOTT

Santa Barbara, California

BECKETT
WRITING
BECKETT

ONE

NARRATRICIDE

One may really indeed say that this is the essence of genius, of being most intensely alive, that is being one who is at the same time talking and listening.

—Gertrude Stein

The rarity of the word "autobiography" in Beckett studies should come as no surprise. For all his protestations of impotence and incompetence, Beckett was an exacting craftsman, and the power of his art seems directly proportional to its thorough transmutation of autobiographical sources. S. E. Gontarski's study of the evolution of Beckett's dramatic manuscripts shows in case after case "the intentional undoing" of personal material, "not so much to disguise autobiography as to displace and discount it."[1] Beckett's own determina-

---

[1] S. E. Gontarski, *The Intent of Undoing in Samuel Beckett's Dramatic Texts* (Bloomington: Indiana University Press, 1985), 3–4. Important recent exceptions are Ann Beer's "Beckett's 'Autography' and the Company of Languages," *Southern Review* 27 (Autumn 1991): 771–791; James Olney's "Memory and the Narrative Imperative, St. Augustine and Samuel Beckett," *New Literary History* 24 (Autumn 1993): 857–880; and Richard Begam's impressive rereading of the "pentalogy," *Samuel Beckett and the End of Modernity* (Stanford: Stanford University Press, 1996). See also Alfred Hornung's "Fantasies of an Autobiographical Self: Thomas Bernhard, Raymond Federman, Samuel Beckett," *Journal of Beckett Studies* 11/12 (1989): 91–107. Two other related approaches to Beckett's work are those of Didier Anzieu and Enoch Brater. Anzieu's psychobiographical study reads Beckett's oeuvre as a continuation of the self-analysis begun when Beckett visited Dr. Wilfred Bion in 1934–36; see Anzieu, *Beckett et le psychanalyste* (Paris: Mentha/Archimbaud, 1992). Brater, in nuanced readings of Beckett's later work argues that Beckett, reinventing

tion to keep silent about himself reinforces this view, and certainly some of the distress that greeted Deirdre Bair's biography of Beckett, whatever the accuracy of its biographical facts, lay in the emphasis it placed on those facts and the corollary implication that, if Beckett's art was not reducible to the story of his life, knowing that story was the main prerequisite to understanding the art.[2]

In this book, I argue that if Beckett's postwar endeavor is not conventional autobiography it is nonetheless best understood not as fiction but as a species of autography (self-writing). My working distinction between autography and autobiography is that autography is the larger field comprehending all self-writing and that autobiography is a subset of autography comprehending narrative self-writing and more specifically that most common narrative, the story of one's life. In this chapter, I locate the comparatively late text *Company* (1980), and by implication the work of Beckett's maturity (especially as it took shape following the death in 1948 of Beckett's reluctant autobiographer, Malone), in another subset of autography. It is a subset that includes texts by Saint Augustine and William Wordsworth and that stands in contrast to the much more fully populated subset (autobiography), for which I have selected Edmund Gosse's *Father and Son* as a representative text. The differences between these subsets are rooted in fundamentally opposed strategies of self-representation and include striking differences between the way the autographers approach narrative and (what is almost the same thing) the way they handle what can be called, broadly, oedipal material. *Company* is a key work for this purpose because it appears to "gravitate," to adapt John Pilling's words,

---

the lyric, spoke to us in his own voice; see Brater, *Beyond Minimalism: Beckett's Late Style in the Theater* (New York: Oxford, 1987) and *The Drama in the Text: Beckett's Late Fiction* (New York: Oxford, 1994).

[2]"I wrote the biography of Beckett because I was dissatisfied with existing studies of his writings. . . . It seemed to me that many of the leading Beckett interpreters substituted their own brilliant intellectual gymnastics for what should have been solid, responsible scholarship; that they created studies that told more about the quality of the authors' minds than about Beckett's writings. This exasperating situation made me aware of the need for a factual basis for all subsequent critical exegesis" (Deirdre Bair, *Samuel Beckett: A Biography* [New York: Harcourt, Brace, Jovanovich, 1978], xii).

"more openly towards the genre of autobiography than anything before it."[3] In my argument, this appearance works to disassemble autobiography altogether while at the same time continuing the autographical project the author has been engaged in all along.

It will help clarify this argument if we shift attention for a moment from issues of literary form to issues of literary response or orientation. Such a shift was implicit when Georges Gusdorf argued in 1956 that there is a gulf separating biography from autobiography. They may be very similarly formed, but the way we read them—what we look for, how we organize them as we read, what kind of significance we find in them—is quite different. To read biographically is to be oriented toward history, toward a sequence of events now past, but to read autobiographically is to be oriented not toward the past but toward a continual revelation of authorial consciousness at the moment of writing.[4] Gusdorf's distinction is acute, though it is not (as Gusdorf would agree) an automatic predictor of how we actually relate to texts that call themselves autobiographies. Even though an autobiographer cannot be trusted as a historian and even though he or she may be much more interesting rhetorically than historically, we do frequently find ourselves reading an autobiography as history. Autobiographers themselves, much more commonly than not, see themselves as engaged in writing history. As the late-eighteenth-century coinage "auto-biography" implies, they see themselves as the biographers of themselves. For this reason, the assurance of historical accuracy quickly became one of the conventions of the genre.[5]

---

[3]John Pilling, " 'Company' by Samuel Beckett," *Journal of Beckett Studies* 7 (Spring 1982): 127.

[4]Georges Gusdorf, "Conditions et Limites de l'autobiographie" in *Formen der Selbstdarstellung,* ed. G. Reichenkron and E. Haase (Berlin: Duncker and Humblot, 1956); translated as "Conditions and Limits of Autobiography," trans. James Olney, in *Autobiography: Essays Theoretical and Critical,* ed. James Olney (Princeton: Princeton University Press, 1980), 28–48.

[5]With deconstruction, confidence in the referential and historical reliability of autobiography has shrunk at times to zero. For a subtly inflected counterargument on the subject of historical reference in autobiography, see Paul John Eakin, *Touching the World: Reference in Autobiography* (Princeton: Princeton University Press, 1992).

UNWRITING HISTORY

At the outset of *Father and Son*, Edmund Gosse declares that "the following narrative, in all its parts, and so far as the punctilious attention of the writer has been able to keep it so, is scrupulously true. If it were not true, in this strict sense, to publish it would be to trifle with all those who may be induced to read it."[6] Gosse tells how he gradually separated his identity from that of his charismatic, fundamentalist father, settling on those key formative moments in the story of his life—the discovery of his father's fallibility, the death of his mother, his baptism—which led to the critical moment at age sixteen when his soul became his own. Leaning out of the window in eager anticipation of some sign at last from the Lord, Gosse receives nothing but the sights and sounds of a summer afternoon. "From that moment forth," he writes, "my father and I, though the fact was long successfully concealed from him and even from myself, walked in opposite hemispheres of the soul."[7]

Gosse, one of the modern architects of the biographical mode, looked on his own life story as an application of that mode to the intimate history of his self. But as readers we have at least two choices. We can accept the document as history (whether accurate or not) and read it as autobiography. Or we can read it autographically. If we choose to do the latter, we read *Father and Son* in a way that I am sure Gosse did not intend us to: that is, read it with an eye not to a history of events now past but to an author doing something in the present at every point in his text. We can see the text, to invoke Elizabeth Bruss's powerful concept, as an "autobiographical act."[8] To read Gosse in this way means seeing his text not as the

---

[6]Edmund Gosse, *Father and Son* (Harmondsworth: Penguin, 1949), 5.

[7]Gosse, *Father and Son*, 207.

[8]Elizabeth Bruss, *Autobiographical Acts: The Changing Situation of a Literary Genre* (Baltimore: Johns Hopkins University Press, 1976). This book by Bruss, particularly her introduction, Gusdorf's essay, and volume 1 of Paul Ricoeur's *Time and Narrative* (trans. K. McLaughlin and D. Pellauer [Chicago: University of Chicago Press, 1984]) are three seminal works behind the approach applied in this book. Two other important studies governed by an idea of autographical action are Paul Jay's *Being in the Text: Self-Representa-*

history of an achieved sense of identity but as an assertion of identity, as a declaration to his readers, including perhaps most importantly the author himself, that the separation from his father recorded in the last sentences of Chapter 11 did in fact take place. Inside this declarative act are tucked others. One very important one is a demonstration of the idea that history can be rendered in the shape of a story. It is an idea that Gosse learned from, among others, his father. Gosse's refinement is to replace his father's creationist masterplot with an evolutionary one.[9] Moreover, as the story asserts the evolution of Edmund as a species superior to that of his evolutionarily unfit father, the narrative itself is a demonstration of Edmund's superiority as a scientist, a case study that accommodates the complexity of life on earth in ways that his brilliant but simplistic father could never do.

One point readily extrapolated from this brief analysis of *Father and Son* is that, though it is possible to read almost any text in the autographical mode (as you could even read my text, right now, in the autographical mode), most texts, even those that are coded as autobiographies, are not *consciously* autographical. However, inti-

---

tion from Wordsworth to Roland Barthes (Ithaca: Cornell University Press, 1984) and Louis Renza's "The Veto of the Imagination: A Theory of Autobiography," in Olney, ed., *Autobiography*, 268–295. For further development of the theoretical distinction between "autobiography" and "autography," see H. Porter Abbott, "Autobiography, Autography, Fiction: Toward a Taxonomy of Literary Categories," *New Literary History* 19 (Spring 1988): 597–615.

A closely related concept is that of "the middle voice," a verbal category that falls between the active and the passive voice. By the act of speaking, the speaker does something but does it for him or herself. In the late 1960s, Roland Barthes revived interest in this ancient linguistic discrimination when he argued that the verb "to write" had evolved a modern usage in the middle voice. See Roland Barthes, "To Write: An Intransitive Verb?" in *The Languages of Criticism and the Sciences of Man: The Structuralist Controversy*, ed. Richard Macksey and Eugenio Donato (Baltimore: Johns Hopkins University Press, 1970), 134–156. See also Emile Benveniste, "Active and Middle Voice in the Verb," in *Problems in General Linguistics*, trans. Mary Elizabeth Meek (Coral Gables, Fla.: University of Miami Press, 1971), 145–151.

[9]This point is developed well in Roger Porter's essay "Edmund Gosse's *Father and Son*: Between Form and Flexibility," *Journal of Narrative Technique* 5 (September 1975): 174–195.

mate the revelations they contain, texts formally designated as auto-biographies are generally governed by a historical—that is, a bio-graphical—orientation.

There are exceptions. Augustine, though he is frequently credited with having invented in his *Confessions* the story form of autobiogra-phy as it is commonly told in the West (a series of formative events leading to a climactic conversion),[10] was equally original in the way he went about undermining that same form. In his meditations on the paradox of the being and nonbeing of time and in the openness and uncertainty of his text, he declares his whole project as work in progress, something happening in a textual present, a prayer in ac-tion. When one compares the extent of nonnarrative to that of nar-rative discourse in the *Confessions,* one sees that the former exceeds the latter by a very wide margin. Paul Ricoeur's brilliant contrast of Augustinian and Aristotelian narrative in *Time and Narrative* shows how they are essentially antitheses, the former dominated by the burden of existential time, the latter in effect an escape from time; the former without an end to give it shape and catharsis, the latter governed entirely by finality.[11] Glancing back at the finality of Gosse's text, one sees that its form has more to do with Aristotle than with Augustine.

Wordsworth's *Prelude* is a text that comes much closer than Gosse's to the *Confessions.* Its originating motives are varied and complex, but its continual return to a voice in the present, its pre-ponderance of nonnarrative over narrative discourse, and its stub-born resistance to completion over the course of fifty years suggest an autographical work in progress governed by the same ontological orientation one finds in Augustine. Most significant in this regard is what Wordsworth, himself a lover of stories, has done to storytelling

[10]For an account of this achievement in its historical context, see Georg Misch's three-volume study, *A History of Autobiography in Antiquity,* trans. E. W. Dickes (London: Routledge, 1950). In his influential 1960 study, *Design and Truth in Autobiography* (Cam-bridge: Harvard University Press, 1960), Roy Pascal used this conception of the Augustin-ian tale as a normative framework within which to examine landmark autobiographical texts.

[11]Ricoeur, *Time and Narrative,* 1:5–87.

in *The Prelude* by, in effect, replacing storytelling with the radically discontinuous mode of the "spot of time." Though there are only two spots specifically referred to as such in the 1805 text, these moments are, to borrow Wordsworth's phrasing, "scatter'd everywhere."[12] As Geoffrey Hartman has pointed out, the earliest manuscripts of *The Prelude* were simply compendia of these moments "massed together and linked desultorily."[13] Later versions of the poem, though they provide increasing structural support, do not violate the essential narrative discontinuity that Wordsworth seems purposefully to have preserved.

The spots of time have been a perennial crux in criticism of *The Prelude*, and perhaps nothing indicates how unsympathetic we are to the autographical indeterminacy they represent than the common assumption that a satisfactory critical accommodation of these spots requires a demonstration of how they belong to a single architectonic unity. Thus, in a famous essay in 1959, Jonathan Bishop in effect normalized *The Prelude* for its readership by restoring a sense of story where the text appears pointedly to have avoided it: "We have a group of memories; these share a vocabulary of imagery, a vocabulary which seems to combine into a story, a story which, so far as it is interpretable, tells of the fears, curiosities, and guilt of childhood. . . . the repetition of language and situation becomes, once it is noted, a clue to something further back."[14] Though Bishop was not in a position to retell the story, just knowing it was there was somehow reassuring. Subsequent interpretations have achieved the same reassurance by accommodating the spots to models of transcendental wholeness. But in doing so, they appropriate Words-

[12]Bk. XI, line 275 (*The Prelude*, ed. Ernest de Selincourt [Oxford: Oxford University Press, 1970], 213). For Wordsworth's full exposition of the concept of spots of time see Bk. XI, lines 258–389 (pp. 213–216).

[13]Geoffrey Hartman, *Wordsworth's Poetry, 1787–1814* (New Haven: Yale University Press, 1964), 212.

[14]Jonathan Bishop, "Wordsworth and the 'Spots of Time,'" in *"The Prelude": A Selection of Critical Essays*, ed. W. J. Harvey and R. Gravil (London: Macmillan, 1972), 148.

worth to a Coleridgean model, and in the process, as Jerome Mc-
Gann in his revisionist critique of romantic scholarship has argued,
they vitiate Wordsworth's originality by glossing over the importance of the nonteleological, the fragmentary, and the accidental in
his work.[15]

Looking more closely at an exemplary passage in Book XI, one
can see how all the rich potential narrative business having to do
with the death of the writer's father—material of which Jean Fran-
çois Marmontel would make such a dramatic, moving, identity-
shaping story in his posthumous *Mémoires d'un père* (1804)—is con-
tracted in *The Prelude* to one point, ten days before his father's
death, when Wordsworth waited impatiently on a high summit in
the fields above the highway for a sight of the horses that would
bring him home:

> on the grass
> I sate, half-shelter'd by a naked wall;
> Upon my right hand was a single sheep,
> A whistling hawthorn on my left, and there,
> With those companions at my side, I watch'd,
> Straining my eyes intensely, as the mist
> Gave intermitting prospect of the wood
> And plain beneath.
>   (Bk. XI, lines 357–364)

The few words of commentary which Wordsworth provides for this
memory (that it appeared as a chastisement, that it has remained a
source of spiritual restoration) do not, as the attention of genera-
tions of commentators indicates, mitigate its insistent accidentality.
It is narrative out of narrative. His very phrase "spot of time" suggests a conversion of the linearity of narrative time to a spatial, spot-
like condition. Wordsworth compounds this effect when, recurring

---

[15]Jerome McGann, *The Romantic Ideology: A Critical Investigation* (Chicago: University
of Chicago Press, 1983), 1–56. McGann has developed a provocative continuation of
this argument in his paper "The *Biographia Literaria* and the Contentions of English
Romanticism," for a copy of which my thanks to the author. See also Anne K. Mellor,
English Romantic Irony (Cambridge: Harvard University Press, 1980), for a similar perspective on other English romantic writers.

briefly to this spot, he bears down on spots within it: "The single sheep, and the one blasted tree, / And the bleak music of that old stone wall" (XI, lines 378–379). He compounds it again when he frames the tableau with an abrupt move to the one conceiving it all in the present, engaged in discourse with his fellow poet Coleridge: "O Friend, for whom / I travel in these dim uncertain ways / Thou wilt assist me as a pilgrim gone / In quest of highest truth" (XI, lines 390–393).[16]

A similar effect of accidental intrusion has continually broken the surface of Beckett's published work since early in the forties. His texts are littered everywhere with the barest fragments of narrative irrelevancy which lead nowhere and, like Wordsworth's, frequently feature objects—a chair, a stone, a dead rat—which augment their alinear, achronological condition. When Beckett composed *Company* in the late seventies, he methodically foregrounded the practice in what, consciously or otherwise, parodies *The Prelude*. *Company* is a baffled present-tense discourse on itself ("What visions in the dark of light! Who exclaims thus? Who asks who exclaims . . ." [C, 16]), intersected at sixteen points by unrelated spots of time rendered in the second person.

> You slip away at break of day and climb to your hiding place on the hillside. A nook in the gorse. East beyond the sea the faint shape of high mountain. Seventy miles away according to your Longman. For the third or fourth time in your life. The first time you told them and were derided. All you had seen was cloud. So now you hoard it in your heart with the rest. Back home at nightfall supperless to bed. You lie in the dark and are back in that light. Straining out from your nest in the gorse with your eyes across the water till they ache. You close them while you count a hundred. Then open and strain again. Again and again. Till in the end it is there. Palest blue against the pale sky. You lie in the dark and are back in that light. Fall asleep in that sunless cloudless light. Sleep till morning light. (C, 25)

---

[16]Wordsworth, *The Prelude,* ed. de Selincourt, 216–217. This frame does not appear in either the earlier two-part MS or the later 1850 MS.

Internally one can note here the contracting of this spot in the continual focusing and refocusing on a single object, the mountain. This object in turn is cast into doubt historically both by the derision of others and by the fact that it emerges in this fragment only as an image of an image, revived in a room in the dark. and moreover as an image that appears to have been created by the sheer effort to see it ("strain again. Again and again. Till in the end it is there"). Finally, the rhyme and alliteration of this passage diminish both narrative and historical attention by accentuating its qualities of sound.

External the spot is further denarrativized by the emphatic blank vacancies of white which set it off in both French and English texts. At the same time, it is dehistoricized by a containing text that replaces the term "memory" with the terms "figment" and "imagining," that further dissociates "remembering" into a voice that "comes to one in the dark," and that—dissociating further still—makes the "one" to whom it comes simply part of a "proposition." The framing action of Wordsworth the maker reflecting in the present on his "dim uncertain ways" to his companion Coleridge has its counterpart in Beckett's frame for this passage: "Deviser of the voice and of its hearer and of himself. Deviser of himself for company. Leave it at that. He speaks of himself as of another. Himself he devises too for company. Leave it at that. Confusion too is company up to a point" (C, 26).

An additional aspect of this spot is that, by invoking the situation of one in the dark (in his room in bed) to whom something imagined comes, it echoes that condition which is the present of this text, announced in its first words: "A voice comes to one in the dark. Imagine." This, too, coaxes us to see this spot of time not as memory but as words tethered to a textual present. The other spots of time which make up the representational moments of this text recapitulate the condition of dark enclosure: "[your] hedgehog in its box in the hutch," you as a lover waiting "in the little summerhouse," you lying on your back with your face "within the tent" of your lover's hair, you as an infant in its crib listening as parental murmurs come down to it, your father on the night of your birth escaping to the dark coach house and further enclosed in his motorcar (his De Dion Bouton) "in the dark not knowing what to think" until the voice of the maid comes to him, in the dark. If all of these moments encourage us to think—and I believe they do, irresistibly—of the fetus in the womb with voices coming to it in the dark, then it is possible to see the entire text with its opening assertion ("A voice comes to one in the dark") as both created and precreative: it exists, is full of voices evoking images, yet is at the same time prenatal, in the womb. In this way, Beckett constructs one of his many transitional spaces and through it expresses the paradox of being on the verge of being.[17]

There is much to pursue along this line, but the main points to be made before we go on are that Beckett, in a text that invites us to think of autobiography, repeatedly sabotages both the narrative character and historical authority of autobiography, and that the "figments" and "imaginings" that emerge in the text are, as it were, unborn. Not going anywhere, they remain bound within that original womb in which the text in effect delivers itself. In this regard, the entire text is a conceptual Möbius strip: "Can the crawling creator crawling in the same create dark as his creature create while crawling?" (C, 52). The question raises the closely allied issue of paternity.

UNWRITING THE FATHER

The spot of time in *The Prelude* which I discussed above occurs at the only point in the poem where Wordsworth refers to his father. Critics have frequently remarked on Wordsworth's "fatherless freedom" (or parentless freedom; references to his mother are almost as rare), but what is striking at this point in the poem is the accentuation of that freedom. Wordsworth, for all his fascination with fathers

---

[17]For applications of D. W. Winnicott's concept of a "transitional" or "intermediate area" to Beckett, see Gabriele Schwab, "The Intermediate Area between Life and Death: On Samuel Beckett's *The Unnamable*," in *Memory and Desire: Aging—Literature—Psychoanalysis*, ed. K. Woodward and M. Schwartz (Bloomington: Indiana University Press, 1986), 205–217; and Patrick J. Casement, "Samuel Beckett's Relationship to his Mother-Tongue," in *Transitional Objects and Potential Spaces: Literary Uses of D. W. Winnicott*, ed. Peter L. Rudnytsky (New York: University of Columbia Press, 1993), 229–245.

and fatherhood in *The Prelude*,[18] refers to his own father only at the very moment when that father left this world. Moreover, as noted above, the whole tale of his father's passing away, with its terrific sentimental capital, is displaced by an accidental scene featuring the poet in isolation together with those single objects (a wall, a tree, a sheep) that echo his singularity. This displacement of the father in a spatialized moment which is, formally, a displacement of temporal narrative itself is a combination at the heart of the autographical subset in which I am placing Beckett.

The oldest narrative of identity, older than the quest, is the narrative of parents begetting children. "In the beginning God created the heaven and the earth" (Genesis 1:1), and He shaped and prepared the latter in numerous details until it was a fitting place for the supreme act of fatherhood (and identity), the act of repeating Himself: "And God said, Let us make man in our own image, after our likeness: and let them have dominion . . ." (Genesis 1:4). Let them have dominion—that is, let them echo our supreme powers of making, shaping, and control—which, in the second act of this narrative, his children do by disobedience (by eating apples, by asserting their difference) and, in the third act, by their own project of begetting, which, in a shadowy and usually suppressed fourth act, produces children rebellious in their own turn. The simplest paradigm of this narrative syntax is found in the "begat structure" of Genesis—"and Irad begat Mehujael: and Mehujael began Methusael: and Methusael began Lamech" (Genesis 4:18)—in which the differences of the nouns of identity alternate with the exact repetition of the verb of creation. Autobiography, conventionally, has internalized this structure and focused on its second act. Thus Benjamin Franklin in his narrative focuses on his flight from the control of his father and brother as an essential preliminary to his self-created difference and dominion over others in Philadelphia. He leaves in the shadows the

---

[18]For Wordsworth's reiterated interest in fatherhood in this poem, see Richard J. Onorato, *The Character of the Poet: Wordsworth in "The Prelude"* (Princeton: Princeton University Press, 1971), 307–332.

son to whom the text was originally addressed (to perfect the author's image in his progeny)—the same son who became, in his
turn, a Royalist. A century later, Edmund Gosse found in Darwinian
evolution, not a repudiation, but a refinement of the Old Testament
syntax of fatherhood, difference, and dominion.

Looking back again at Augustine, one can see a number of ways
in which the *Confessions* undoes this syntax. Worthy of special note
among them is the way Augustine deals textually with his procreative father. Whatever tale of conflict with his father there may have
been to tell, it is, as in Wordsworth, replaced by an almost complete
textual erasure of that father. In one of the very few references to
him, Augustine features his father's delight upon discovering, at the
public baths when his son was sixteen, "the signs of active virility
coming to life in me." "And this was enough," he continues, "to
make him relish the thought of having grandchildren."[19] In this way,
his father is very closely identified with the linear paradigm of generation and mastery. The key act of Augustine's conversion is his commitment to chastity. Abandoning the instrumentality of procreation,
he demonstrates his commitment to a "Father" outside of time and
therefore outside of narrative, a father for whom even the term "father" itself is a probe in the dark, "for even those who are most
gifted with speech cannot find words to describe you."[20] But then,
in the *form* of his self-writing, Augustine went even further by creating a discourse that features the presentness of all its elements. The
text is a radical act of unmastery and openness, swamped from beginning to end by unanswerable questions, identifying its narrative
fragments with the absolute present of its creation, addressing the
Unnamable and meditating on its own unnamability. It is that rare
form of vulnerable autographic awareness which is repeated in
Wordsworth's erasure both of his procreative father and of the linear

---

[19]St. Augustine, *Confessions*, trans. R. S. Pine-Coffin (Harmondsworth: Penguin, 1961), 45.

[20]Ibid., 23.

procreation of narrative. It is, in effect, an autographical attempt to pull time up into oneself.[21]

Samuel Beckett, in real life childless by choice, has made the horror of fatherhood a theme that recurs throughout his oeuvre. "Children, babies," says the voice of "The Expelled," "I personally would lynch them with the utmost pleasure" (STN, 15–16); Molloy would happily be rid of his balls, those "decaying circus clowns" (TN, 36); Hamm "bottles" his "accursed progenitor" (En, 9, 24) and orders the death of a flea for fear that humanity might start from there all over again. What my argument does is link this theme to Beckett's own autographical attack on narrative. It is a link one finds everywhere, as for example in "The End" when, in a narrative non sequitur, the reader is suddenly apprised of the existence of progeny: "One day I caught sight of my son. He was striding along with a briefcase under his arm. He took off his hat and bowed and I saw he was as bald as a coot. I was almost certain it was he. I turned round to gaze after him. He went bustling along on his duck feet, bowing and scraping and flourishing his hat left and right. The insufferable son of a bitch" (STN, 58). Not only does each detail here (his briefcase, his baldness, his bowing and scraping) pointedly work to disjoin the son from what we know of the father, but the episode itself in its intrusiveness, its sharp disjunction from all that goes before and comes after, works to unwrite narrative.

In one of the longer spots of time in *Company*, Beckett symbolizes by overlaid images the complete, troubling narrative chain of Genesis. The passage is devoted to a meeting or tryst in a summerhouse on a "Cloudless May day." In a kind of prelude, the voice begins by describing the hearer as a child who sits with his father in the summerhouse, engaged in an elementary form of role modeling:

The waist of his trousers unbuttoned he sat on the one ledge turning the pages. You on the other with your feet dangling. When he chuck-

---

[21]Fascinating in this light is Wordsworth's further displacement of his own fatherhood with the tale of Vaudracour and Julia in Book IX, a substitution usually accounted for by other motives (cowardice, prudishness, concern to protect the identities of others).

led you tried to chuckle too. When his chuckle died yours too. That you should try to imitate his chuckle pleased and tickled him greatly and sometimes he would chuckle for no other reason than to hear you try to chuckle too. (C, 39)

This passage is conventionally cute but at the same time disturbing, particularly in the way it invokes, in the last sentence, the drive for self-replication. It brings to mind *Molloy's* Jacques Moran and his keen desire that his son (Jacques, Jr.) take his exact imprint, especially as they undertake the arduous narrative of linear pursuit: "I wanted him to walk like his father, with little rapid steps, his head up, his breathing even and economical, his arms swinging, looking neither to left or right, apparently oblivious to everything and in reality missing nothing" (TN, 128).[22]

In the episode in *Company*, after this prelude, the tryst between lovers is recorded, and then, in a closing passage, the voice aligns father, lover, and the possibility of progeny in a spatial conflation of the master narrative of identity:

The ruby lips do not return your smile. Your gaze descends to the breasts. You do not remember them so big. To the abdomen. Same impression. Dissolve to your father's straining against unbuttoned

---

[22]Jacques Moran is so fully embedded in the oedipal matrix that he not only expects absolute authority but honors the rebellion that is its inevitable complement: "If I had been my son I would have left me long ago. He was not worthy of me, not in the same class at all" (TN, 104). Appropriating his son's knife, he remarks, "He would doubtless at that moment with pleasure have cut my throat, with that selfsame knife I was putting so placidly in my pocket. But he was still a little on the young side, my son, a little on the soft side, for the great deeds of vengeance" (TN, 131).

Thomas J. Cousineau, in his Lacanian reading of *Molloy*, sees both principal figures of the text as prisoners of "oedipal logic": Moran of the *Nom du père*, Molloy of the pre-oedipal yearning for the womb. Answering the question Why does Moran's narrative follow Molloy's? Cousineau proposes that Moran at the end of the book has the possibility not only to free himself of the Law of Youdi but also to opt *not* to connect with Molloy and the yearning for stasis and death. Cousineau's is an original departure from most readings of the structure of *Molloy*, but in its very argument it reinstates a progressive linear orientation that can itself be linked to oedipal logic ("It now remains for Moran to free himself and his language from the marks of fear and subservience which point to their origin but not to their destiny"). See Cousineau, "*Molloy* and the Paternal Metaphor," *Modern Fiction Studies* 29 (Spring 1983): 91.

waistband. Can it be she is with child without your having asked for as much as her hand? (C, 42).

In dissolving to the father's unbuttoned waistband from the lover's swelling womb, the scene expresses the condition of being locked fore and aft in an implacable biological chain of identity. One becomes a link in this chain by the agency of one's own natural desires and in spite of one's best intentions.[23]

The moment ends with a shot of the fictive hearer sitting in an attitude of symbolic rejection of this master narrative: with "eyes closed and your hands on your pubes." But, as I have been arguing, not only is fatherhood thematically rejected, but the moment itself participates in an erasure of fatherhood's formal analogue— narrative. Only by laying waste story itself does one create the opportunity of finding oneself outside an ancient story that absorbs all identity into its relentless functioning. Like all the other narrative seeds that we have been calling spots of time, this tableau is also labeled, not a memory, but an "imagining," sealed from narrative intercourse with the others, packed away in thick swathes of blank space and then packed still further in layers of discursive insulation that repeatedly stress its fabricated, propositional, wholly unverifiable nature.

An important tangential point in this analysis is that the erasure of fatherhood in this subset of autography is at a Copernican remove from the oedipal struggle with the father. Take, for example, the baptism scene in Gosse's *Father and Son*. Before the eyes of the assembled congregation, the ten-year-old prodigy descends into the baptismal tank, his tiny feet splashing, held in the "Titanic arms" of the minister, and emerges an insufferable little Baptist. It was, as the author remarks, "the central event of my whole childhood."[24]

---

[23]This construction is given emphasis in the French translation: "A son ventre. Même impression. Il se fond dans celui de ton père débordant de la ceinture déboutonnée" (*Compagnie* [Paris: Minuit, 1980], 57). Where in the English text the filmic locution "dissolve to" foregrounds the constructedness of this "memory," "se fond dans" sacrifices that foregrounding to stress the organic connection of the two images.

[24]Gosse, *Father and Son,* 129.

Immersion in the model of fatherhood allowed him to proceed to those other narrative points well beyond the evolution of his particular father and finally to recount the scene itself with that fatherly distance and compassion that forgives as it diminishes his childlike father. Absolutely according to form, the attack on the father confirms the model of fatherhood *and* the narrative syntax from which it is inseparable.

"You stand at the tip of the high board," says the voice in *Company:*

> High above the sea. In it your father's upturned face. Upturned to you. You look down to the loved trusted face. He calls to you to jump. He calls, Be a brave boy. The red round face. The thick mustache. The greying hair. The swell sways it under and sways it up again. The far call again, Be a brave boy. Many eyes upon you. From the water and from the bathing place. (C, 18)

Putting this scene in its entirety (as it is here) beside Gosse's baptism makes the contrast vivid. In *Company,* we have, in essence, an action that does not take place—no jump occurs. Nor, and this is equally important, is it the record of a refusal to jump (nothing in the scene indicates such a construction either). It is the not-taking-place of a following of a father's command. It is the not-taking-on of an identity ("*Be* a brave boy"). It is the nonoccurrence of a baptism of total immersion with a father before the witness of many ("Many eyes upon you"). Moreover, regardless of what we may dig up in the way of biographical details from Beckett's past, this nonoccurrence does not happen in any past time, in any "then" of narrative, but is a textual nonevent in a textual present. And its internal repudiation of any belonging in any story is compounded by its condition as a "spot" of time, externally sealed from meaningful, sequential narrative connection with any of the other spots in *Company.*

WRITING FOR COMPANY

In summary, what I am proposing is a fundamental categorical shift in our reading of Beckett, one that moves him out of fiction altogether and relocates him in that rarely occupied subset of autography which I have identified with key texts by Augustine and Wordsworth. These texts are as distant from fiction as they are from conventional autobiography insofar as conventional autobiography is as given to the comforts and authorial distance enabled by fictional form as are traditional novels. Beckett's subset is writing governed not by narrative form or any species of tropological wholeness but by that unformed intensity of being in the present which at every point in the text seeks to approach itself. Writing under such governance, Beckett must, to use Gontarski's phrase, "undo" autobiography. Yet this undoing is not to the end of fictional creation but to the end of being Beckett, Beckett as it were *avant la lettre*, Beckett before he is Beckett.[25]

Company, which appears at first glance to come much closer to autobiography than does Beckett's other work, actually serves to make clearer what he has been doing all along. As to what inspiration or crisis brought *Company* into existence late in the seventies, we can only speculate. Deirdre Bair has suggested that the publication of her biography of Beckett in 1978 may have had a significant influence on this particular text. I think she is quite possibly right, though we differ on the character of that influence. Bair suggests that her biography may have liberated Beckett to the extent that "he can now admit to a truthful use of biographical self-analysis as the material for his fiction without any further need to hide behind layers of disguised prose devices."[26] In my view, if Bair's biography

---

[25]This formulation, together with the implication that *Company* takes place in a womb, are in close accord with the words attributed to Beckett by Lawrence Harvey to the effect that "life on the surface was 'existence by proxy' " and that "along with this sense of existence by proxy goes 'an unconquerable intuition that being is so unlike what one is standing up,' an intuition of 'a presence, embryonic, undeveloped, of a self that might have been but never got born, an *être manqué.*' " In the context of a whole range of current discourse on Beckett, but particularly discourse starting from poststructuralist assumptions, Beckett's alleged words represent a problem that is usually ignored. I take up this issue further in the next chapter. See Lawrence E. Harvey, *Samuel Beckett: Poet and Critic* (Princeton: Princeton University Press, 1970), 247.

[26]Deirdre Bair, " 'Back the Way He Came . . . or in Some Quite Different Direction': *Company* in the Canon of Samuel Beckett's Writing," *Pennsylvania English: Essays in Film and the Humanities* 9 (Fall 1982): 18.

is at all involved, then *Company* is best seen as a response or emergency action, occasioned by the imminence of a narrative presenting itself as the story of Samuel Beckett's life. In the preface to her biography, Bair in passing remarks of her subject, "I am sure he did not want this book to be written and would have been grateful if I had abandoned it."[27] There was much more than simple human reticence or shyness in this desire, for if my argument is correct, then her work would have threatened roughly forty years of concentrated endeavor.

In proposing this argument—that for many years Beckett was consciously engaged in autography—I have also proposed that in Beckett's subspecies of autography the whole structure of oedipal conflict undergoes erasure. The signs of originary force which so absorbed Beckett's attention throughout his life achieve a configuration, not within a dialectic of parent and self, but outside of it. A major step in this process is disassembling narrative itself, disassembling, that is, the formal equivalent of generative fatherhood. This, in turn, means undoing the illusion of sequential time. I have focused on how Beckett carries on the formal efforts of Augustine and Wordsworth to, as it were, pull time up into the text. I have done so by concentrating on that special feature, the spot of time. In this regard, it is significant that the penultimate spot in *Company* is a meditation on a watch—literally a spot of time—defamiliarized to the monotonous circular ballet of the second hand and its shadow (C, 57–59).

This perspective on Beckett's art might well, among other things, displace the common oedipal narrative of Beckett's relations with Joyce—that is, the tale of the supremely competent father and his defiantly incompetent son. It would revalue the impact on Beckett of *Finnegans Wake*, a work that in its own way sought to pull time up into itself. Though I would not argue that *Finnegans Wake* is the

---

[27]Bair, *Samuel Beckett*, xii. *Company* was begun in 1977 as Bair's biography was being readied for publication. For a different perspective on *Company* as a reply or reaction to Bair's biography, see Ann Beer, "No-Man's Land: Beckett's Bilingualism as Autobiography," in *Biography and Autobiography: Essays on Irish and Canadian History and Literature*, ed. James Noonan (Ottawa: Carleton University Press, 1993), 170–171.

kind of conscious autography which I am arguing Beckett's work is, the two artists' mutual experience of the continuing incompletion of Joyce's second epic over roughly a decade was perhaps the outstanding artistic fact of their relationship. In other words, the tale of the supreme artist (creator of finished masterpieces) and his rebellious ephebe (arch botcher) is replaced by a long tableau of shared company in the shadow of a project outside the closure of time and fictional form. And though Joyce finally did (as Beckett would with his own work) see the text bound and published, he wrote it in such a way that readers would continue experiencing forever what he had experienced for the last fourteen years of his life. He had succeeded in creating an art without end. Work forever in progress, it was work that, to use Beckett's continual refrain, "must go on."

If this proposal regarding Beckett's relationship with Joyce is more speculative than real, the necessarily in-progress character of Beckett's art is an unavoidable consequence of my argument. For to end would be either to give way to the illusion of auto-biography or to switch over altogether to fiction. For all his great gift for artistic form, Beckett continually avoided formal completion. And though, like Joyce, he saw his works bound and published, these "finished" works contain everywhere notes and questions for the author.[28] Moreover, as I argue in the next chapter, by repeating names, images, and motifs from one work to another—sufficiently developed to be recognizable, insufficiently developed to connect—Beckett was constantly reinventing his entire oeuvre. *Company*, in particular, as both John Pilling and Enoch Brater have shown with impressive documentation, is a kind of Beckett "compendium" or "palimpsest."[29] There is the constant sense of a continuation, together with

---

[28]"Impending for some time the following. Need for company not continuous. Moments when his own unrelieved a relief. Intrusion of voice at such. Similarly image of hearer. Similarly his own. Regret then at having brought them about and problem how dispel them. Finally what meant by his own unrelieved? What possible relief? Leave it at that for the moment" (C, 31).

[29]Pilling, " 'Company,' " 127–131; Enoch Brater, "The *Company* Beckett Keeps: The Shape of Memory and One Fabulist's Decay of Lying," in *Samuel Beckett: Humanistic Perspectives*, ed. Morris Beja et al. (Columbus: Ohio State University Press, 1983), 157–171.

the absence of any clear repetition. Additions to the oeuvre are as unexpected and disorienting as they are, in retrospect, somehow fitting. What appears an extravagant concern for originality is a key part of the effort to avoid the development of tropes from within, tropes however peculiar to his own work which would still occlude the possibility of, to ill-express it, the closest possible encounter. For one function of strangeness in Beckett's work is to keep readers (including, while he was alive, Beckett himself) in quest of its deviser.

This last consideration brings us to Beckett's special earnestness, his intensity and focus. Few writers have approached his austerity of purpose. If I am right, what is involved here is more than his being peculiar or compulsive or even what is called a "dedicated artist." To say of Beckett that his art was his life is to give new meaning to an old cliché. It is to explain why, outside of his art, as in it, he was so hesitant to talk of his life. For to engage in autobiography, however casually, would have been to threaten that ongoing enterprise which was the very closest approach to what autobiography presumes. As Opener says in *Cascando,* a radio play written late in 1961, it was what he lived on:

> They say, That is not his life, he does not live on that. They don't see me, they don't see what my life is, they don't see what I live on, and they say, That is not his life, he does not live on that.
> [*Pause.*]
> I have lived on it . . . till I'm old. (CSPL, 140)

In consequence, what autography also means in Beckett's case is an art of extreme vulnerability. Instead of an artist above his work, paring his fingernails, we have an artist seeking to approach unmediated contact. As one of his voices says, he is "devising it all for company" (C, 8 et passim). The phrase can be taken in several ways. Beckett told John Calder in 1976 that "in old age work would be his 'company.' "[30] And the last words of *Company* are "And you as you always were. Alone." It is important never to underrate the feeling

[30]Beer, "Beckett's 'Autography,' " 771.

of utter isolation which runs through Beckett's work. But one of the ways to read "devising it all for company" is in the spirit in which Wordsworth addressed his poem to Coleridge and Augustine addressed his work to God. These autographical texts, by creating the possibility of contact, create the possibility of company.

I will come back to the meaning of "company" in Beckett's work in my last two chapters. The object of this book is to show how Beckett's art can be read as a continuous autographical project. Central to this argument is the way in which so much of Beckett's artistic effect is a production of strangeness. This same quality in Beckett is highly susceptible to methods of reading, like those of the Russian formalists, which are predicated on a concept of aesthetic defamiliarization *(ostranenie)*. This formalist strain, as is well known, contributed much to the New Criticism, a way of reading which starts with the abolition of autobiography and which has, in its turn, inspired so much of the American response to Beckett, including my own earlier work. Gontarski's argument in *The Intent of Undoing*—that Beckett undoes autobiography, converting its raw material to art—can be seen as a shoring up of this American formalist critique of Beckett. If my present reading of Beckett represents a sharp divergence from this critique, it also has points of compatibility with it, including shared roots in a formalist aesthetic of defamiliarization.

Finally, as I have suggested in this chapter, once the stakes of his project became clear, it was clear also that the achievement of a successful autography required of Beckett what I have been calling "narratricide." Two major steps toward this end occurred at approximately the same time in his career (1948–50): the writing of a play in which "nothing happened" *(Godot)* and the exhaustion of the quest narrative in *The Unnamable*. In the fourth and fifth chapters, I take up Beckett's first fully postnarrative art. The immediate business of the next two chapters is to take a closer look at Beckett's way of making strange, to place it in combination with the earnestness referred to above, and to weigh how well or ill these two qualities fit with the construction of a postmodern Beckett. The goal is to acquire not a label for Beckett but a keener sense of the difference of his art.

Two

Beckett and
Postmodernism

Then on! then on! Where duty leads,
My course be onward still.
—Bishop Reginald Heber

From early in the 1960s, Beckett has been a site of the modernist/
postmodernist turf war. Unlike Virginia Woolf (modernist) or John
Cage (postmodernist), Beckett has remained a categorical rift, giving
the lie to categories.[1] Nonetheless, after a spate of early readings
(often inflected by Beckett's connection with Joyce and Proust) casting him as a modernist or late modernist or, at times, the "Last

---

[1]To the student of categorical consciousness, Beckett reveals the semantic porousness
of categories. Even those who might agree on a category for him more often than not
disagree on why he fits. Both Hugh Kenner and Irving Howe have called Beckett the "Last
Modernist," but they assign him the label for strikingly different reasons. Again for different reasons, David Lodge called Beckett "the first important postmodernist writer," and
Ihab Hassan suggested the publication date of *Murphy* (1938) as a beginning date for
postmodernism, while Marjorie Perloff located Beckett in a still-lengthening strain of
modernism which began with Rimbaud. See Hugh Kenner, "Modernism and What Happened to It," *Essays in Criticism* 37 (April 1987): 97; Irving Howe, *The Decline of the New*
(New York: Harcourt, 1970), 33; David Lodge, *The Modes of Modern Writing: Metaphor,
Metonymy, and the Typology of Modern Literature* (Chicago: University of Chicago Press,
1977), 12; Ihab Hassan, *Paracriticisms: Seven Speculations of the Times* (Urbana: University
of Illinois Press, 1975), 44; Marjorie Perloff, " 'The Space of a Door': Beckett and the
Poetry of Absence," in *The Poetics of Indeterminacy: Rimbaud to Cage* (Evanston, Ill.:
Northwestern University Press, 1983), 200–247.

Modernist," momentum has passed to the other side as the post-modernist categorizers have steadily gained the high ground. Their advantage of armament has come from the fit between Beckett's writing and poststructuralist theory, a fit so snug that Beckett has provided, to use Herbert Blau's word, a "gloss" on deconstruction.[2] Michel Foucault appropriated voices from *The Unnamable* and *Texts for Nothing* to abet his attack on essentialistic constructions of authorship.[3] And for Gilles Deleuze and Félix Guattari, Beckett has exemplified such concepts as "schizophrenic disjunction," "schizoid sequences," and "territorial assemblages."[4]

Since 1980, a steady production of essays has argued that Beckett's art is, in the words of Stephen Barker, "writing of and for deconstruction."[5] There have also been book-length studies, beginning with Angela Moorjani's *Abysmal Games in the Novels of Samuel Beckett* in 1982 and steadily increasing into the nineties with books by Richard Begam, Steven Connor, Peter Gidal, Sylvie Debevec Henning, Leslie Hill, Carla Locatelli, Thomas Tresize, and David Watson that have elaborated a postromantic, posthumanist, post-Heideggerian Beckett. Connor's book *Samuel Beckett: Repetition, Theory and Text* had a special impact when it appeared in 1988 because it not only made the case for Beckett as postmodern *"bricoleur"* but situ-

[2]Herbert Blau, *The Eye of Prey: Subversions of the Postmodern,* Theories of Contemporary Culture 9 (Bloomington: Indiana University Press, 1987), 65–103.

[3]Michel Foucault, "What Is an Author?" in *Language, Counter-Memory, Practice: Selected Essays and Interviews,* ed. Donald F. Bouchard, trans. Bouchard and Sherry Simon (Ithaca: Cornell University Press, 1977), 138, and "The Discourse on Language," in *The Archeology of Knowledge,* trans. A. M. Sheridan Smith (New York: Harper, 1972), 215.

[4]Gilles Deleuze and Félix Guattari, *Anti-Oedipus: Capitalism and Schizophrenia,* trans. Robert Hurley et al. (Minneapolis: University of Minnesota Press, 1983), 76, 324; *A Thousand Plateaus: Capitalism and Schizophrenia,* trans. Brian Massumi (Minneapolis: University of Minnesota Press, 1987), 503. More recently, Deleuze has contributed a long essay, "L'épuisé," on Beckett's late work for television; Samuel Beckett, *Quad et autres pièces pour la télévision* (Paris: Minuit, 1992), 55–106.

[5]Stephen Barker, "Conspicuous Absence: Trace and Power in Beckett's Drama," in *Rethinking Beckett: A Collection of Critical Essays,* ed. Lance St. John Butler and Robin J. Davis (London: Macmillan, 1990), 201.

ated his work in opposition to the essentializing activities of the Beckett critical establishment. And now Jacques Derrida himself, in an interview published in 1992, has described Beckett as "an author to whom I feel very close, or to whom I would like to feel myself very close; but also too close"—so close, in fact, that he has avoided dealing analytically with Beckett, having felt "as though I had always already read him and understood him too well."[6]

But Beckett remains a categorical rift. The deconstructive Beckett is a modernist Beckett or, rather, what John Fletcher almost called him, a "postmodern modernist."[7] His deconstructive art not only grew out of, but sustained, salient elements of a modernist frame of mind, of which perhaps the most consistent is reflected in the fact that, where the postmodern terms of choice are "difference" and

[6]Jacques Derrida, "This Strange Institution Called Literature," in *Acts of Literature*, ed. Derek Attridge (New York: Routledge, 1992), 60–61. The books referred to are Angela Moorjani, *Abysmal Games in the Novels of Samuel Beckett*, North Carolina Studies in the Romance Languages and Literatures, no. 219 (Chapel Hill: University of North Carolina Press, 1982); Richard Begam, *Samuel Beckett and the End of Modernity* (Stanford: Stanford University Press, 1995); Steven Connor, *Samuel Beckett: Repetition, Theory and Text* (Oxford: Blackwell, 1988); Peter Gidal, *Understanding Beckett: A Study of Monologue and Gesture in the Works of Samuel Beckett* (London: Macmillan, 1986); Sylvie Debevec Henning, *Beckett's Critical Complicity: Carnival, Contestation, and Tradition* (Lexington: University Press of Kentucky, 1988); Leslie Hill, *Beckett's Fiction: In Different Words* (Cambridge: Cambridge University Press, 1990); Carla Locatelli, *Unwording the World: Samuel Beckett's Prose Works after the Nobel Prize* (Philadelphia: University of Pennsylvania Press, 1990); Thomas Tresize, *Into the Breach: Samuel Beckett and the Ends of Literature* (Princeton: Princeton University Press, 1990). Though there is some debate as to whether Lacan is properly described as poststructuralist, I have included David Watson's excellent Lacanian study, *Paradox and Desire in Samuel Beckett's Fiction* (New York: St. Martin's Press, 1991), which, as I read it, falls on the poststructuralist side of the ledger.

[7]Fletcher's exact words are: "Like Matisse in the 1950s, Beckett stands dominant today as one of Modernism's great survivors, postmodernly modern to the last." John Fletcher, "Modernism and Samuel Beckett," in *Facets of European Modernism*, ed. Janet Garton (Norwich: University of East Anglia, 1985), 216. In a spirited rejection of the whole modernist/postmodernist dispute, P. J. Murphy makes the case for a "post-avant-gardiste" Beckett. This is a Beckett who, in his engagement with traditional issues of the relations of art and life, escapes the predictable bromides and sterile formalism to which, in Murphy's view, participants on either side of the debate would consign him (Murphy, *Reconstructing Beckett: Language for Being in Samuel Beckett's Fiction* [Toronto: University of Toronto Press, 1990]).

"deconstruction" the modernist terms were "opposition" and "resistance." Even before the terms of postmodernism (including the
term "postmodernism" itself) had gained currency, something very
similar to the contrast between difference and opposition was in-
voked by Irving Howe in an already nostalgic essay, published just
prior to the American efflorescence of poststructuralist theory and
titled "The Culture of Modernism." Howe singled out Beckett as
the last modernist, underscoring Beckett's fidelity to the modernist
spirit of opposition and his consistent refusal to decline into one or
another mode of intellectual or aesthetic fixity (primitivism, nihil-
ism, political ideology) or, worse still, to sell out to a commercial
culture in which "the decor of yesterday is appropriated and slicked
up; the noise of revolt, magnified in a frolic of emptiness; and what
little remains of modernism, denied so much as the dignity of opposition."[8]

In so defining modernism, Howe sought to identify as its consistent deep structure what was most dramatically expressed in the
concept of an avant-garde: exceptional fidelity to the spirit of opposition. As such, modernist art carried the spirit of opposition everywhere into the form as well as the content of art. At the same time,
it fell short of an all-embracing irony; it preserved, in Howe's terms,
the focused intent of earnest opposition.[9] Decades later, Fredric
Jameson used the same idea to distinguish the modernist from the
postmodernist. In Jameson's version of postmodern art and culture,
the modernist device of parody gives way to pastiche, a value-neutral
mashing together of styles, "without any of parody's ulterior motives, amputated of the satirical impulse, devoid of laughter and of
any conviction that, alongside the abnormal tongue you have mo-

---

[8]"A lonely gifted survivor, Beckett remains to remind us of the glories modernism once
brought" (Howe, *The Decline of the New*, 33).

[9]Alan Wilde, for example, uses the term "absolute irony" to group Beckett and others
who have advanced to "the furthest perceptual thrust of the modernist movement"
(Wilde, *Horizons of Assent: Modernism, Postmodernism, and the Ironic Imagination* [Balti-
more: Johns Hopkins University Press, 1981], 40).

mentarily borrowed, some healthy linguistic normality still exists. Pastiche is thus blank parody, a statue with blind eyeballs."[10] The importance of maintaining this distinction in the case of Samuel Beckett is not to make another contribution to the war of labels. Rather, by identifying the limits of a postmodernist reading of Beckett, we can gain a purchase on several key aspects of his autographical investment in his work and see how this investment colored his approach to the artistic business of making strange.

AN ART OF THE OEUVRE

The great challenge faced by an art founded on the principle of opposition is finding ways to resist the neutralizing effect of repetition, whether repetition is imposed from without or arises from within. From without, repetition is inflicted through the various cultural agencies of appropriation, duplication, and veneration. Lionel Trilling noted in 1961, in his anxious reflections on the teaching of modern literature, that the familiarity bred and enforced by canonization robs the modernist "classic" of the very element that originally gave it life.[11] But the normality enforced by cultural repetitions parallels what modernists themselves often sensed as a threat from within: the danger of self-repetition. In Howe's words, "Modernism

---

[10]Fredric Jameson, *Postmodernism; or, The Cultural Logic of Late Capitalism* (Durham, N.C.: Duke University Press, 1991), 17. Though Jameson has, in this book, softened his critique of postmodernism, the passage cited traveled pretty much unchanged from an earlier essay. Andreas Huyssen has mounted a counterargument by identifying true postmodernism with the spirit of the avant garde and its revival in the sixties; see Andreas Huyssen, *After the Great Divide: Modernism, Mass Culture, Postmodernism* (Bloomington: Indiana University Press, 1986). For a broader defense of the political viability of postmodernism see Linda Hutcheon, *A Poetics of Postmodernism: History, Theory, Fiction* (London: Routledge, 1988).

[11]Lionel Trilling, "On the Teaching of Modern Literature," in *Beyond Culture* (New York: Viking, 1965), 3–30.

does not establish a prevalent style of its own; or if it does, it denies itself, thereby ceasing to be modern."[12]

It is here that the anxiety of modernism closely matches the poststructuralist absorption with the problematic relations of repetition and difference. The dilemma of naming articulated by Howe and Trilling is the same dilemma that led Jean-François Lyotard to his elegant inversion of terms whereby modernism would denote namable—that is, repeatable—styles (for example, cubism) and postmodernism their unnamable, as yet to be repeated, precondition (Picasso and Braque, reacting to the now recognizable, and hence modernist, style of Cézanne, but not yet arrived at cubism).[13] But despite Lyotard's privileging of the term "postmodern" (arguably a move that, by the very act of making it, defeated its purpose), modernists themselves frequently sought to practice an oppositional art so thoroughgoing as to elude the classifiable. This quality lies as much behind Friedrich Nietzsche's ideal of the constancy of willed self-transformation or behind the mutability of Proust's characters as it does behind the succession of new formal departures that characterize such modernist oeuvres as those of Virginia Woolf, James Joyce, Gertrude Stein, and Thomas Mann.

This importation of the principle of resistance into one's own evolving oeuvre was brought to what may well be (and remain) its historical apex by Beckett. It is implicit in the constant formal experimentation that marks his work from the start, a restlessness that would indicate, among other things, a continual search for new ways to begin. It shows up also in Beckett's deployment, almost everywhere in his work, of a process of self-resistance we can call recollection by invention. This is a technique of deliberate metamorphosis, a kind of remembering by misremembering in successive works of

[12]Howe, *The Decline of the New*, 3.

[13]"A work can become modern only if it is first postmodern. Postmodernism thus understood is not modernism at its end but in the nascent state." "Answering the Question: What Is Postmodernism?" trans. Régis Durand in Jean-François Lyotard, *The Postmodern Condition: A Report on Knowledge*, Theory and History of Literature 10 (Minneapolis: University of Minnesota Press, 1984), 79.

elements from those that went before. It is the quiet, baffled epony-
mous hero of *Watt* (composed 1943–45), making his thundering
entrance in Beckett's next novel, *Mercier and Camier,* or Malone,
revived after his death at the end of *Malone Dies* to move in orbit in
the discourse of *The Unnamable,* or the "great wild black and white
eye, moist . . . to weep with" in *The Unnamable* (TN, 359) recovered
in the "great moist cleg-tormented eyes" of Christy's hinny in *All
That Fall* (CSPL, 13). The device riddles the oeuvre, and can be
found not simply in people and body parts but themes, words, turns
of phrase, structural devices.[14]

A concentrated refinement of modernist practice, the device not
only has the look of the postmodern but, up to a certain point, a
textbook availability to poststructural analysis. What I am calling
recollection by invention is similar to what Steven Connor in his
study of Beckett called, drawing on the terminology of Gilles Deleuze, "clothed" (as opposed to "naked") repetition. Naked repetition is so blatant a repetition it gives the illusion of some essential
reality. It is what Molloy called "the principle of advertising"—"If I
go on long enough calling that my life I'll end up by believing it. It's
the principle of advertising" (TN, 53). By contrast, clothed repetition puts difference on display; it is repetition that signals the impossibility of repetition. Even as it indicates what is repeated, it ensures
its absolute indeterminacy.[15] I shall return to Connor's important

---

[14]Harold Bloom's appropriation of Søren Kierkegaard's phrase "recollecting forward"
bears affinities with what I am calling "recollection by invention." But I hesitate to invoke
Bloom's theories of poetic succession because they are so bound up with the idea of an
agon. As I argued in the last chapter, however adequate such theories may be to the early
Beckett, he was by mid-career working his way outside of the oedipal sequence. Recollection by invention plays a central role in that nonprogressive orientation to his art. See
Harold Bloom, *The Anxiety of Influence* (London: Oxford University Press, 1973), 82.

[15]Connor, *Samuel Beckett,* 5–9 et passim. For "clothed," Deleuze uses, alternatively,
"vetu," "Masqué," "déguisé," and "travesti." Considering the concept involved, this series could go on forever. For the opposed concept, fittingly, only one term is used: "nu";
see Gilles Deleuze, *Différence et répétition* (Paris: Presses Universitaires de France, 1968),
36–39. The wording in my text slightly adapts both Connor and Deleuze for my own
stress in the analysis that follows. For further treatment of repetition in Beckett, see
Moorjani's *Abysmal Games* and Locatelli's *Unwording the World.*

study later, but first I want to address this process of recollection by invention which was, I think, Beckett's most significant refinement of modernist oppositional practice. It allowed him to create and maintain a web of resistances out of which his art gained much of its life. The Beckett oeuvre operates as a language, but one that seeks never to allow us to forget that meaning is a matter of difference and deferral. Beckett always situated his art against our expectations, but it is in the preemptive vigilance he exercised on his own work that he raised to a new level the oppositional character of classical modernism.[16]

In *Happy Days*, well on in Act I, Winnie, finding herself incapable of putting her parasol down, says, "No, something must happen, in the world, take place, some change, I cannot, if I am to move again" (HD, 36); shortly thereafter her parasol bursts into flame. Again, late in Act II, Winnie says, "No, something must move, in the world, I can't any more" (HD, 60); shortly thereafter Willie, for the first time in the play, comes from behind the mound and out into full view. Both events are rich parodies, drawing oppositional life from a variety of conventions: the answered prayer, the *deus ex machina*, the catastrophe (flames, possible death-dealing by Willie), and most broadly the dramatic mythos itself (Aristotelian action). But they also take place in an aesthetic field that had been recently fashioned by Beckett's own work for the theater, most notably by *Waiting for Godot*. By the fall of 1961, when *Happy Days* was first performed, *Godot* was in serious danger of becoming a classic, having advanced to that status through what could be called the law of retrospective

---

[16]Recollection by invention closely resembles common accounts of the working of intertextuality. The best definition of the latter, in my view, is provided by Gerald L. Bruns: "To write is to intervene in what has already been written; it is to work 'between the lines' of antecedent texts, there to gloss, to embellish, to build upon invention. All writing is essentially amplification of discourse; it consists in doing something to (or with) other texts" (Bruns, *Inventions: Writing, Textuality, and Understanding in Literary History* [New Haven: Yale University Press, 1982], 52–53). As Bruns acknowledges, there are degrees of intertextual subtlety. Beckett is nothing if not extraordinarily adept in his interventions in antecedent texts. But the further distinction we are working with here is the conscious application of this procedure to one's own work.

comparative advantage.[17] Beckett had become "the author of *Godot*," the man who wrote the play in which "nothing happens, twice."[18] *Happy Days*, then, creates its effects not simply against Greek tragedy and Protestant devotional practice or (to go on) against *Hamlet, Romeo and Juliet, Cymbeline, Paradise Lost,* Gray's "Ode on a Distant Prospect of Eton College," and *The Rubaiyat of Omar Khayyam*—to name a few of the classics against which the play also situates itself (one *never* "loses one's classics")—but also against the emerging classic *Waiting for Godot*.

In such a context, *Happy Days* is the play in which something happens, twice. Like other surprising features of the play (Winnie's femininity, her relentless cheerfulness), the structure of the play itself draws energy from *Godot's* countervailing field of influence. The absolute absence of the long-awaited one in *Godot* is undercut in the later play first by an unaccountable flame (bringing incidentally to mind storied flames in which the deity appears or from which it speaks) and second by the vivid manifestation of Willie, "dressed to kill." By means of these inventions the earlier play is recollected in the later. The effect is not to subvert (*Godot* is neither overthrown nor corrupted), much less to revert (the deity is not recovered), but rather to sustain in the later play the effects (among them, the condition of unknowing) which are so powerfully evoked in the earlier one. One has only to imagine a *Happy Days* in which Willie never appears and is never seen by Winnie to appreciate at once how boldly opportunistic Beckett's oppositional art is (the fine embellishments of Willie's hairy arm, his newspaper, the words he says, Winnie's ability to rap him on the skull) and how oppressive *Godot* might have become in the oeuvre of a lesser artist.

Beckett's art, then, fuels itself. And the brilliance with which it

---

[17]"They begin . . . by saluting play A as 'awful.' When play B comes along, that too is awful, not nearly as good as A. Play C is then dismissed as awful, worse than B, which though good was not a patch on A, which in the interval has become a masterpiece." Opinion of Alan Schneider as rendered by Beryl S. and John Fletcher in their *A Student's Guide to the Plays of Samuel Beckett* (London: Faber, 1985), 89.

[18]Perhaps the most widely cited description of *Godot*, this was first employed by Vivian Mercier in "The Uneventful Event," *Irish Times,* February 18, 1956: 6.

burns is directly proportional to the threat of familiarity from which it seeks to escape. Familiarity and habit were defined as threats to art in Beckett's earliest published critical writing: the essay "Dante . . . Bruno . Vico . . Joyce" (1929) and the monograph *Proust* (1931), both written when he was in his twenties. At the time, he was advancing an aesthetic argument implicit in the art of the two modernist masters (Joyce and Proust) who had had the greatest influence on him and who, in their turn, were recapitulating an antagonism to habit one can find as far back as Baudelaire's concept of *modernité*. As Beckett pursued his own craft over the succeeding decades, he turned this modernist screw ever tighter, bearing down with increasingly keen attention on the emergent familiarity of his own work and on the opportunities it afforded for occasions of renewed surprise. In this context, the device of recollection by invention—calling attention to what you thought you remembered as Beckett, but bringing it to mind as different—played a critical role. In consequence, the gathering intertextual complexity of Beckett's oeuvre is marked by a double action: *Happy Days* takes its life in opposition to *Godot* and in so doing gives new life to the earlier play. For this reason I prefer to the term "repetition" the Augustinian term "recollection" (or "re-collection") with its connotation of the recursive action that Augustine wondered at in the working of memory and that he found expressed in the Latin word *cogitare*.[19] By his inventions, both grand and subtle, Beckett augmented the double action of recollection. In this way, he was always writing everything he had written.

THE TROPE OF ONWARDNESS

Such an approach to one's art, with its continual recursive motion, puts into question the idea of the progress or development of an oeuvre. By the time he had begun his theatrical work in earnest,

[19]St. Augustine, *Confessions,* trans. R. S. Pine-Coffin (Harmondsworth: Penguin, 1961), 218–219.

Beckett had become fully absorbed by this question. His early writing shows signs that he had already begun imagining his work as a total oeuvre, but it was in the forties that his collected achievement began to take on its unusual combination of coherence and unravelment. In the same decade, Beckett began to introduce into his work with increasing frequency the Victorian trope of onwardness. This trope is worth dwelling on not only because it foregrounds the question of whether oeuvres progress but because the trope itself, in Beckett's hands, is yet another element that participates in the complex web of resistances which Beckett created through the method of recollection by invention. The textual history of the trope is closely bound up with that of the dead metaphor of progress. Its prehistory seems to lie mainly in the language of combat, a usage that is itself revived, often with symbolic suggestiveness, in nineteenth-century literature of the battlefield ("En avant, Gaulois et Francs!"; "Forward, the Light Brigade!"). In the nineteenth century, it can be found spread out over a great range of discourse—poetry, devotional literature, political oratory, social commentary, the novel. In its characteristic manifestation, the trope was distinguished by three features: (1) the exhortative mood, bearing with it the sense of obligation, duty, and moral imperative ("Onward!"); (2) linear directionality, or the sense of a progressive, usually ascending, advance toward an objective that lies ahead, both in space and time; and (3) processionality, or an orientation toward the ennobling and arduous process of advance rather than the final objective, which, like the end of a story, is less interesting in itself than in what it enables. It was the sufficiency of the process of onwardness which made, in an age that glorified the exploratory voyager, Robert Scott's doomed 1912 expedition to the South Pole a kind of apotheosis of the trope.

All the major Victorian poets yield examples of the trope of onwardness:

> To strive, to seek, to find, and not to yield

> Not enjoyment, and not sorrow,
> Is our destined end or way;
> But to act, that each tomorrow

> Find us further than to-day.
>
> *Roam on! the light we sought is shining still*
>> Call me rather, silent voices,
>> Forward to the starry track
>> Glimmering up the heights beyond me
>> On, and always on!
>
> On and on, anyhow onward . . .[20]

In cadence and diction, this poetic language matches very closely that of nineteenth-century Christian hymnology ("Onward, Christian soldiers") as well as the political and social rhetoric of a society that conceived of itself as engaged in righteous movement and in which one's individual being found its validation in the degree to which one shared or imitated that movement:

> A sacred burthen is this life ye bear,
> Look on it, lift it, bear it solemnly,
> Stand up and walk beneath it steadfastly;
> Fail not for sorrow, falter not for sin,
> But onward, upward, till the goal ye win.[21]

Modernist parody made considerable capital out of the trope of onwardness, and in so doing thematized modernism's rejection of both linearity and the Victorian moral imperative. A brilliant subversion of the trope occurs in Woolf's *To the Lighthouse* in her representation of Mr. Ramsay's intellectual expedition to the end of the alphabet ("On, then, on to R").[22] The chapters of Joyce's *Portrait of*

---

[20]Respectively, Tennyson's "Ulysses," Longfellow's "A Psalm of Life," Arnold's "Thyrsis," Tennyson's "Silent Voices," Browning's "Martin Relph."

[21]Frances Anne Butler [Fanny Kemble], "Lines Addressed to the Young Gentlemen Leaving the Academy at Lennox, Massachusetts," in *Poems* (London: Henry Washbourne, 1844), 126.

[22]Virginia Woolf, *To the Lighthouse* (New York: Harcourt, 1927), 55. In a series of deft strokes, Woolf plays Mr. Ramsay's expedition off against Scott's: "Who shall blame him, if, standing for a moment, he dwells upon fame, upon search parties, upon cairns raised by grateful followers over his bones? Finally, who shall blame the leader of the doomed expedition, if, having ventured to the uttermost, and used his strength wholly to the last ounce and fallen asleep not much caring if he wakes or not, he now perceives by some

the Artist as a Young Man present Stephen's immersion in successive transformations of the figure: "A wild angel had appeared to him, the angel of mortal youth and beauty, an envoy from the fair courts of life, to throw open before him in an instant of ecstasy the gates of all the ways of error and glory. On and on and on and on!"[23] The long last chapter of *A Portrait* can be read as one final, difficult gestation of the figure, which at the very end makes its appearance in a dingy, battered improvisation: "Away! Away! . . . Welcome, O life! I go to encounter for the millionth time the reality of experience and to forge in the smithy of my soul the uncreated conscience of my race."[24] Coming now from Stephen's pen, the trope may well announce in its parodic style the birth of Stephen's own modernist awareness.

Beckett's adaptation of the trope began implicitly in *Watt*, the novel he wrote during World War II, with the imperative yet obscurely destined journeying of its protagonist; was sustained in the same way in *Mercier and Camier*, the *Nouvelles*, and *Molloy*; and finally given explicit development toward the end of *Malone Dies*. The striking variation on the trope that Beckett introduced through Malone is its reflexive application to the writing of which it is a part. Nor is it just any writing, but a life's work, an oeuvre. Malone, struggling to bring on the catastrophe of his story before expiring himself, exhorts his pen to greater effort: "On. One morning Lemuel, . . ." and later, "But what matter about Lady Pedal? On" (TN, 280, 281). Here, among the last fragments of consecutive narrative in his work, Beckett introduces the trope almost as if to signal his own emergent sense of an oeuvre. From then on, Beckett so frequently restated the trope that it became one of the commonest Beckettian markers. In the very next book of the trilogy, *The Unnamable*, the trope was transferred from the task of narration to that of self-formulation:

---

pricking in his toes that he lives, and does not on the whole object to live, but requires sympathy, and whisky, and someone to tell the story of his suffering to at once? Who shall blame him?" (57).

[23]James Joyce, *A Portrait of the Artist as a Young Man* (New York: Viking, 1968), 172.

[24]Ibid., 252–253.

strange pain, strange sin, you must go on, perhaps it's done already, perhaps they have said me already, perhaps they have carried me to the threshold of my story, before the door that opens on my story, that would surprise me, if it opens, it will be I, it will be the silence, where I am, I don't know, I'll never know, in the silence you don't know, you must go on, I can't go on, I'll go on. (TN, 414)

In the late text *Worstward Ho* (1983), Beckett built a forty-page tone poem out of the trope, beginning with a fanfare so brazen as to suggest not a little self-conscious irony: "On. Say on. Be said on. Somehow on. Till nohow on. Said nohow on" (WH, 7).[25] The title of this piece, at first blush a bad joke, sustains the figure's Victorian embeddedness, evoking both the Westward course of Empire and, more specifically, Charles Kingsley's classic tale of adventure and combat on the Spanish Main.[26] This example and others throughout Beckett also recover the Victorian counterversion of the trope of onwardness: the urge for stasis, for abandoning the march, feeling the imperative as a whip. Among Victorians, the counterversion was given early expression in such poems as Tennyson's "The Lotos-Eaters" ("Time driveth onward fast/And in a little while our lips are numb. / Leave us alone") and was later elaborated by Ernest Dowson, Algernon Charles Swinburne, and William Butler Yeats. In 1951, Beckett translated a distilled example of the counterversion by the short-lived, late-nineteenth-century Mexican *poèt maudit* Manuel Gutiérrez Nájera in his poem "To Be":

> There is no pause.
> We crave a single instant of respite
> and a voice in the darkness urges: "On!"[27]

---

[25]Ruby Cohn has touched on the resonance of Beckett's use of "on" in *Worstward Ho:* ". . . 'no' reverses to a polyvalent 'on.' And that monosyllable—on—may serve as the watchword of Beckett's ever searching, ever exploring 'wordward ho.' "*A Casebook on "Waiting for Godot,"* ed. Cohn (London: Macmillan, 1987), 13.

[26]For a fuller exposition of the complex directionality of Beckett's title, see Enoch Brater, "Voyelles, Cromlechs, and the Special (W)rites of *Worstward Ho,*" in *Beckett's Later Fiction and Drama: Texts for Company,* ed. James Acheson and Kateryna Arthur (London: Macmillan, 1987), 167–168.

[27]*Mexican Poetry: An Anthology,* ed. Octavio Paz, trans. Samuel Beckett (New York: Grove, 1985), 136.

In the trope of onwardness, Beckett appears to have come upon
something that matched his obsessions so closely that it may have
presented a serious threat to the oppositional character of his art,
something on the order of an invariant repetition. That this was not
going to be the case can be seen by noting how, once Beckett had
fastened it to the business of narrative composition at the end of
Malone, he had, within a matter of months, redeployed it in Pozzo
and Lucky as an outrageous caricature of the Westward course of
Empire (complete with baggage, bearer, and whip). In all productions of *Godot* that I have seen, the two enter from stage left, which
is appropriate as their progress would then correspond (for the audience) to the cartographical index of westward movement. That they
should enter from the same side twice suggests the possibility that
in the interval they went clear round the world. Pozzo's first word
is "On!" announcing the arrival of the metaphor even before his
appearance on stage (WG, 15).[28] And as he departs in the first act,
raising the cry with which he entered, Pozzo seems to infect the
waiting, unjourneying pair with the trope.

POZZO: I need a running start. *(Having come to the end of the rope,
            i.e. off stage, he stops, turns and cries.)* Stand back! *(Vladimir
            and Estragon stand back, look towards Pozzo. Crack of whip.)*
            On! On!
ESTRAGON: On!
VLADIMIR: On!
            Lucky moves off.
POZZO: Faster! *(He appears, crosses the stage preceded by Lucky. Vladi-
            mir and Estragon wave their hats. Exit Lucky.)* On! On!
                                                              (WG, 31)

---

[28]As he does on occasion, Beckett winks at the reader in his stage directions; "Pozzo:
(Off) On!" This binary joke is transformed and revived at the end of the play:

VLADIMIR: Pull on your trousers.
ESTROGON: What?
VLADIMIR: Pull on your trousers.
ESTRAGON: You want me to pull off my trousers?
VLADIMIR: Pull ON your trousers.
                                                              (WG, 60)

Part of the comedy here turns on the imitation of a wagon train and the colonial departure for long expeditions to distant lands, embellished with nice touches in the standing back of onlookers and the waving of hats. And part of the comedy turns on the stark severity with which Estragon and Vladimir have been deprived of any vestige of forward movement. Nevertheless, the trope expands over the course of the play to cover not only movement but the endurance of its lack, the sheer deprivation of physical onwardness. Vladimir, concluding his final soliloquy, exclaims, "I can't go on!" (WG, 58); and in the last lines of the play he is echoed by Estragon: "I can't go on like this" (WG, 60). In yet another elaboration of the figure, Beckett enfolds within Pozzo's march of physical mastery a reapplication of the trope to the march of intellectual inquiry in Lucky's oration: "I resume alas alas on on in short in fine on on abode of stones . . ." (WG, 29).

In at least three different ways, then, *Godot's* deployment of the figure of onwardness recalls by resisting the way in which he had made use of it in *Malone Dies* several months earlier. In the following years, Beckett was to redeploy the trope again and again, each time altering it or introducing new elements. In *Endgame,* a play that takes place entirely within its denouement, onward becomes both the mysterious working of time ("Something is taking its course") and the effort to bring time to an end, to "finish," as in Hamm's motif—"We're getting on"—which calls to mind the business of aging (getting on). In *All That Fall,* the trope is reworked as leading and being led on, keyed to John Henry Newman's nineteenth-century variant of the trope which Maddy Rooney tries to sing: "Lead, Kindly Light, amid the encircling gloom, / Lead Thou me on!" In *Happy Days,* the figure is split, its imperative mood given to the bell that rouses Winnie when she nods off and the sign of onwardness given to the earth, which rises to swallow her.[29] In

---

[29]Productions have frequently, and rightly, suggested in their management of the decor that Winnie is not so much sinking into the earth as being engorged by a rising mound. This is also a recollection and resistance of the drowning that concludes "The End" and that seems figuratively to conclude *Malone Dies:* not water but dry sand; not sinking but being pursued by the upward moving earth. This reorientation of the vectors of force is

Krapp's Last Tape, the trope receives its most thoroughgoing revision. Here the forwardness of time is played off against an insistent drive backward and inward. With bold economy, the play aligns the quest backward in time with Krapp's male drive, which would take him, through the eyes and womb of his lover, to his first home. "Onward!" becomes "Let me in," and the moment in the play which finally absorbs our attention is a counterversion of the trope, the anti-onward, a point of fetal stillness in random movement, repeated three times: "my face in her breasts and my hand on her. We lay there without moving. But under us all moved, and moved us, gently, up and down, and from side to side" (CSPL, 60, 61, 63).[30]

By keeping our attention on the trope and having us experience something of its infinite variability, Beckett approaches what the more discursive postmodern theorist falls short of. Deleuze's metaphor—"clothed" or "masked" repetition—contains, despite its deviser's best intentions, essentialistic implications (what is it that is clothed?) that Beckett could avoid in his successive distortions of the trope of onwardness. There is, in fact, nothing under the trope. This absence is what gives it its great flexibility. And the theater that Beckett began seriously to develop late in the 1940s, precisely because it

---

given an additional twist by Winnie in her reflections: "Yes, the feeling more and more that if I were not held—*(gesture)*—in this way, I would simply float up into the blue. *(Pause.)* Don't you ever have that feeling, Willie, of being sucked up? *(Pause.)* Don't you have to cling on sometimes, Willie?" (HD, 33–34).

[30]When I first made this argument, Ruby Cohn pointed out to me that, in Beckett's French version of *Krapp,* "Let me in" is rendered not in the imperative but in the past perfect *(passé composé):* "M'ont laissé entrer." "Let me in" could conceivably be spoken in performance as "[They] let me in." As the years go by, this reading seems to me more in accord with the context. But it is worth noting that the instruction preceding the line in English—"*(Pause. Low.)*"—becomes in French merely "*(Pause.).*" The English Krapp speaks with a different voice at this point; the French Krapp does not. So there may be two different linguistic events here, performed by two different characters. The point is grist for the argument that Beckett's art works against itself and that even as a self-translator he practices an art of subtle misremembrance. For added support, see Ann Beer, "Beckett's 'Autography' and the Company of Languages," *Southern Review* 27 (Autumn 1991): 771–791. On the general subject of Beckett's self-translation and the complexity of transformation it produced, see Brian T. Fitch, *Beckett and Babel: An Investigation into the Status of the Bilingual Work* (Toronto: University of Toronto Press, 1988).

was a medium ill-disposed to any representation of voyaging (on stage, all ships stand still), provided a "dramatic" enlargement of Beckett's capacity to exploit the vital emptiness of the trope of onwardness. If the characters in much of his prose fiction (Watt, Mercier and Camier, Molloy and Moran, and the narrators of the *Nouvelles*) are on the move, the characters in Beckett's work for the stage are most emphatically going nowhere. What stunned the world in 1953 was the radical plotlessness of Beckett: sheer Heideggerian "thrownness" displaced any sense of origins or historical chains of cause and effect. *Godot, Endgame, Krapp,* and *Happy Days* (despite its two surprises) were plays in which nothing really happens at all.

Beckett's method of recollection by invention, in its refinement of modernist opposition, is the continual and vigorous reconstruction of tropological emptiness. Onwardness is only one of many blanks around which Beckett's texts, translations, and productions hover, but the process I have outlined here shows why Beckett had to keep on writing. Going on, he warded off encroachments on these vital absences. The threat of content is ever-present, lying in wait upon an author's death, silence, or naked self-repetition. Beckett's oeuvre, then, operates like the life of Krapp, whose successive self-recordings and transcriptions (like his author, Krapp works in more than one medium) alter as they recall what went before and are in turn recalled and altered by those to come. Pressing on, Beckett kept the shape of his oeuvre, and the relations of all its elements, at play. Such a going on is both a going back and also a kind of spreading out. His oeuvre itself transmutes the trope of onwardness.

The argument so far, then, is that if Beckett's work glosses deconstruction, it was a modernist scribe who wrote the gloss. What Beckett did, more thoroughly than any modernist, was so to concentrate and extend the modernist spirit of opposition that it spread everywhere in his language. In the process, Beckett turned the spirit of opposition most keenly upon himself. As he constructed his language in successive works, he had to be ever alert against its potentially deadening or imprisoning effects, an object that required, in its turn, keeping that language from coming to an end. The function of writing was to avoid having written. Like Proust before him, who argued that great authors are always writing the same book, Beckett made his "work" of art his uncompletable oeuvre.

Of course, the best intentions of any author are no proof against the readership. In the last chapter of his book on Beckett, Steven Connor develops a stinging critique of the immense structure of critical discourse which had grown up around Beckett's work over the previous three decades. Abetted, he argues, in curious ways by Beckett himself, this "discursive formation" has in its cultural effect run exactly counter to the kind of complex indeterminacy I have just been discussing. According to Connor, discourse about Beckett has served the function of completing Beckett, in effect taming him, by making and maintaining a "Beckett" who, by the very unity of being implicitly attributed to him, reaffirms the essentialistic assumptions of the humanistic tradition. "What gives Beckett criticism such importance and cultural centrality is the continued reassertion in that discourse of the myth of the author as creator, source and absolute origin." Beckett's long and difficult management of the repetitions in his work is thus converted, in the interests of cultural authority and power, to a more limited and less disruptive kind of repeatability: "The discourse of Beckett criticism has a special, representative place within discourses of culture as a whole, for it is a site in which cultural values of great importance may be repeated and recirculated with authority. What is extraordinary is that all the breaks which Beckett's writing practice makes, or attempts to make, with these traditions and the power relations they encode can be so effectively contained and rewritten as repetitions."[31]

The argument Connor makes is a powerful one, and touches on many all-too-familiar aspects of Beckett criticism. But to begin with, it is not at all clear that what Connor criticizes can, finally, be avoided. He himself does not avoid it. His book is yet one more act of veneration; it is a reading, offered up, of culturally important texts, all of which are attributed to the same man. It presumes to its own superior penetration, presumes to have found a truth about these texts which has been hidden from others. Most insidiously,

---

[31]Connor, *Samuel Beckett*, 191, 199.

the book's consistent use of the name Samuel Beckett (along with grammatically appropriate pronouns) as a person and a maker of texts and its blazoning of that name in the title and on the cover only encourages us to persist in our essentialistic habits—which is not so much to criticize Connor as to say that, like the rest of us, he inhabits, and is inhabited by, our language and our culture. But a more important point can be made in this context, and it brings us back to the issues of repetition and onwardness in Beckett. The point begins with a question: What are the limits of any critique of origins, authority, or unity of being? To which the best, or fairest, answer would have to be: We do not know. This answer is not insignificant, for it implies that it may well be a mistake to find in Beckett any foreclosure of our vital ignorance in this matter. "The key word in my plays," he once told an interviewer, "is 'perhaps.' "[32] So far my argument has carried us in one direction. I have used Beckett's treatment of the Victorian trope of onwardness to show how the modernist spirit of opposition, by harnessing the method of recollection by invention, could be pursued with near infinite variety. In the process, by subjecting the trope to an elaborate, multifaceted, potentially endless deconstruction, Beckett made apparent, far more persuasively than could any discursive analysis, the absence at its center. At the same time, by exploding the idea of onwardness, he completed the job that modernists had begun in ridding plot of linear causality.

PERSISTENT SINGULARITIES

But Beckett did only half a job on the narrative tradition. If, with the turn to the writing of plays in the 1940s, he obliterated plot, he did not obliterate character. This is the second most interesting thing about Beckett's plays. In Ruby Cohn's words, "One has to be blind not to distinguish Hamm from Dan Rooney; deaf not to know

---

[32]Quoted in Tom F. Driver, "Beckett by the Madeleine," *Columbia University Forum* (Summer 1961): 23.

Mouth from M. Vladimir and Estragon are not identical twins . . . .
On the rare occasions when Beckett speaks of his characters, he calls
them 'my people.' Not symbols, or objects, or fictions, but *people*."[33]
Yet we *have* been curiously blind to this conventionality of Beckett's,
and to how strange it is that our leading exponent of the disintegration of the self should have produced some of our most memorable
characters. The fact is finessed, overlooked, accommodated, argued
around, probably because it is difficult to integrate with the "Beckett" that has been created by our collective discourse and in particular by the postmodern drift of that discourse.

That Beckett should have contributed so richly to the art of characterization is not out of keeping with modernism, whose major
figures have given us unsurpassed examples of the art (the Duc and
Duchesse de Guermantes, the Baron de Charlus, Molly and Leopold
Bloom, Stephen Dedalus, Mr. Ramsay, Gentleman Brown). If Beckett's characters appear on the verge of extinction—going blind, confined to wheelchairs, sucked inexorably into the earth—their imper-
ilment only sets off their vigor. And for better or worse, it is more
than likely a nostalgia for character among even the most sophisti-
cated of theatergoers which has given Pozzo, Hamm, Krapp, and
Winnie the secure place they occupy in the stage repertoire. It may
well be the same frame of mind which leads scholars of Joyce to
celebrate Bloomsday.

Was it nostalgia that animated Beckett himself when, at the moment he abolished character from his prose fiction he reinstated it
so brilliantly on the stage? It has frequently been noted that when
Beckett moves to a new genre or medium he appears to revert to an
earlier stage of aesthetic development. Thus one might argue that
the characters in these first plays are a consequence of such a rever-
sion. But the argument cannot account for the number of these
characters—Estragon, Hamm, Krapp, Maddy Rooney, Winnie—in
play after play. They appear in plays, moreover, that consistently
show the most radical departure from tradition in the handling of

[33]Ruby Cohn, *Just Play: Beckett's Theater* (Princeton: Princeton University Press,
1980), 13.

other aspects of the medium—action, decor. If one seeks to perfect the argument by pointing to the abandonment of character after *Happy Days* and by contending that this theatrical austerity was where Beckett was headed—that his more recent work is a purer manifestation of what he has been trying all along to do—one makes *Godot, Endgame,* and *Krapp* somehow more primitive than the later *Footfalls* and *Rockaby.* Such an argument imposes a progressive teleology, a literalization of the trope of onwardness, on an oeuvre that, as I have argued, cannot support it.

I see no way around this fact: Beckett's "people" are characters, and they are as fully and legitimately Beckett's as anything he has created. The point introduces an important qualification to the argument I have been making, for character—a recognizable integrity of being maintained over time—is itself a literal kind of onwardness. And in case after case, the imminent extinction of the character intensifies our focus on its capacity to "carry on." The fact that during this same period (1948–61) Beckett was writing prose fiction (in such texts as *The Unnamable, Texts for Nothing,* and *How It Is*) in which traditional characterization is subjected to the most ruthless disintegration cannot be taken to deny or diminish the importance of the characters in his plays. Such a denial would be to argue, as some have, that the prose is somehow closer to the real Beckett.[34] Such privileging of the prose fails to account for Beckett's continued productivity in theater and his extension to works in that medium of the same earnest care he devoted to his other work. More important, it slights the self-resistant nature of Beckett's art: the way, always, it pushes against itself. It is much more likely that the theater and the prose took fire from each other and that his characters burn as brightly as they do because modes of disintegration were pursued with such determination in the prose.

Of course, the plays can be, and have been, read as prose texts. And read closely, and analytically, these characters crumble into dust. Theodor Adorno, for example, reads *Endgame* as Beckett's

---

[34]"For [Beckett] the 'important writing' always means prose" (Deirdre Bair, *Samuel Beckett: A Biography* [New York: Harcourt, Brace, Jovanovich, 1978], 562).

abandonment of the last outpost of Western individualism. Beckett abandons it, he argues, "like an outmoded bunker": "*Endgame* takes for granted that the claims of the individual to possess autonomy and ontological status have become implausible. . . . The position of the Absolute Subject, once cracked open as the manifestation of the transcendent whole which engendered it, can no longer be defended."[35] But Adorno's is a textual reading. As such, it is not wrong, but only half right. It fails to take into account what happens when the play is performed. And one of the things which happens is that the discontinuities that riddle the parts of Clov and of Hamm are bound together by the force of individual performance. This binding up of the character happens time and again. And if the actors (whether Roger Blin and Jean Martin or Patrick Magee and Stephen Rea) are good enough, the audience falls for it, as it should.

Mikhail Bakhtin may or may not be right when he writes that "drama is by nature alien to genuine polyphony,"[36] but it would appear that theater's capacity to showcase a voice—or its tendency to make one voice dominate, as Bakhtin maintains is the case in Shakespeare's plays—may in fact have been part of what drew Beckett to the theater.[37] Take what may be the most "polyphonic" role Beckett ever composed for the stage, that of Pozzo:

> (*Lyrically.*) The tears of the world are a constant quantity. For each one who begins to weep somewhere else another stops. The same is true of the laugh. (*He laughs.*) Let us not then speak ill of our generation, it is not any unhappier than its predecessors. (*Pause.*) Let us not

---

[35]Theodor W. Adorno, "Towards an Understanding of *Endgame*," in *Twentieth-Century Interpretations of Endgame*, ed. B. G. Chevigny, trans. Samuel M. Weber (Englewood Cliffs, N.J. : Prentice-Hall, 1969), 90. This essay was originally published as "Versuch das Endspiel zu verstehen," in Theodor W. Adorno, *Noten zur Literatur*, vol. 2 (Frankfurt am Main: Suhrkamp Verlag, 1961).

[36]Mikhail Bakhtin, *Problems of Dostoevsky's Poetics*, trans. R. W. Rotsel (Ann Arbor, Mich.: Ardis, 1973), 28; see also 13–14.

[37]Bert States refers to a "processing consciousness" that dominates such plays as *Endgame* and *Krapp's Last Tape*, though he finds it absent in *Waiting for Godot*. See *The Shape of Paradox: An Essay on "Waiting for Godot"* (Berkeley: University of California Press, 1978), 11.

speak well of it either. *(Pause.)* Let us not speak of it at all. *(Pause. Judiciously.)* It is true the population has increased. (WG, 22)

The nothingness that Adorno quite rightly speaks of is brilliantly rendered in Pozzo's sudden moves from voice to voice. Especially in the multivocality of his tyrants, Beckett expresses the dissolution of character as a property of character. But coming upon the different individual voices in this passage as one reads silently to oneself is not the same experience as listening to an actor bind them together from first to last, stamping them all with his own voice and appearance. It is in fact the persistence of shape and sound on stage which brings out the discontinuities in these lines and makes them so funny. Walter Benjamin may have had this effect in mind when he wrote that "the character of the comic figure is not the scarecrow of the determinist; it is the beacon in whose beams the freedom of his actions becomes visible."[38] The point to stress here is that the unpredictable breaks that are at once the signs of this freedom and the cause of humor are not just any breaks; they are seen rather to belong to the character. This quality of belongingness is what an actor enhances, and it must have been an important consideration for Beckett when he turned to the physicality of theater and what he has called its comparative "clarity."[39]

From the opening of *En attendant Godot* at the Théâtre de Babylone in 1953, critics have remarked on the way Beckett consistently took advantage of theater's physical presence. Alain Robbe-Grillet, in a review of *Godot's* first run, likened the effect to Heidegger's description of life on earth as a kind of raw thereness.[40] Though Beckett's experimentation with character evolved away from the em-

---

[38]Walter Benjamin, "Fate and Character," in *Reflections,* trans. Edmund Jephcott (New York: Harcourt, 1978), 310. Mary McCarthy developed a similar critique of Bergsonian theory in her essay "Characters in Fiction," in *The Humanist in the Bathtub* (New York: Signet, 1964), 195–216.

[39]Paul-Louis Mignon, "Le théâtre de A jusqu'a Z: Samuel Beckett," *L'avant-scène du théâtre* 313 (June 15, 1964): 8.

[40]Alain Robbe-Grillet, "Samuel Beckett; or, Presence on the Stage," reprinted in *For a New Novel,* trans. Richard Howard (New York: Grove, 1965), 111–125.

phatic "types" he developed in the fifties, the theater remained a medium in which he was able, through the use of voice and image, to bring out similar kinds of durable individualities. Through the agency of persistent physicality, he bound confusion over time. Anyone who has heard Billie Whitelaw carry the lines of more recent plays, including *Not I* and *Rockaby*, has seen how Beckett designed his work to concentrate our attention on that persistence. What I am arguing is powerfully expressed in the image of P, the victim protagonist of Beckett's 1972 play *Catastrophe*, who, outlasting the canned applause that concludes the play, seems to outlast the play itself. The same interest in the persistence of character and voice (including its persistence beyond the formal limits of art) is reflected in Beckett's cultivation over the years of a select group of exceptional actors whom he not only directed but at times heard in his mind when composing the parts they play. If, as Connor suggests, one consequence of the cultivation of this elite group was to augment the illusion of godlike authority in Beckett's own person,[41] the roots of this practice and its continuation seem to lie in Beckett's fascination with the persistence through discontinuity of that individually distinctive integrity of being which is most notably manifest in what is called character.

As for the issue of personal author-ity, and more specifically that of origin-ality, here too, as I have noted above, our discourse ought to acknowledge our collective ignorance. If there are myths that have controlled the way we speak of authorship and originality, and that deserve exposure, there is still much regarding these two subjects which we do not yet understand. One recurring aspect of current discourse about them is a tendency to merge the issues of personal authorship and sociocultural authority. That a community can enforce a view of the world, can read a text to find in it what it wants, can make an acceptable hero where it needs one, can convert complex and nuanced revisions into naked repetitions, can subvert the subversive, normalize it, and then draw its sting by venerating it— that a society can do all this, painlessly, and in ways that we subtly

---

[41]Connor, *Samuel Beckett*, 192–193.

and not so subtly collaborate with, is a slow death that must continually be brought to our attention. But such culturally authorized
and enforced impositions ought not to be confused with the force
that brings any new text into existence. And if there are myths of
personal origin and authorship which abet the tyranny of cultural
authority, the final returns on the subject of origins and authoring
are not yet in.

All of which is to say that Beckett's own persistence, as writer and
director, his determination to have things his way, can be read as an
allegiance to his own individually distinctive productivity, which
may or may not, finally, have originated in himself but which was
always vigorously subversive. Nor was his author-itarianism the behavior of a stubborn, rigid old man who would freeze his work by
converting it into a set of naked repetitions. As Connor himself
points out, Beckett, even in directing his work, was always altering
it. An important example Connor introduces is Beckett's 1985 revision of *What Where* for German television *(Was Wo)*, which elimi-
nated the megaphone and confined itself to the faces of the actors.[42]
Connor takes issue with the essentialistic account of this transformation given by Martha Fehsenfeld, who argues that Beckett was moving toward a truer rendering of his original idea—that it was meant
to be a television play all along. Connor's stress on Beckett the
"freely-ranging" *bricoleur*, engaged in a continual process of discovery, is in keeping with the importance of continual self-resistance in
creation which I have been arguing here. More grist that Connor
could have used for his argument is the Paris production of *Quoi où*
in April of the next year. This version, directed by Pierre Chabert
and also endorsed by Beckett, replaced the inquisitor (Bam), as well
as the megaphone, with a circular orange light; more strikingly, it
dropped the mime element and doubled the speed of performance.
In the process, according to Enoch Brater, it introduced an effect of
farce which had been carefully avoided in the German version.[43] The

---

[42]Ibid., 200.

[43]Enoch Brater's discussion of all three versions of *What Where* can be found in his
Beyond Minimalism: Beckett's Late Style in the Theater (Oxford: Oxford University Press,

sequence of these productions is powerful evidence that Beckett, in his translations and re-productions, as in the successive works of his oeuvre, was never going anywhere in particular.

But what Connor fails to remark in Fehsenfeld's report is what one can find in all reports of Beckett at work: his intense concentration on doing the thing right. If Beckett's revisions were not going anywhere in particular, they were nonetheless very much in pursuit of what works. The other side of *bricolage*—its veiled aspect—is rejection: rejecting one thing after another until the rare right thing turns up: "Then Sam said, 'keep his eyes closed the whole time,' and that was the answer to it."[44]

For the 1988 Charles Eliot Norton Lectures at Harvard, John Cage chose to read from a composition made up of 487 quotations, selected by chance and then disassembled and recombined with the assistance of a computer program based on the I Ching. Part of the way through the second lecture, a tape recorder in the auditorium suddenly began to make a racket, which continued until the machine was found and turned off. Cage read steadily through the noise. Asked about it afterward, he said that "the incident occurred just at a point when he had thought he would like some musical accompaniment."[45] His was a different frame of mind from that of the man who clutched Alan Schneider's arm during a London production of *Waiting for Godot* and whispered, "It's ahl wrahng! He's doing it ahl wrahng!"[46] Beckett's was a modernist ego. And for all his devotion

---

1987), 152–164. For another view of the Paris production, see S. E. Gontarski, "*What Where II:* Revision as Re-creation," *Review of Contemporary Fiction* 7 (Summer 1987): 120–123. Martha Fehsenfeld's richly detailed account of the making of *Was Wo* can be found in "Everything Out but the Faces: Beckett's Reshaping of *What Where* for Television," *Modern Drama* 29 (June 1986): 229–40. Finally, Beckett himself can be seen commenting on yet another version of *What Where* in the video documentary *Waiting for Beckett* (New York: Global Village, 1993).

[44]Cameraman Jim Lewis quoted in Fehsenfeld, "Everything Out," 236.

[45]Mark Swed, "John Cage: A Rebel Sets Up in Ivied Halls," *Los Angeles Times*, November 13, 1988, Calendar Sec.: 70.

[46]Alan Schneider, "Waiting for Beckett: A Personal Chronicle," *Chelsea Review* 2 (September 1958): 8.

to "failure," he manifested a desire for exacting artistic control which was in the same tradition of Paterian ascesis which ran through Joyce.

Beckett's allegiance to what goes by the name of Beckett was what lay behind his interventions against staging *Endgame* in a subway or having women play the roles in *Godot*.[47] These interventions were efforts to prevent the pastichification of Beckett, his dismemberment and redistribution into the bad infinity of postmodern endlessness. No doubt he made mistakes, ran the risk of thwarting the bold but workable inventions of others; but going his own road Beckett sought to continue writing his autograph, remaking his oeuvre in his own way. In so doing, he lived the kind of persistence through difference which he re-created throughout his career and which he constructed for us so vividly in his dramatic characters and voices.

If this assessment is correct, then the kind of persistence I have been featuring in Beckett himself, as in his characters and voices, is a different kind of onwardness from that discussed in the first part of this chapter, which, being a trope, was entirely a matter of language and therefore necessarily (and vitally) hollow at its core. Important as this insight is, a view of Beckett which features primarily the Beckett of linguistic and tropological subversion may fail to account for the intense earnestness that distinguishes him from so many of his postmodern contemporaries. This earnestness is most comprehensible, I believe, when one considers the other Beckett that I have been holding up to view in the second part of this chapter. This other Beckett would appear to give the lie to the argument, so frequently made in studies of Beckett, that in his fictional world "the only principle of consistency is that all possibilities are possible."[48] Though the possibilities in Beckett's artistic world seem indeed to be endless, they could never consist of all possibilities no more than they could have been just any possibilities. They are instead Beckett's

---

[47]See Linda Ben-Zvi's shrewd conjectures regarding the importance of Beckett's gender assignments in "Women in *Godot*," *Beckett Circle* 10 (December 1988): 7.

[48]Judith Dearlove, *Accommodating the Chaos: Samuel Beckett's Nonrelational Art* (Durham, N.C.: Duke University Press, 1982), 28.

possibilities and, as such, sharply constrained by the persistence of his signature. In this way, both of the Becketts I have featured in this chapter are inseparable components of the same postmodern modernist, the endless complexity generated by the one serving only to sharpen the intent scrutiny of the other in its fascination for breath, for what pushes the words out into the air, sustaining them there in a voice we recognize. This is the same modernist who sustained Beckett's own unmistakable voice as it found its way from one very different piece to another.

THREE

THE WILD BEAST OF EARNESTNESS

Out of the ground up rose
As from his Laire the wilde Beast where he wonns
In Forrest wilde . . .

—*Paradise Lost*

THE RELUCTANT POSTMODERN

"There is something in the deep seriousness of Beckett's attitude toward art that looks suspiciously modernist. The least that can be said is that he does not fit in comfortably with the playful self-reflexivity of many of his present-day colleagues."[1] So described by Breon Mitchell, Beckett would also appear less compatible than, say, John Cage (or John Ashbery or Alain Robbe-Grillet or Steve McCaffery or David Antin or the L*A*N*G*U*A*G*E writers) with the entirely external and relational concept of power developed at length by Foucault and seconded eloquently by Deleuze. Power in this conception is a field existing *in* no place, always dispersed, always "outside." Any notion of interiority we may entertain, of force arising from within, is simply an illusion "we must conjure up . . . in order

---

[1]Breon Mitchell, "Samuel Beckett and the Postmodernist Controversy," in *Exploring Postmodernism*, ed. Matei Calinescu and Douwe Fokkema (Amsterdam and Philadelphia: J. Benjamins, 1987), 114.

to restore words and things to their constitutive exteriority."[2] This way of looking at power has been a central perception of those who theorize the postmodern field. But such a view of power has not been entirely incompatible with a less playful, more earnest, version of art and the artist. In fact, running on parallel tracks with the elaboration of this conception of power has been the posthumanist construction of a Beckett much less playful than the postmodern stuntman. Often as agonized as earlier (existentialist) versions of Beckett, this Beckett is a reluctant postmodern—a Beckett fully persuaded of the Foucauldian insight, yet unable entirely to abandon the idea of extralinguistic, originary force. This Beckett knew, but knew under protest, that the trace of being in the text does not refer back to some pretextual presence but is instead a Derridean *tracé*,—in Stephen Barker's words, "an active force in the written text, a metaphoric force, a force of cross-reference and lateral exchange, of linearity, of association with context, of order and disruption."[3] This Beckett understood the Lacanian paradox that, as David Watson puts it, "the subject is a retrospective effect of the discourse it utters," yet he set this assumption "in a tension of 'reversibility' with its opposite, an interplay between two incompatible necessities."[4] By pulling the focus back to language, such critics as Barker and Watson, Leslie Hill, and Thomas Tresize, like Connor, avoid the failing of earlier critics who "read the late texts," in Hill's words, "as proof of a rendez-vous with ultimate verities."[5] Stepping beyond the limitations of the phenomenological tradition, they avoid falling into "the great trap of what Nietzsche

---

[2]Gilles Deleuze, *Foucault,* trans. Seán Hand (Minneapolis: University of Minnesota Press, 1988), 43.

[3]Stephen Barker, "Conspicuous Absence: Trace and Power in Beckett's Drama," in *Rethinking Beckett: A Collection of Critical Essays,* ed. Lance St. John Butler and Robin J. David (London: Macmillan, 1990), 186.

[4]David Watson, *Paradox and Desire in Beckett's Fiction* (New York: St. Martin's Press, 1991), 40, 92.

[5]Leslie Hill, *Beckett's Fiction: In Different Words* (Cambridge: Cambridge University Press, 1990), 174.

calls 'metaphysical comfort.' "[6] For this Beckett, agony is a kind of residue, a yearning that lives on in the language. Again, the argument gains its strength from its tight fit with so much of Beckett's thematics: "it's the voice that does that, it goes all knowing, to make me think I know, to make me think it's mine" *The Unnamable*, (TN, 410).

There are, nonetheless, two difficulties with this version of Beckett. One is Beckett's consistent expression in his occasional comments outside his art, if not of a conviction, of a fascination regarding what might lurk in the *hors-texte*, that terrain which Lacan acknowledged and at the same time strictly admonished his colleagues to post with the sign "Don't touch."[7] In this regard, Beckett was in closer sympathy with his modernist masters than were many of his contemporaries. This continuing fascination suggests that he may not have outgrown his early enthusiasm for the sudden intrusions of involuntary memory, or for the program he articulated at the age of thirty-one in a letter to Axel Kaun: "As we cannot eliminate language all at once, we should at least leave nothing undone that might contribute to its falling into disrepute. To bore one hole after another in it, until what lurks behind it—be it something or nothing—begins to seep through; I cannot imagine a higher goal for a writer today" (D, 171–172).

The letter to Axel Kaun has become a crux since it was translated by Martin Esslin and published in 1983. The principal question has been, Does Beckett express here a romantic, or Heideggerian, nostalgia for a transcendent, prelinguistic reality and, if so, does he maintain or abandon it? In current debate, nostalgia is a loaded term, suggesting a retrograde attachment to an illusory real. But Beckett does not express an attachment to illusion; rather, he expresses an openness to the possibility of extralinguistic personal force. This atti-

---

[6]Barker, "Conspicuous Absence," 186. For an upbeat departure among postmodernist readings of Beckett see Richard Begam's intensely Derridean *Samuel Beckett and the End of Modernity* (Stanford: Stanford University Press, 1996).

[7]Jacques Lacan, "The Function and Field of Speech and Language in Psychoanalysis," in *Ecrits: A Selection*, trans. Alan Sheridan (New York: Norton, 1977), 57.

tude is quite compatible with The Unnamable's suspicion of the knowing voice. More important, it is not only compatible with a thoroughgoing skepticism, but a necessary component of it. Certainly, to elide one or the other noun of Beckett's "something or nothing" in the letter to Axel Kaun would be to understate his skepticism. The fascination with an *hors-texte* which he expresses in this letter is a fascination with possibilities, not an assertion of actualities. By contrast, a skepticism that accepts the absolute absence of knowledge outside of the text is to that extent not skepticism but certainty. In its finality, it assures. However bleak, such an absolute stance conveys greater "metaphysical comfort" than does the full import of the adverb "perhaps," which, as noted above, Beckett has called the most important word in his work.

Just as Beckett's modernist oppositional stance persisted into the rich postmodern elaboration of his art, so the Beckett of *Proust* and the author of the letter to Axel Kaun in 1937 would appear to have persisted in the Beckett who, in his fifties, spoke urgently to Lawrence Harvey of "Being" as an intuited "presence, embryonic, undeveloped, of a self that might have been but never got born, an *être manqué*," for the pursuit of which "the slightest eloquence becomes unbearable."[8] At the age of sixty-two, the same Beckett spoke to Charles Juliet of the obligation he felt to find and bring back to life an "*être assassiné*," killed before he was born, yet whom he had always felt buried inside him: "I have always felt that there was within me a murdered being. Murdered before my birth. I had to find this murdered being again. To try to bring him back to life. . . ."[9] These sentiments, expressed outside of his art, are fully compatible with the radically dissociative language of the postmodern Beckett: ". . . it's the fault of the pronouns, there is no name for

---

[8]Lawrence E. Harvey, *Samuel Beckett: Poet and Critic* (Princeton: Princeton University Press, 1970), 247, 249.

[9]"J'ai toujours eu la sensation qu'il y avait en moi un être assassiné. Assassiné avant ma naissance. Il me faillait retrouver cet être assassiné. Tenter de lui redonner vie. . . ." (quoted in Charles Juliet, *Rencontre avec Samuel Beckett* [Paris: Éditions Fata Morgana, 1986], 14).

me, no pronoun for me, all the trouble comes from that, that, it's a kind of pronoun too, it isn't that either, I'm not that either, let us leave all that, forget about all that, it's not difficult, our concern is with someone, or our concern is with something, now we're getting it, someone or something that is not there . . ." (*The Unnamable,* TN, 404).

The second difficulty with the darker poststructuralist reading of Beckett as I have described it is the difficulty raised in the last chapter: its failure to elucidate the proprietary care Beckett exercised over the things he created. What motivated this care? In the often insightful reading of Leslie Hill, the inferred motivator is a gray concept of "indifference": "Beckett writes in the name of something which has no name, but to which he struggles to give a name. That something is what throughout this book, for my part, I have named: indifference. Yet indifference is not stasis. It is the infinity of difference, the erasure of identity and the still turbulence at the centre of language and the body."[10] Conceived thus, Beckett's texts orbit this center, betraying in their constant play of difference the authority of this nameless organizer. As in other readings on this side of the postmodernist divide, this one describes a sad travail in which the "author" is imprisoned: "The force of indifference in Beckett's writing cannot be incorporated. That is its definition. This is why . . . there is no exit from the labyrinth."[11]

What we do not get, here as elsewhere, is the Beckett who said, "They're doing it all wrong!" This is the Beckett who produces difference in such a way that, though we could not predict the differences as they arise, we recognize them as Beckett's differences once we see them. If an infinite Beckett could produce difference infinitely, he would nonetheless do so with fierce exactitude. Everything he made would bear the marks of the austere self-discipline we might expect to find among the highest of high modernist writers. Despite such fluid aesthetic journeys as that from *What Where* to

---

[10]Hill, *Beckett's Fiction,* 162.

[11]Ibid., 163.

Was Wo to *Quoi où*, Beckett treated each individual work in the series as an object of art, something to be hammered out, appreciable in its fine coordination of detail. The relation between Beckett's obvious love of his art as art to his "gloss" on deconstruction is something that has never been clearly worked out.

THE METAPHYSICAL AESTHETE

Taken together, these two objections I have raised to the construction of the alternative postmodern Beckett seem to stand at opposite removes from one another. On the one hand, there is the metaphysical questor, impatient with surface truth, at once plagued and riveted by the idea of a hidden, unimagable, possibly interior, possibly nonexistent, originary force or being. On the other hand, there is the artist of a thousand details, devoting himself with loving attention to the physical and verbal articulation of his work as finished art. Indeed, they seem as ill suited to each other as either of them seems to a reading predicated on poststructuralist assumptions. But they obviously did cohabit in the same mind. How does one read the inscribed effects of that cohabitation?

A playful allusion in *Malone Dies* can provide some service to this end. It is lodged in a resonant and often cited early passage of the novel. The passage concludes with what appears to be a capsule autobiography of Beckett himself as he was when he passed through the critical transformation of his art after the war:

> I began again. But little by little with a different aim, no longer in order to succeed, but in order to fail. Nuance. What I sought, when I struggled out of my hole, then aloft through the stinging air towards an inaccessible boon, was the rapture of vertigo, the letting go, the fall, the gulf, the relapse to darkness, to nothingness, to earnestness, to home, to him waiting for me always, who needed me and whom I needed, who took me in his arms and told me to stay with him always, who gave me his place and watched over me, who suffered every time I left him, whom I have often made suffer and seldom contented, whom I have never seen. (TN, 195)

Thematically the passage is an excursion into darkness and nothingness to an unseen and unvoiceable presence. But syntactically, au-
rally, and intertextually, it is a stunning performance, as original and
polished in its wonderful Miltonic travesty ("struggled out of my
hole, then aloft through the stinging air towards an inaccessible
boon") and its variety of rhythmic combinations (culminating in an
extended series of "who"s and "whom"s) as one finds anywhere in
Beckett's work. As such it embodies the combination I have been
dwelling on: an anguished fascination with extratextual originative
power; a loving attendance on the text itself.

The allusion I referred to above comes just before this passage, as
Malone opens his topic: "Live and invent. I have tried. I must have
tried. Invent. It is not the word. Neither is live. No matter. I have
tried. While within me the wild beast of earnestness padded up and
down, roaring, ravening, rending" (TN, 194). It is the phrase "the
wild beast of earnestness" which tugs at the ear, allusively. It is very
like the kind of allusive fun in dark prose to which Beckett was
frequently prone ("the hardy laurel," "night's young thoughts"). In
a passage written *de profundis* and devoted to "earnestness," Beckett
calls up an early modernist precursor, his fellow Anglo-Irishman
and forerunner at Portora Royal School, the author of *The Importance of Being Earnest*. The marquess of Queensberry referred to
Oscar Wilde as "that beast Wilde," an epithet that stuck.[12] In context, Malone's autobiographical words might serve as much for
Wilde as for Beckett: "The grown-ups pursued me, the just, caught
me, beat me, hounded me back into the round" (TN, 195).

So there is a good chance that Beckett wanted us to think of
Wilde in this passage devoted not so much to the importance as to
the inevitability of being earnest (which was what Wilde's play was
about, too). Wilde is a suggestive figure to keep in our minds when
we think of Beckett. He combined in one career an art of extraordinary polish and a personal depth that, complex to begin with, ar-

---

[12]Richard Ellmann, *Oscar Wilde* (New York: Random House, 1988), 569. Henry James,
for example, referred to Wilde as "an unclean beast"; see Leon Edel, *Henry James: A Life*
(New York: Harper and Row, 1985), 273.

rived in time at torment (in a case of almost too expressive timing, his greatest triumph, *The Importance of Being Earnest,* opened at the very moment of his fall from grace). The dance of personal pronouns in *The Unnamable* was anticipated by Wilde's enactment of his own identity as a dance of antitheses—English/Irish, masculine/ feminine, Protestant/Catholic, socialist/dandy—which gave the lie to the notion of a namable self. Beckett's remarkable answer to the question Are you English? could well have been Wilde's: "Au contraire."[13] The French amplification of this mazelike response was, likewise, a complicating dimension of Wilde, who, like Beckett, lived in France, died in France, and composed significant original art in French.[14]

Another point rarely touched on is how closely Wilde's aesthetic dicta parallel Beckett's own comments on art. Beckett, for example,

---

[13]Richard Ellmann, *Samuel Beckett, Nayman of Noland* (Washington, D.C.: Library of Congress, 1986), 5. Ellmann also suggests several other ways of aligning Beckett and Wilde, most notably their propensity for "self-cancellation" (21–24). For an interesting elaboration of Wildean doubleness in the context of the issue of Irish identity, see Declan Kiberd, *Anglo-Irish Attitudes* (Derry: Field Day Pamphlets, 1984), 6–10.

[14]In an unpublished paper, "The Unimportance of Being Godot," P. J. Murphy shrewdly notes that the dialogue of *Godot* echoes passages such as the following in *The Importance of Being Earnest:*

ALGERNON.	Do you know it is nearly seven?
JACK [*irritably*].	Oh, it is always nearly seven.
ALGERNON.	Well, I'm hungry.
JACK.	I never knew when you weren't. . . .
ALGERNON.	What shall we do after dinner? Go to a theatre?
JACK.	Oh, no! I loathe listening.
ALGERNON.	Well let us go to the club?
JACK.	Oh, no! I hate talking.
ALGERNON.	Well, we might trot round to the Empire at ten?
JACK.	Oh, no! I can't bear looking at things. It is so silly.
ALGERNON.	Well, what shall we do?
JACK.	Nothing.
ALGERNON.	It is awfully hard work doing nothing.

Oscar Wilde, *"The Picture of Dorian Gray" and Other Writings,* ed. Richard Ellmann (New York: Bantam, 1982), 419. Wilde also wrote a diptych of poems titled "Eleuteria." Could Beckett have picked up the title for his 1947 play, *Eleutheria,* from Wilde? Like Beckett's, Wilde's "Eleuteria" thoroughly problematizes its titular subject (freedom).

wrote of painting that it is for "the inoffensive crank who spends his
time in galleries, in the museum, even in churches, as others do in
the cinema, with the hope—please take note—of enjoying himself.
He has not wish to be instructed, the pig, nor to be improved. He
thinks only of his pleasure."[15] Wilde's view that "thought and language are to the artist instruments of an art" is very close to Beckett's
comment on *Footfalls* that "the words are only the excipient [i.e. the
sugar on the pill]; the pacing is far more important."[16] Wilde's view
that "from the point of view of form, the type of all the arts is the
type of the musician" is echoed by Beckett's complaint that "pro-
ducers don't seem to have any sense of form in movement. The kind
of form one finds in music."[17] Wilde's indifference to the truth or
falsity of John Ruskin's views compared to the "music" of his prose
aligns itself with Beckett's expressed preference for the shape of ideas
over their content.[18]

There is no denying Beckett's aestheticism. Like its apparent alter-
ego—Beckett's earnest pursuit of inaccessible being—this overriding
concern for shape and for the music of what he wrote marked his
work to the end. Together they make an odd couple. In the pursuit

---

[15]"l'inoffensif loufouque qui court, comme d'autres au cinema, dans les galleries, au
musée et jusque dans les églises avec l'espoir—tenez-vous bien—de jouir. Il ne veut pas
s'instruire, le cochon, ni devenir meilleur. Il ne pense qu'a son plaisir" (D, 120).

[16]Wilde, *The Picture of Dorian Gray*, 3; Beryl S. Fletcher and John Fletcher, *A Student's
Guide to the Plays of Samuel Beckett* (London: Faber, 1985), 225.

[17]Wilde, *The Picture of Dorian Gray*, 4; Beckett cited by Charles Marovitz in "Paris
Log," *Encore* 9 (March–April 1962): 44.

[18]Oscar Wilde, "The Critic as Artist," in *The Artist as Critic*, ed. Richard Ellmann (New
York: Random House, 1969), 341–408; Harold Hobsen, "Samuel Beckett; Dramatist of
the Year," *International Theatre Annual* 1 (1956): 153. Hobsen quotes Beckett as follows:
"I am interested in the shape of ideas even if I do not believe them. There is a wonderful
sentence in Augustine. I wish I could remember the Latin. It is even finer in Latin than
in English. 'Do not despair; one of the thieves was saved. Do not presume; one of the
thieves was damned.' That sentence has a wonderful shape. It is the shape that matters."
For a compendium of Beckett's expressions of similar or related sentiments, see Dougald
McMillan and Martha Fehsenfeld, *Beckett in the Theatre: The Author as Practical Playwright and Director, vol. 1: From "Waiting for Godot" to "Krapp's Last Tape"* (London:
Calder, 1988), 13–16.

of the former, as he told Lawrence Harvey, "the slightest eloquence becomes unbearable." Yet Beckett is always and everywhere eloquent. He not only knew this, he cultivated his eloquence. Perhaps, in the context of his remark to Harvey, Beckett meant by "eloquence" what goes by its name in the marketplace—the familiar language and cadences of culturally acceptable eloquence—not language like this: "Sleep if maintained with cacodemons making waking in light and dark if this maintained faint sweet relief and the longing for it again and to be gone again a folly to be resisted again in vain" (*All Strange Away*, CSPR, 127). But this passage is assuredly eloquent. Moreover, with its stark absence of assisting pronouns and copulative verbs, its wonderful collisions ("Cacodemons making waking") and its faintly punning serial rhyme involving two "maintained"s, three "again"s, and a final "in vain," it is eloquence that tells us at all times who wrote it—tells us while it surprises us.

Such eloquence was so important for Beckett that he introduced his eloquent precursor in a pun (a signature pun, again, both elegant and corny) in the extended passage, cited above, on the dark descent to unimagable, ungraspable origins. In this reading, Wilde's presence in that passage does not support a linear narrative charting a trajectory from an art of brilliant wit and musical effects to a sadder and wiser art *(de profundis)*, keyed to nonlinguistic originary power. It attests instead to their coexistence. Such a reading is borne out by the presence, noted above, of Beckett's own elegant art announcing itself everywhere in the passage from start to finish, at times in not-distant variations of Wilde himself: "I wonder why I speak of all this. Ah yes, to relieve the tedium."

I have been speaking of two arts, two Becketts, two Wildes. But in the case of Beckett, both art and artist, I am arguing in this book that there is one art, analytically separated here into two coexistent phases. Beckett's "aestheticist" attention to the felicities of his work was an attention to something quite amazing, of whose true nature he had no idea but that it seemed to belong to him alone. In his few cautious words on Beckett, Derrida would seem to concur. He suggests that we shelve any serious pursuit of Beckett's "thematics" as, finally, an exhausting and fruitless endeavor, and direct our attention instead to the art: "The composition, the rhetoric, the construction and the rhythm of his works, even the ones that seem the most 'decomposed,' that's what 'remains' finally the most 'interesting,' that's the work, that's the signature, this remainder which remains when the thematics is exhausted (and also exhausted, by others, for a long time now, in other modes)."[19] I believe that he is right about where the action is in Beckett. As action, it was a kind of autographical music, the significance of which far exceeded the satisfactions of formal control and the pleasures of artful repetition. Beckett's aestheticism was so strong because it kept him apprised of his own originality. It was the recursive action of that tracery of form, playing itself out in a continually self-reconstructing oeuvre, which raised, over and over, the possibility of something wild and originary, yet persistent: an exotic and willful singularity working somewhere on the other side of language.

---

[19]Jacques Derrida, "This Strange Institution Called Literature," in *Acts of Literature,* ed. Derek Attridge (New York: Routledge, 1990), 61.

FOUR

ENGENDERING KRAPP

Then I'll let down my trousers and shit stories on them.
—*The Unnamable*

AUTOGRAPHICAL THEMATICS

Paraphrasing Antonin Artaud, Jacques Derrida described art as pure crap. "The work, as excrement, is but matter without life, without force or form. It always falls and collapses as soon as it is outside me. This is why the work—be it poetic or other—will never help me stand upright. . . . The work always being the work of death."[1] In this view (common in current discourse), our words depart from us as inert things, a waste product in which we can find no reassuring signs of our belonging. Roland Barthes called it "the negative where all identity is lost."[2] Michel Foucault called it "the singularity of [the writer's] absence."[3] Beckett called it "wordshit" (STN, 118).[4]

---

[1]Jacques Derrida, *Writing and Difference*, trans. Alan Bass (Chicago: University of Chicago Press, 1978), 183.

[2]Roland Barthes, "The Death of the Author," in *Image-Music-Text*, trans. Stephen Heath (New York: Hill and Wang, 1977), 142.

[3]Michel Foucault, "What Is an Author?" in *Language, Counter-Memory, Practice: Selected Essays and Interviews*, ed. Donald F. Bouchard, trans. Bouchard and Sherry Simon (Ithaca: Cornell University Press, 1977), 117.

[4]Beckett's scatology has inspired a growing body of commentary. Notable examples are David Lloyd's "Writing in the Shit: Beckett, Nationalism, and the Colonial Subject," in his *Anomalous States: Irish Writing and the Post-Colonial Moment* (Durham, N.C.: Duke

> A voice, a small voice, the same voice only small, it sticks in the
> throat, there's the throat again, there's the mouth again, it fills the
> ear, there's the ear again, then I vomit, someone vomits, someone
> starts vomiting again, that must be how it happens, I have no expla-
> nations to offer, none to demand, the comma will come where I'll
> drown for good, then the silence . . . . (*The Unnamable*, TN, 408–409)

As logorrhea, it was imagined in its purest form when Beckett staged
a detached mouth in a play pointedly titled *Not I.*

An earlier culmination was Beckett's compact anatomy of autobiography, *Krapp's Last Tape* (1958). In the 1940s, Beckett had richly
problematized autobiography in the *Nouvelles* and the trilogy, but
the tape recorder he used in *Krapp's Last Tape* was a stroke of genius
which allowed him to stage the self-estrangement he had elaborated
in prose. Krapp has spent the better part of a life excreting dead
selves, coffined separately year by year in cardboard boxes that Beckett later changed to tins so that they would clatter on the floor when
Krapp sweeps them off the table. They pile up, they get in the way,
and, played back, sound strange and repellant. So the whole project
of self-recording, as Sylvie Debevec Henning describes it (echoing
Derrida), is a misdirected investment in crap: "The creation of a
work of art—even one based on self-recollection—remains always a
form of self-alienation. The work is expelled from the writer; it
stands away from him; it confronts him like a double."[5]

But if one turns from Krapp's relationship with his tapes to Beckett's relationship with *Krapp*, the contrast is sharp. From its first
production in 1958 at the Royal Court Theatre, Beckett followed his
creation with close solicitude. He was deeply involved in both the

University Press, 1993), 41–58; William Hutchings's " 'Shat into Grace' or a Tale of a
Turd: Why It Is How It Is in Samuel Beckett's *How It Is*," *Papers on Language and Literature* 21 (Winter 1985): 64–89; and Jonathan Weinberg's "It's in the Can: Jasper Johns and
the Anal Society," *Genders* 1 (March 1988): 40–56. For a compilation of Beckett's figures
of excretion see Susan Brienza's "Krapping Out: Images of Flow and Elimination as Creation in Joyce and Beckett," in *Re: Joyce 'n Beckett,* ed. Phyllis Carey and Ed Jewinski
(New York: Fordham University Press, 1992), 117–146.

[5]Sylvie Debevec Henning, *Beckett's Critical Complicity: Carnival, Contestation, and Tradition* (Lexington: University Press of Kentucky, 1988), 154.

1960 and 1970 Théâtre Récamier productions of *La dernière bande,*
directing the latter; he directed *Das letze Band* at the Schiller-Theater
Werkstatt in 1969; he contributed notes for the 1972 BBC television
version of *Krapp;* he attended rehearsals of the Royal Court revival
of the English stage version in 1973; he worked closely with Pierre
Chabert in the 1975 Théâtre d'Orsay production of *La dernière
bande;* he directed Rick Cluchey in Berlin in 1977. For these productions, his notes and alterations of the play are extensive and lovingly
precise.[6] In other words, where Krapp aborts his last tape and sweeps
all the others on the floor, Beckett pays close and sustained attention
to the product of his pen, translating it, staging it, improving it in
myriad subtle ways. Where Krapp expels, Beckett mothers.

Of course, Krapp is jettisoning overt autobiography while Beckett
is caring for art. Yet the burden of *Krapp's Last Tape* is to reject not
simply the recording of a life but a life devoted to art. The work of
art to which Krapp devoted his life and for which he said "Farewell
to Love" has amounted to "seventeen copies sold." Krapp refers to
it with an amused contempt. At sixty-nine, his emotional center of
gravity is not his art but what he sacrificed at thirty-nine to pursue
it. The record of his moment of commitment to his art—"that
memorable night in March, at the end of the jetty" (CSPL, 60)—has
become unbearable. The energy in his life is now absorbed in his last
moments of love as they are recorded on tape. Near the end, Krapp
the artist, the counter-Krapp, makes one final stir ("Sometimes
wondered in the night if a last effort mightn't") and is immediately
silenced by Krapp, who barks at him in the second person as he
would at one of his taped selves: "Ah finish your booze now and get
to your bed. Go on with this drivel in the morning. Or leave it at
that. [*Pause.*] Leave it at that" (CSPL, 63).

The poignancy of the play arises from its capacity to maintain

[6]See James Knowlson, "*Krapp's Last Tape:* The Evolution of a Play, 1958–75," *Journal
of Beckett Studies* 1 (Winter 1976): 50n. For a full treatment of Beckett's extensive involve-
ment with productions of this play, see Dougald McMillan and Martha Fehsenfeld, *Beckett in the Theatre: The Author as Practical Playwright and Director* (London: Calder, 1988),
241–311, and James Knowlson, ed., *Samuel Beckett: Krapp's Last Tape,* Theatre Workbook
1 (London: Brutus Books, 1980).

our attention on how much Krapp's life sacrifice weighs in the balance. As such, it requires keeping out of our awareness the Beckett who energetically translated, improved, directed, adapted, and generally cared for it. By keeping Beckett out of view, we can be *with* Krapp, feel his immersion in hopelessness and regret, fully perceive that extinction is imminent, that life is now past and, worse, that it might have been richer but for that misstep when Krapp committed himself to a delusive system founded on the value of works. Yet the play itself is firmly situated within that system. How, then, is this work valuable for Beckett? If, as Derrida argues and Beckett's thematics confirm, the work of art is always "the work of death," can one argue that there is a pleasure of autographical action in Beckett's work and that, despite his gloomy thematics, it inscribes itself even in a play that rejects this pleasure absolutely? Do we in some way experience as part of the play this other version of the artist, writing his signature in counterpoint with his despairing subject? We can answer these questions by placing *Krapp* beside a text that Beckett, within a few years of writing it, wanted very much to expel.

Eleutheria[7] was Beckett's first complete play, a play about a family named Krap, which he wrote in the early months of 1947, eleven years before *Krapp's Last Tape*. Both the original French text and an American translation have now been published, but of all Beckett's "failures" (a term he tended to apply to everything he wrote), *Eleutheria* was the one he most steadfastly withheld from publication.[8] This is because it failed in a way that his other, later, work did

---

[7]Most critical references to this play have included an *accent aigu* over the third "e" (*Eleuthéria*), and it is so spelled in the Michael Brodsky translation (Foxrock). In the Minuit edition of the original French text, however, there is no accent. As there is also no accent on the title page of Beckett's manuscript for the play (now at the University of Texas) or in photocopies of two different typescripts (at Dartmouth and the University of California at Santa Barbara, respectively), or in excerpts published in a special 1986 issue of *Revue d'esthetique* devoted to Beckett and approved by the author, I have chosen to omit the accent.

[8]On the cover of the original manuscript, Beckett wrote: "Prior to Godot, 1947. Unpublished, jettisoned." On a photocopy of one of the typescripts, Beckett also wrote: "Never attempted English translation. . . . Never edition of any kind if I can help it.

not. Understanding that failure can shed light on his success. At the same time, it can throw into sharp relief the transformation of dramatic method which Beckett effected in the intervening eleven years and his autographical investment in that transformation. *Eleutheria* provided an extended opportunity for Beckett to start thinking through the connections between dramatic form and his own special content. When he came to revive Krap as Krapp, he pushed against his first play, recollecting as always to invent. But in this instance Beckett, in effect, wrote the earlier play out of his oeuvre. In the process, *Krapp* became Beckett's implicit statement on dramatic method. Above all, it solved in rich and wonderful ways the problems of narrative and the representation of time which had plagued *Eleutheria.*

TIME AND NARRATIVE

At first glance, the two plays could hardly be more different. Where *Krapp* is a one-act solo and a masterpiece of compression, *Eleutheria* is a sprawling three-act play, over 150 pages long, with seventeen characters. Where the young Krapp was an aspiring writer with a "fire burning" in him, the young Victor Krap is a Bartleby-like character who refuses to act according to any recognizable motivation. A narratological crux, he comes to dominate the play.

There are signs in the manuscript—doodles and crossings out—that Beckett found the play increasingly difficult to write.[9] The problem of composition was doubtless identical to the problem put forward in the text itself: How does one write a drama that has for its central dramatic interest a failure of dramatic interest? In the text,

Samuel Beckett / Paris / March 69." Both of these copies of *Eleutheria* are held in the Humanities Research Center at the University of Texas, Austin; see *No Symbols Where None Intended: A Catalogue of Books, Manuscripts, and Other Materials Relating to Samuel Beckett in the Collections of the Humanities Research Center,* Selected and Described by Carlton Lake (Austin: University of Texas Humanities Research Center, 1984), 51–52.

[9]Deirdre Bair, *Samuel Beckett: A Biography* (New York: Harcourt, Brace, Jovanovich, 1978), 362–363.

the principal critic-antagonist is a glazier who springs up like a genie
at the beginning of Act II, immediately after Victor gratuitously
flings his shoe through the window. The Glazier, a man of the people, a man with a trade, goal-oriented, cannot resist turning from
his work to interject his withering contempt for Victor's dramatic
implausibility.

VITRIER.	Vous savez, il est temps que vous vous expliquiez.
VICTOR.	M'expliquer?
VITRIER.	Mais oui. Ça ne peut pas continuer comme ça.
VICTOR.	Mais je n'y comprends rien.
GLAZIER.	You know, it is time that you explained yourself.
VICTOR.	Explain myself?
GLAZIER.	Well, yes. It cannot go on like this.
VICTOR.	But I am at a loss to understand. (El, 84/81)[10]

Lacking self-accountability and recognizable human motivations,
Victor can chart no narrative course for this play. In the Glazier's
words, he is (like his name) a kind of oozing ("une sorte de suinte-
ment" [El, 84/81]). As such, he anticipates *Godot*'s "Tout suinte"—
"Everything oozes" (WG, 39).[11] The ultimate model of narrative failure, oozing received its final oxymoronic reinvention in *Worstward
Ho*'s "Somehow ooze on" (WH, 39).

Yet many threads run between this long, convoluted, and self-
afflicted play and the taut, lyrical piece Beckett wrote eleven years
later. They are threads that at once unite and disunite the two plays,
beginning with a shared surname that recurs, yet doesn't recur (with
an extra "p," Krapp is Krap with a difference). In 1975, Beckett told

[10]The English translations here and below are Michael Brodsky's; his page references
appear after the slash. It is important to bear in mind that Beckett himself translated all
his other French texts or worked closely with those who did. These were not so much
translations as fresh work. One liability of the rush to bring out an English version of
Eleutheria is that it did not allow time for a more thorough vetting in this very important
dimension of Beckett publication.

[11]Samuel Beckett, *En attendant Godot*, ed. Germaine Brée and Eric Shoenfeld (New
York: Macmillan, 1963), 69.

Pierre Chabert: "I thought of writing a play about the situation in reverse. Mrs. Krapp, the girl in the boat, would be prowling around behind him, and his failure, and his solitude would be just the same."[12] But Beckett had already written the other version in *Eleutheria's* Henri Krap, husband of Violette Krapp, father of Victor Krap.[13] A more successful novelist than Krapp (he is a member of the "Institute"), he writes nonetheless in the excremental mode [au genre merde]" (El, 43/35). Like Krapp in his last moments, Henri Krap on his own last night on earth rejects both art and autobiography. Asked if he would now try his hand at a small volume of memoirs [un petit livre de Mémoires]," he replies, "Cela me gâterait l'agonie [That would spoil the death throes]" (El, 44/35). His failure and solitude are comparable to those of Krapp, more exacerbated than relieved by Mme Krapp, "cette catastrophe" (El, 57/52).

Henri Krap is one of Beckett's first sustained looks at aging. In his aged infirmity, he belongs to a series of preemptive encounters with old age which Beckett began in his *Nouvelles* right after the war ("I don't know when I died. It always seemed to me I died old, about ninety years old . . . " ["The Calmative," STN, 27]). Often, in these works—as with the pairing of the two Kraps, *père et fils*— different strata of time are juxtaposed in the same space: Molloy preceding and at the same time somehow inside of a more fit but rapidly deteriorating Moran, who in turn is accompanied by his son, Jacques, Jr.; the youth Saposcat of *Malone Dies* metamorphosed into the ancient MacMann; Pozzo and Lucky aging markedly in the space of a day; the ancient Nagg and Nell permanently on stage in *Endgame* with their son, Hamm. In this sequence, *Krapp's Last Tape* is both a culmination, providing the most compact "anatomy" of time to date, and an anticipation of the even more compact anatomies of *That Time* (wr. 1974–75) and *A Piece of Monologue* (1979).

---

[12]Quoted in Knowlson, *Samuel Beckett: Krapp's Last Tape*, 87.

[13]This observation was first suggested by James Knowlson; see James Knowlson and John Pilling, *Frescoes of the Skull: The Later Prose and Drama of Samuel Beckett* (New York: Grove, 1980), 90.

In its treatment of aging and memory, *Krapp's Last Tape* has often been aligned with *Remembrance of Things Past,* and Krapp cast as a battered Hibernian Marcel.[14] But if Beckett was adapting the temporal thematics of Proust, he did so by way of a narrative strategy more like that of Dickens's *A Christmas Carol.* Scrooge, who is curiously like Krapp (aged, cranky, self-centered, intent on keeping the complications of human contact at bay), is allowed, like Krapp, to see strata of his life in rapid juxtaposition. But *A Christmas Carol* has what *Krapp* does not: an escape clause, whereby Scrooge can elude his fate. Seeing the future before it arrives gives Scrooge a choice of life lines. At the eleventh hour, he opts for the right one. Thus, though Dickens disrupts narrative, the disruption reaffirms narrative linearity. Krapp, a tragic version of Scrooge, is also keenly aware of time's linearity, so keenly aware that he literally hangs onto his tape recorder (as Beckett instructed Martin Held) before being dragged off by the Reaper. But, unlike *A Christmas Carol, Krapp's Last Tape* never abandons its equally insistent alinear polytemporality. If its final image is Krapp-69, its final voice is Krapp-39.

Again, a rough sketch of the single (yet most multiple) Krapp can be found in *Eleutheria's* curious identification and disjuncture of the old and young Kraps.[15] Both plays in this regard reflect a narratricidal need to undo the masterplot of death and procreation. From internal evidence, it is clear that, by the time he wrote *Eleutheria,* Beckett had

---

[14]Abetting this alignment is the final scene of *Remembrance,* when Marcel returns as an old man, older than the Marcel who writes. The importance of Proust in *Krapp* was first developed in Arthur Oberg's "*Krapp's Last Tape* and the Proustian Vision," *Modern Drama* 9 (1966): 333–338. This essay has been brought together with Rosette Lamont's "Krapp, Anti-Proust" in Knowlson, *Samuel Beckett: Krapp's Last Tape,* 151–173.

[15]A number of touches suggest that father and son, for all their differences, somehow share an identity. We do not hear Victor speak until his father is dead. Mme Krap calls her husband "Victor" at one point ("Victor?" M. Krap replies, "Je ne m'appelle pas Victor [I'm not Victor]" [El, 58/54]), and she refers to both of them as "crapule" (El, 31/19, 59/54) ("Moi aussi? [Me too?]" asks M. Krap [El, 59/55]). In Act II, before Mme Meck informs Victor of his father's death, she says, "Vous êtes mort [You are dead]" (El, 79/75). Both men are writers; both are absorbed by the question of the viability of suicide; both are equally incomprehensible to Victor's fiancée, Olga Skunk; and both share a similar distance from the other characters. Indeed, Victor and Henri seem characters from another genre who find themselves by some unaccountable accident in a farce.

come to see the expectations of narrative form as embedded in the model of lineage—the begat model of descent from father to son (see Chapter 1). This embeddedness is markedly developed in the role of the Glazier, the play's conservative internal critic, who arrives on the scene equipped not only with the tools appropriate to his trade but with a son as well.[16] Apprenticed to his father, Michel obediently takes orders in ritual preparation for his eventual promotion to the adult model awaiting him (on the job, his father admonishes his son to address him as "Monsieur," though on break he is permitted to call him "Papa"). Together as they work, by paternal command, father and son sing a rousing hymn to the progress of the nation:

La France est belle
Ses destins sont bénis,
Vivons pour elle,
Vivons unis.
Passons les monts, pa . . .
Beautiful is France,
Her destinies are blessed,
As one we advance,
As hers we live best.
Over the mountains, o———
(El, 90/89–90)

Out of this matrix of self-perpetuation and the ideal of productive onwardness come, quite naturally, the Glazier's exhortations to Victor regarding his appropriate narrative course:

Tout sacrifier, à l'idée fixe, au sacerdoce! Là alors vous commencez à vivre. . . . Vous êtes le pauvre jeune homme, l'héroïque jeune homme. On vous voit crevant comme un chien à trente ans, à trente-

---

[16]Further expression of the power of the reproductive drive is figured in Dr. André Piouk. Dr. Piouk's solution to the problem of humanity, to which he has given extensive thought, is universal extermination. His plan includes the execution of all women guilty of childbirth and the promulgation of homosexuality ("et en donnerais moi-même l'exemple [and myself set the example]" [El, 50/43]). But it is revealed early in the play that Dr. Piouk, who has just married Mme Krap's sister, is intent on producing his own child ("pour qu'il reçoive le flambeau de mes mains [that it should receive the torch from my hands]" [El, 51/44]). Throughout Acts II and III, the randy doctor is in hot pursuit of the beautiful Olga Skunk.

trois ans, vidé par vos labeurs, par vos découvertes, rongé par le radium, terrassé par les veilles, par les privations, mort en mission,
fusillé par Franco, fusillé par Staline.

To sacrifice everything, to the *idée fixe*, to the priesthood! At that
point you begin to live. . . . You are the poor young man, the heroic
young man. You are seen croaking like a dog at thirty, at thirty-three,
drained by your labors, by your discoveries, eaten away by radium,
laid low by sleepless nights, by the privations, dead on mission, shot
by Franco, shot by Stalin. (El, 89/87–88)

Correspondingly, Victor's dramatically unsatisfying nonpattern
of anarratological movement, his oozing, is of a piece with his non-
relation to the paternal home. Both belong to the narratricidal matrix. As such, they do not arise from oedipal strife but rather displace
it. As I argued in Chapter 1, patricide and its symbolic tokens are an
integral part of the lineal masterplot. By contrast, Victor's departure
from home two years before, though it is treated as an affront by
everyone except his father, is not meant as one. It is, rather, an
unraveling of relationship. Appalled, the Glazier has his own son
solemnly swear that he will not grow up to be like Victor ("Tu ne
seras pas comme ça quand tu seras grand, dis, Michel? . . . Oh non,
papa" [El, 86/84]).

By seeking to kill off the narrative masterplot, Victor seeks somehow to step outside of time. Forced to speak on threat of torture,
Victor says that what he would really like is to be dead and to know
it at the same time. Suicide is not an option because if he were
actually dead he wouldn't know it. This is the one thing he has
against death. "Je veux jouir de ma mort. C'est là la liberté: se voir
mort [I want to squeeze pleasure out of my death. That's where
freedom lies: seeing oneself dead]" (El, 149/166). Later, he says that
viewing his father's dead body convinced him beyond doubt that
this was an impossibility. "On ne peut pas se voir mort. C'est du
théâtre [One cannot see oneself dead. It's theatrics]" (El, 150/168).[17]

---

[17]This impossible idea haunted Beckett into his old age, emerging in the last words of
his late prose text *Ill Seen Ill Said:* "Farewell to farewell. Then in that perfect dark foreknell
darling sound pip for end begun. First last moment. Grant only enough remain to devour

Something like seeing oneself dead may well have been the object of Beckett's representations of aging and death which began in the 1940s. They were a way of being through with it all before it is finished, of standing both within and outside of the finishing of it. From this perspective, compressing the story of father and son into the life of a single figure, then interleaving its temporal strata so that the interplay of contrasts almost dominates the play's effect, made *Krapp's Last Tape* Beckett's closest approach to date to this seemingly impossible combination. Viewing *Krapp*, we experience time as an arrow and, at the same time, experience it as a medley of tiny epochs of time in an intricate nonlinear array.

The displacement of the oedipal masterplot which this redistribution of time entails is also reflected in the way Krapp-39 on the jetty before the stormy Irish Sea gives way to an idyll of lovers adrift on a still pond. They belong to two opposed temporal constructions, the one keyed to the ideal of onwardness, the other to stasis. The abrupt passage from one to the other provides the most energetic moment of *Krapp's Last Tape*. Here again are instances in which key elements of *Krapp* seem to grow from seeds sewn in *Eleutheria*. Krapp-39's stormy sea is foreshadowed at the beginning of the earlier play's third act as Victor talks in his sleep under the stress of a nightmare:

Non . . . non . . . trop haut . . . rochers . . . mon corps . . . papa . . . sois brave . . . brave petit . . . je suis brave . . . un brave petit . . . brave petit. *(Silence. Il s'agite. Plus fort:)* Brasse . . . profondeur cinq brasses . . . à marée basse . . . mer basse . . . profonde . . . profonde, onde profonde. *(Silence. Entre le Vitrier. Il va vers le lit.)* Là les yeux . . . mille navires . . . les tours . . . circoncises . . . feu . . . feu . . . *(Silence.)*

No—no—too high—rocks—my body—papa—be brave—good little boy—I am brave—a good little boy—good little boy. (A silence. He tosses and turns. Louder) Fathom—full fathom five—at low tide—low water—deep—deep—deep surge. (Silence. Enter the Glazier. He

all. Moment by glutton moment. Sky earth the whole kit and boodle. Not another crumb of carrion left. Lick chops and basta. No. One moment more. One last. Grace to breathe that void. Know happiness" (ISIS, 59).

goes toward the bed) There the eyes—a thousand ships—the
towers—circumcised—fire—fire. (A silence) (El, 119/125)[18]

In Victor's dreaming, Beckett amplifies the associations of male heroic endeavor by stressing the roughness of a sea full of rocks and
big waves, then binds these associations with heroic narrative by
annexing the epic text of the *Iliad* (filtered through Marlowe): "a
thousand ships—the towers—circumcised—fire—fire." In these few
words, Beckett highlights the epic setting out upon the sea and
makes Marlowe's "topless towers of Ilium" even more emphatically
phallic as "circumcised" towers.

Eleven years later, when Krapp-69 stumbles on Krapp-39's account of the "memorable equinox" in March, this whole complex
of associations is recollected in a striking reinvention:

at the end of the jetty, in the howling wind, never to be forgotten,
when suddenly I saw the whole thing. The vision at last. . . . great
granite rocks the foam flying up in the light of the lighthouse and the
wind-gauge spinning like a propeller, . . . unshatterable association
until my dissolution of storm and night with the light of the understanding and the fire (CSPL, 60)

The oozing protagonist of *Eleutheria*, fearful of the paternal masterplot, is replaced at this point by a hero of whom the Glazier might
have been proud. The image of fire which, in the earlier sequence,
was mechanically tacked on in what seems a separate dream sequence is here closely bound up in a single coherent tableau with
images of wind, waves, and rocks. The whole complex is dominated
by the phallic tower of the lighthouse. This figural endorsement of
male heroism marks Krapp-39's personal commitment to the manly

[18]Brodsky's "good little boy," though it works idiomatically for "brave petit," sacrifices
the exhortation to be a man which is contained in "brave boy." This latter construction
is congruent with Beckett's late version of the same tableau in *Company* (discussed in
Chapter 1) where "the loved trusted face" of his father beckons the child to jump into
the sea: "Be a brave boy" (C, 180). Brodsky has also freely evoked Ariel's song on the
presumed death of Ferdinand's father in *The Tempest*—"Full fathom five thy father lies"
(I.ii.396)—in his translation of "profondeur cinq brasses." Whether Beckett would have
done so is very much open to question, but that the death of his father would have
provoked Victor's nightmare seems quite plausible.

linear saga of onwardness, a life dedicated to his "work" with its requisite sacrifice of happiness (also a necessary part of the heroic model).[19] The other significant water passage in *Eleutheria* occurs near the end of Act I as M. and Mme Krap reminisce about her attempts to abort Victor and their decision to keep him. "Nous étions sur l'eau," Henri recalls. "Je ne ramais plus. L'onde nous berçait. *(Pause.)* Lui aussi, l'onde le berçait. *(Pause.)* Tu es sûre qu'il est de moi? [We were on the water. . . . I was no longer rowing. The waves rocked us. (Pause) He too was rocked by the waves. (Pause) You are sure that he is mine?]" (El, 62/58). This fragmentary passage featuring love on calm waters, together with the gentle rocking of Victor still in the womb, was stunningly reconfigured in *Krapp's Last Tape:*

—upper lake, with the punt, bathed off the bank, then pushed out into the stream and drifted. She lay stretched out on the floorboards with her hands under her head and her eyes closed. Sun blazing down, bit of a breeze, water nice and lively. I noticed a scratch on her thigh and asked her how she came by it. Picking gooseberries, she said. I said again I thought it was hopeless and no good going on and she agreed, without opening her eyes. [*Pause.*] I asked her to look at me and after a few moments—[*Pause.*]—after a few moments she did, but the eyes just slits, because of the glare. I bent over her to get them in the shadow and they opened. [*Pause. Low.*] Let me in. [*Pause.*] We drifted in among the flags and stuck. The way they went down, sighing, before the stem! [*Pause.*] I lay down across her with my face in her breasts and my hand on her. We lay there without moving. But under us all moved, and moved us, gently, up and down, and from side to side. (CSPL, 61)

As in the stratification of Krap(p)s, the pairing of these two sets of passages is at once eerily balanced yet intricately reworked. The character of their reworking brings out not simply Beckett's far more austere sense of dramatic compression but a much more complex

---

[19]The linkage of a specifically narrative enterprise with this collection of images was made explicit in an earlier version of the text: "unshatterable association till my dying day of *story* and night with the light of understanding and . . ." (emphasis mine; cited in Bair, *Samuel Beckett,* 351).

vision. In the earlier play the linear heroic is disowned throughout, either made into a nightmare or given affirmative voice by a character wholly other than Henri and Victor, such as the Glazier. In the later play, the linear heroic is absorbed into the character, Krapp, and staged through his voice at thirty-nine. For Krapp-39, the vision of the tower amid the rocks and stormy sea is the foundation point for his new sense of self. Conversely, the moment of erotic love on calm waters which Henri Krap recalls fondly, if briefly, during his final hours on earth becomes the wholly absorbing moment for Krapp-69. Where the passage in *Eleutheria* is brief and threaded with farce,[20] the later passage is an extended idyll of extraordinary beauty.

Two contrasting moments, widely separated in *Eleutheria*, are expanded in *Krapp* to the point where their opposition virtually dominates the play. The economy of the later play is such that the two kinds of water are placed literally side-by-side, the one setting off the other in one of drama's most abrupt transitions:

> unshatterable association until my dissolution of storm and night with the light of the understanding and the fire—[Krapp *curses louder, switches off, winds tape forward, switches on again*]—my face in her breasts and my hand on her. We lay there without moving. But under us all moved, and moved us, gently, up and down, and from side to side. (CSPL, 60)

In *Krapp's Last Tape*, calm overwhelms storm, enacting in the process the abandonment of oedipal linearity in narrative which Beckett had accomplished over the preceding ten years. The progressive mystique of onwardness played out in the words of Krapp-39 at once gives way to and is absorbed by an idyllic art, going nowhere in particular: "gently, up and down, and from side to side."

This imagistic and emotional movement of the play into a nonprogressive stasis works in close harmony with the conversion of linear time into a medley of tiny epochs, which I discussed above. Yet what is to prevent one from arguing that this whole movement

---

[20]In answer to M. Krap's question, Mme Krap says she is 70 percent sure that Victor is his child. There is also erotic by-play regarding Henri's "knife," which I have suppressed here in the interest of focus.

of the play, together with its attempted escape from linear time, is simply towed in the wake of Krapp's regressive symptomatology? Critics have often been hard on Krapp, reading his fate as a cautionary tale about masturbatory self-absorption. Krapp is "self-centered" and so fails at love.[21] He is a "possessive" and "narcissistic spirit," seeking a "nourishment of the selfish ego."[22] He is "psychologically maladaptive"—"just pre-mirror stage."[23] Though such readings usually point to the love that Krapp has abandoned as the road he should have taken, we may plausibly see the final sequence itself not as a break from this maladaptive narcissism but as a continuation of it. Though he repudiates the windy and complacent rhetoric of onwardness which characterized his voice thirty years earlier, Krapp turns to the past with a focus so acute it seems to seek a point before the life he lived. The power of the love to which Krapp had said farewell is figured as the possibility of reentry ("Let me in") and of union in a place of gentle amniotic motion: "my face in her breasts and my hand on her. We lay there without moving. But under us all moved, and moved us, gently, up and down, and from side to side." These are the only lines that are repeated three times in the play and they express very powerfully the emotional magnet of an end to toil and uncertainty not too different from the one offered by Old Nick, who stands invisibly behind Krapp's left shoulder.[24]

Life in the womb—"the only endurable, just endurable, period of my enormous history" as Molloy calls it (TN, 18)—is a powerful

---

[21]Henning, *Beckett's Critical Complicity*, 153.

[22]Jon Erickson, "Self-Objectification and Preservation in Beckett's *Krapp's Last Tape*," in *The World of Samuel Beckett*, ed. Joseph H. Smith (Baltimore: Johns Hopkins University Press, 1991), 190–191.

[23]Debra Malina, "Whom Else: Gendered Consciousness and Wholeness in *Krapp's Last Tape* and *Rockaby*," *Modern Drama* 35 (1992): 397.

[24]In the German versions of *Krapp* directed by Beckett, Krapp darted two separate looks over his left shoulder. Beckett told Martin Held that "Old Nick's there. Death is standing behind him and unconsciously he's looking for it" (Knowlson, "*Krapp's Last Tape:* The Evolution of a Play," 54–55).

draw felt widely in Beckett's oeuvre. Victor Krap, who was rocked in the womb as his parents rocked gently on the waves, curls up on his bed at the end of *Eleutheria*. If Beckett's art developed in the eleven years since *Eleutheria*, did it work out of, or more deeply into, this obsession? Is the gradually perfected narratricidal beauty of Beckett's art governed, in the last analysis, by a yearning for an impossible return? This question marks a good point to move to one more element of *Eleutheria* reworked in *Krapp's Last Tape*.

SCRIPT INTO SCORE

Late in Act I, we learn that Henri Krap loves music, and in Act III we learn that his son actually makes a kind of music. Jacques, the Valet, reveals that the explanation for Victor's behavior which the Glazier has been trying to pry out of him was granted freely to the servants on the day before. Clear at the time, it is not something that Jacques can render in his own words ("Ce n'est pas une chose qu'on peut raconter"). It was, he says, "un peu comme la musique [a little like music]." The Glazier is outraged: "La musique! . . . Que de crimes! . . . Ah, je l'entends, votre musique. Vous étiez tous saouls naturellement [Music! . . . How many crimes! . . . Ah, I hear it, your music. You were all plastered, naturally" (El, 126/133–134). Climbing on stage some moments later, Spectateur finds it insufferable that this key to the entire drama has been kept offstage ("dans les coulisses" [El, 134/144]).

In the later play, too, there is music kept in the wings. Krapp-39, listening to the silence, speaks of how old Miss McGlome would always sing "songs of her girlhood" at this hour of the night. "Shall I sing when I am her age, if I ever am?" he asks and answers: 'No [*Pause.*] Did I sing as a boy? No. [*Pause.*] Did I ever sing? No" (CSPL, 58).[25] At thirty-nine, Krapp gives pride of place to melo-

---

[25]Shortly thereafter, in Beckett's original version, Krapp-69 bursts into *"quavering song"*: "Now the day is over . . . " (59). Later, Beckett found the dramatic irony of this song too flat-footed and dropped the singing, though not the passage on old Miss McGlome.

drama and cliché ("at the crest of the wave—or thereabouts," "the miracle that . . . the fire that set it alight"). At sixty-nine, he growls and croaks, an awkward and unmusical man, expelling hard pellets of sound. But over the course of its development, the play recovers an involuntary music of Krapp-39. What that earlier Krapp had "chiefly to record" was his memorable equinox, its fustian language now painful to the ears. When he came closest to speaking a prose "a little like music," he did so without knowing it, setting it aside as he set aside the love it memorialized. It is this musical prose that Krapp at sixty-nine seizes on. The earlier Krapp had described himself as "separating the grain from the husks" and then later asked, "The grain, now what I wonder do I mean by that" (CSPL, 57). Krapp-69, separating the grain from the husks, finds unerringly the genuine note.

However one conceives the older Krapp's state of mind in seizing this passage from his tapes—regret, tragic awareness, self-pity, regressive yearning for an impossible return—it is no less the case that he has at the same time found the indisputably musical language of his earlier self. In doing so, he serves not only his own agenda but Beckett's as well, an agenda that both includes and surpasses Krapp's. Krapp, focused intently on one point in his life, craves an exact repetition of the words that bring him back to it. If we feel with Krapp, we at the same time enjoy a music that is compounded from the words he focuses on, enhanced and made more beautifully complex by being repeated at varying lengths. So the answer to the question above is No. The play is not towed in the wake of a regressive narcissism, but includes that state of mind in a production that stays fully in the present.

Little wonder that Beckett took such care with the play. It celebrates itself, and not simply in its final passages. Throughout the play, the rasping voice and ungainly gestures of the aged Krapp counterpoint the much more robust notes of Krapp-39. Listening closer still, one can find an additional complexity of rhythmic interest within these two voices. In an early study of Beckett's theater, Alec Reid shows clearly how three "distinct sound-patterns"— narrative, lyrical, and sardonic—play off against each other in the

lines of Krapp-39.[26] Reid's enduringly useful short study is keyed to
George Devine's exhortation to think of "a Beckett play . . . as something like a musical score wherein the 'notes,' the sights, the sounds,
the pauses, have their own special inter-related rhythms, and out of
their composition comes the dramatic impact."[27]

Eleutheria shows many signs that Beckett had some idea of trying
to compose a script that was at the same time a score. To this apparent end, he deployed the devices of interruption, stychomythia, con-
versational breakdown, and symmetries between the acts.[28] But over
the course of this long and densely populated play, this aspect of its
effects dissipates. The theory and practice of a drama that works like
music and a script that works as a score are still at a rudimentary
stage of development in *Eleutheria*. In *Krapp,* by contrast, the deployment of a tape recorder was a masterstroke in the art of interruption, allowing extraordinary flexibility in the making of a script
into a score. The machine not only permitted the interplay of two
voices, old and young but, in the inevitable pauses that come with
taping, produced still other rhythms quite different from those of
ordinary speech.

> Everything there, everything on this old muckball, all the light and
> dark and famine and feasting of . . .
> > [*hesitates*] . . .
> the ages! [*in a shout.*] Yes!
> > [*Pause.*]
> Let that go! Jesus! Take his mind off his homework! Jesus!
> > [*Pause.*
> *Weary.*] Ah well, maybe he was right. [*Pause.*] Maybe he was right.

---

[26]Alec Reid, *All I Can Manage, More Than I Could: An Approach to the Plays of Samuel Beckett* (Dublin: Dolmen Press, 1968), 21–24.

[27]Quoted in Reid, *All I Can Manage,* 35.

[28]Mme Krap visits Victor's room in Act I; Victor visits the Krap drawing room in Act II. At the beginning of Act II the Glazier walks in holding Victor's shoe; at the beginning of Act III, Jacques, the Valet, walks in with Victor's shoe. Each act ends with a kiss between males: Act I, Henri Krap kissed by Jacques; Act II, the Glazier by his son; Act III, Victor by the Glazier (on the hand).

> [*Broods. Realizes. Switches off. Consults*
> *envelope.*]
> Pah! [*Crumples it and throws it away.*
> *Broods. Switches on.*]
> Nothing to say, not a squeak. What's a year now? The sour cud and
> the iron stool.
> [*Pause.*]
> Revelled in the word spool.
> [*With relish.*]
> Spooool! (CSPL, 62)

SEPARATING THE GRAIN FROM THE HUSKS

Early in the 1950s, probably no later than 1952, *Eleutheria* had fallen
so far in Beckett's opinion that he no longer considered it viable
either for production or publication.[29] If he agreed in his very last
years to allow his long-time American publisher, Barney Rosset, the
right of publication, there is no indication even in the accounts favorable to Rosset that Beckett was at all enthusiastic about the prospect. At that stage, he was doubtless motivated by generosity and
loyalty to a good friend in trouble.[30]

---

[29]In the late forties, Beckett had made efforts through his agent to interest publishers
in the play, and it was both *Eleutheria* and *En attendant Godot* that Suzanne Deschevaux-
Dumesnil left with Roger Blin in the spring of 1950. That Blin chose to produce *Godot*
seems finally to have been dictated by the fact that, with only four characters, barely any
stage decor, and no costuming expense, it was a cheaper work to do. The rest is history.
(See Bair, *Samuel Beckett*, 403; S. E. Gontarski, "Introduction," *Eleuthéria*, x–xi). Still, the
impending publication of *Eleutheria* was announced, along with that of *L'innommable,* in
Minuit's first editions of *Molloy* and *Malone meurt,* 1951 and early 1952, respectively. As
L'innommable appeared on schedule in the following year, one can assume that, by 1952
at the latest, Beckett had asked Jérôme Lindon to withhold *Eleutheria* from publication.
In a conversation with me, Monsieur Lindon has affirmed that Beckett's request came
almost immediately after the play was given to him in 1951.

[30]Grove Press was founded by Rosset in the early 1950s and brought out the first
English edition of *Waiting for Godot* in 1954, at least two years before there was any
significant American market for Beckett's work. In 1985, Grove was purchased by Ann
Getty. The name of the press was changed to Grove Weidenfeld, and in the following year
Rosset was let go. It was shortly thereafter, in April 1986, that, according to Rosset, Beckett

In 1952, with a production of *Godot* now in the works, Beckett must have had a strong sense of the vital difference he had achieved in his second play. In effect, *Godot* inverted the priorities of his theater. Where his first play is dominated by a figure of authority, however antiheroic, his second takes place in the vacuum left by that figure's departure. Whatever authority one attributes to Godot, the whole point about him, as legions of commentary have strained to reiterate, is that he is not there. Conversely, the music that is kept off-stage in *Eleutheria* pervades *Godot*. In consequence, *Godot* is not something, to use Jacques' swords, that can be recounted. It is a score for a strange new music: a duet for two voices, with Pozzo and Lucky *obligato*. And though, as I argued in Chapter 2, it is saturated with the vestiges of onwardness and the teleology of a resting place in some final point of Authority, these are all set to a music that spreads interest out causing us to forget just where it was we wanted to go.

In 1958, when Beckett started the "Magee Monologue" that became *Krapp's Last Tape,* he had written, in addition to *Godot, Fin de partie (Endgame),* the radio play *All That Fall,* a piece called *Rough for Theatre,* and two mimes. By that time, he had seen four of these pieces performed and had acquired a strong sense of his theater. So, when he picked up the name Krapp again in an intricate and deftly reelaborated set of recollections from *Eleutheria,* it was not to confer on the earlier play a dignity of status. Instead, he used one play to write out the other. By pushing off from *Eleutheria* in *Krapp,* Beckett consolidated his dramatic art. In place of the delicate reciprocity of exchange characteristic of works in Beckett's later oeuvre, the two plays combined to make an argument. McMillan and Fehsenfeld

---

gave him the typescript of *Eleutheria.* In this account, Beckett even began the task of translation, only to give up shortly afterward. Beckett then gave Rosset something new, his last major work, *Stirrings Still,* which Rosset published under the Blue Moon imprint in 1988. Rosset, however, has never conceded that the gift of *Stirrings Still* canceled out the permission to publish *Eleutheria* (Matthew Flamm, "The Godot-Father II: Barney Plugs Beckett," *New York Observer,* October 3, 1994: 1, 20). For a fuller account of this episode of publishing history from a point of view favorable to Rosset, see the introductory material by Martin Garbus and S. E. Gontarski in the Foxrock edition of *Eleuthéria* (iii–xxii). For a different perspective, see Jérôme Lindon's *Avertissement* to the Minuit edition (7–11).

have called *Eleutheria* "Beckett's own full statement on dramatic method."[31] But it turned out not to be a full statement. Its very lack of fullness was, in fact, a symptom of its problem. An often brilliantly staged discussion in progress, it failed to arrive at a formal response to Victor's, and Beckett's, practical dilemma. In particular, it did not realize its dramatic potentiality for something "like music" which Beckett had begun energetically to realize in *Godot* and *Endgame* and which he rendered in its most concentrated form to that date in *Krapp's Last Tape*.

The trajectory of *Eleutheria* is toward the loss of form altogether. As Spectateur realizes after he has climbed on stage, there is something strangely enervating about the atmosphere on that side of the pit (El, 132/142). At one point, the characters even come to a halt, "*comme envahi par un sentiment de fatigue et de fatuité* [as if overrun with a feeling of fatigue and fatuity]" (El, 139/153). Even the Glazier, who stands for the dignity of narrative and lineal descent, finds his best efforts undermined. At the end of Act II, he asks his son if he is happy and discovers that, no, his son is not happy. As if the gravitational pull of Victor Krap has already drawn him out of the orbit of his father, Michel declares to the Glazier's surprise that what he likes best is lying in bed like Victor (El, 114/122). In the final act, we learn that Michel has stayed home in bed that day. And by the end of the play, the Glazier himself has fallen prey to Victor's irresistible spirit of entropy; he abandons his job and leaves his tools with Victor. The final image is that of Victor alone on his bed with his back to the audience.

One irony of this development is that, for all its raggedness and enormous clutter, together with its stiff theoretical resistance to narrative, *Eleutheria* is not only governed by a narrative line but arrives at narrative finality. It is as if Beckett had sought to expose that hidden end point past all digression, diversion, or arabesque which many theorists have argued narrative always wants to find.[32] From

---

[31]McMillan and Fehsenfeld, *Beckett in the Theatre*, 29–30.

[32]See Jean-Paul Sartre, *La nausée* (Paris: Gallimard, 1938), trans. Lloyd Alexander, as *Nausea* (Norfolk, Conn.: New Directions, 1969) and *Qu'est-ce que la littérature?* (Paris;

the start of the play, that end point is always anticipated in Victor's presence. Even in Act I, when Victor has no lines and no interaction with the other characters, he is still present on the stage, a ghostly anticipation of the play's conclusion. In this way, Beckett dramatized Derrida's equation of art with excrement. More thoroughly than Alfred Jarry's *Ubu roi*, to which it owes much, the play is written "au genre merde." In its final resting place at the end of Act III, the play has achieved an art that is "matter without life," falling and collapsing upon itself. It is, in short, a play in which Krap is Victor. But in this, its success, must have lain the failure of *Eleutheria* for Beckett. To take a line from Victor's description of his life, it is a play devoured by its liberty ("mangée par sa liberté" (El, 146/162). Over this triumph of the formless looms the threat of sentimentalism and self-pity, which is all one has in the kingdom of shit. How Beckett must have cringed in later years at Victor's self-righteousness: "Ma vie sera longue et horrible. *(Pause.)* Mais moins horrible que la vôtre [My life will be long and horrible. (Pause) But less horrible than yours]" (El, 162/184). He must have cringed, too, at his final stage direction: ". . . *il se couche, le maigre dos tourné à l'humanité* [he gets into bed, his scrawny back turned on mankind]" (167/191).[33]

Gallimard, 1947); trans. Bernard Frechtman *What is Literature?* (New York: Harper, 1965); Frank Kermode, *The Sense of an Ending: Studies in the Theory of Fiction* (London: Oxford University Press, 1976); Roland Barthes, "Introduction à l'analyse structurale des recits," *Communications* 8 (1966): 1–27. "Introduction to the Structural Analysis of Narratives," trans. S. Heath in *Image-Music-Text* (New York: Hill and Wang, 1977), 29–124. In a response to these and other theorists of narrative, D. A. Miller, in *Narrative and Its Discontents: Problems of Closure in the Traditional Novel* (Princeton: Princeton University Press, 1981), challenges the notion of closure's dominion. He does this by shifting attention from narrative to the narratable, which, in his words, "inherently lacks finality" (xi). Yet Miller does acknowledge the continual effort to get to the end, to bring to a close, which seems to accompany narrative, however frustrated it may be by activity "possible only within a logic of insufficiency, disequilibrium, and deferral" (265). Shortly after Miller's study, Peter Brooks published *Reading for the Plot: Design and Intention in Narrative* (New York: Knopf, 1984), in which he developed an "erotics" of narrative which complicates Miller's model but which also, following Sigmund Freud's *Beyond the Pleasure Principle,* asserts the final governance of the death instinct.

[33]In 1986, Beckett permitted publication of sizable passages from *Eleutheria* in a special Samuel Beckett issue of *Revue d'esthetique*. These included the conclusions of both the first and second acts. But neither the conclusion of Act III nor any of Victor's moralizing

In the same way, Krapp-69 cringed at Krapp-39. Doubtless, Beckett's play about rereading arose in part from his own experience of rereading. In all productions of *Krapp's Last Tape*, Beckett strictly admonished, there was to be no sentimentalism, a state of mind entirely relegated to his creature ("Scalded the eyes out of me reading *Effie* again, a page a day, with tears again" [CSPL, 62]). The distance that failed in *Eleutheria* was firmly established in *Krapp*. Yet it was a distance in the service of a greater intimacy, achieved when Beckett absorbed the story of Krapp into the music of Beckett. Playing the Wilde beast of earnestness, Beckett engendered life out of crap. Material that has everything to do with death, dying, collapse, the loss of form was set to music in *Krapp*. Like the inimitable and highly personal music of Victor which so delights the servants, it was a music never heard before, because it was a music that could come from only one person.[34]

How successful was Beckett in his autographical project? It is, of course, impossible to say. Referring to *The Unnamable* many years later, he told André Bernold: "It has become completely foreign to me. I don't know this author [Ça m'est devenu complètement étranger. Je ne connais pas cet auteur]."[35] But the decade that followed *The Unnamable* was, for Beckett, a period of intense reflection on his art. In its extraordinary compression and musicality, *Krapp's Last Tape* consolidates the view that emerged from that reflection. It was a view in which music, both as a formal principal and an idea, played a much more central role than it had played in the work of earlier decades.[36]

---

rhetoric in Act III is among them ("*Eleutheria:* Extrait du manuscrit inédit," *Revue d'esthetique*, n.s. [1986]: 111–134).

[34]Beckett's most focused reflexive treatment of the relations of music and verbal material is found in the two radio plays *Words and Music* and *Cascando*, which followed within four years of *Krapp's Last Tape* (1961 and 1962, respectively). With the discord of Words and Music which concludes the first of these, and the harmony of Voice and Music which concludes the second, the two plays recapitulate the movement from *Eleutheria* to *Krapp* which I have sought to demonstrate in this chapter.

[35]Quoted in André Bernold, *L'amitié de Beckett* (Paris: Hermann, 1992), 92.

[36]In his remarkable memoir, André Bernold also reports that Beckett, asked what he would have done had he not been a writer, replied that he would have listened to music (ibid., 93).

As for *Eleutheria*, it is indeed a remarkable play, hardly the dismissible text that some have made it out to be.[37] As McMillan and Fehsenfeld have pointed out, its intertextual connections are rich and meaningful.[38] Beckett's ferocious wit crackles on almost every page. And for all its length and complication and clutter, there are the signs everywhere of the author's concentrated attention on his material. All of which makes Beckett's suppression of the play even more significant. It shows how much was at stake for him in the fashioning of his oeuvre. At one point in *Eleutheria*, Spectateur checks the program to see who wrote this dud ("ce navet"): "Béquet, Béquet," he exclaims, "ça doit être un juif groenlandais mâtiné d'Auvergnat [that's got to be a Jew from Greenland crossed with an Auvergnat]" (El, 136/148). I like to think that when he brought Krap back to life, the extra "p" Beckett added to the end of the name chimed with the extra "t" in his own name, lost and unsounded in *Eleutheria*.

---

[37]Bair, *Samuel Beckett*, 363.

[38]McMillan and Fehsenfeld, *Beckett in the Theatre*, 29–45.

FIVE

ORIGINAL MUD

others knowing nothing of my beginnings save what they could glean
by hearsay or in public records nothing of my beginnings in life
—*How It Is*

Beckett consolidated his autographical project when he released his
art from the teleology of narrative. This key element in his evolving
strategy abetted the inclination to turn attention from the end, narrative's yet-to-be-revealed, to the autograph as it unfolds. In Beckett's writing, this change did not happen all at once. His attack on
narrative began with his first works, was developed with high sophis-
tication in the prose of the 1940s, and reached one culmination in
the trilogy. But, as I noted at the end of Chapter 1, if there were two
giant steps he took, the first was the writing of *Godot* in the fall of
1948. Composed within months of completing *Malone Dies (Malone
meurt)*—a text that had concluded with the death of a narrator trying desperately to kill the children spawned by his narrative—*Godot*
was the first successful application of the art I have sought to encap-
sulate in my discussion of *Krapp's Last Tape*. The second giant step
was the writing of *Texts for Nothing (Textes pour rien)* in 1950–51
after the completion of *The Unnamable (L'innommable)*.

It was at these points, the one in drama and the other in prose
fiction, that Beckett took the final steps in easing the deep structure
of his work from the dominion of narrative. Beckett's second major
prose work after the trilogy, *How It Is* (composed from 1958–1960
as *Comment c'est*), despite its account of a universal journey in the

87

mud, confirms and continues the postnarrative art of the *Texts*. The two works have been kept separate in the criticism of Beckett but were in fact companion pieces in the same intimate way that all of Beckett's mature work is companionable. Despite bleak comments about the future of his art which he made to Israel Shenker in the mid-fifties, Beckett did not evacuate from the *Texts* to be born again with *How It Is,* except insofar as being born again was an integral part of the formal artistic process in both works. At the same time, these works developed an invigorated (and complementary) thematics of the mystery of origins, including their own.

BEGINNING AGAIN

From its publication, *Texts for Nothing* has suffered from comparative neglect. One of the orphans in Beckett's oeuvre, it has been adopted by few critics, and its individual texts are rarely anthologized.[1] Yet its language and thematics are quite close to those of the volume that precedes it. The opening lines of the *Texts* are a wry continuation of the last lines of *The Unnamable:*

> . . . perhaps they have carried me to the threshold of my story, before the door that opens on my story, that would surprise me, if it opens, it will be I, it will be the silence, where I am, I don't know, I'll never know, in the silence you don't know, you must go on, I can't go on, I'll go on. (TN, 414)

> Suddenly, no, at last, long last, I couldn't anymore, I couldn't go on. Someone said, You can't stay here. I couldn't stay there and I couldn't go on. (STN, 75)

---

[1] John Pilling and P. J. Murphy are among the rare critics who have promoted the *Texts*, each devoting full chapters to make up for this neglect. Theirs are the only text-by-text analyses of this work which I know of. See James Knowlson and John Pilling, *Frescoes of the Skull: The Later Prose and Drama of Samuel Beckett* (New York: Grove, 1980), 41–60; and P. J. Murphy, *Reconstructing Beckett: Language for Being in Samuel Beckett's Fiction* (Toronto: University of Toronto Press, 1990), 34–52. Among its rare republications are those of Texts 4, 8, and 13 in *Monologues de minuit,* ed. Ruby Cohn and Lily Parker (New York: Macmillan, 1965), 117–132.

But in these opening words, Beckett is again recollecting by inventing and, in this instance, continuing by discontinuing. *Texts* starts
with a stop ("I couldn't move any more") and then continues
throughout its sixty pages in a constancy of stopped starts:

> How can I go on, I shouldn't have begun, no, I had to begin. Some-
> one said, perhaps the same, What possessed you to come? I could
> have stayed in my den, snug and dry, I couldn't. My den, I'll describe
> it, no, I can't. It's simple, I can do nothing any more, that's what you
> think. I say to the body, Up with you now, and I can feel it struggling,
> like an old hack foundered in the street, struggling no more, strug-
> gling again, till it gives up. (STN, 75)

It is more than likely that it is not the difficulty of the *Texts*—the
uncertainty and drift of its prose—but this absolute frustration of
structural "onwardness" which accounts for the neglect into which
this beautiful work has fallen. The prose of *The Unnamable* (comparable to that of the *Texts*) culminates the steady, inexorable progress
of the trilogy, a progress that contextualizes its obscurity and, in so
doing, to a certain extent naturalizes it. In other words, even as he
set out in the 1940s on his deconstruction of the Victorian trope of
onwardness, Beckett reinvigorated the trope through the narrative
structure of his prose work. *Watt, Mercier et Camier,* the *Nouvelles,*
and the trilogy, all conform to the quest structure, despite the mani-
fold incompetence of the questors. If the trilogy is not impeccably
linear, if it enacts a gradual progress of unraveling and disembodiment rather than the triumphant arrival at a goal, it nonetheless
collaborates in its progressive disembodiment with the linear orientation that the mind craves in narrative.

The power of that appeal is reflected in the abundance of linear,
end-oriented readings which have been laid over the Beckett oeuvre
since people began writing about him in the late fifties. In many of
these readings, *Texts for Nothing* marks a pause in the story of the
oeuvre. It has seemed a succession of misfires or last sputterings
from the trilogy, flung together in an aftertext marking the end of
what has been called Beckett's "great creative period" (1945–50).[2]

---

[2] "The thirteen *Textes pour rien* . . . which Beckett himself considers a failure, clearly
prolong the inquiry of *The Unnamable*" (Michael Robinson, *The Long Sonata of the Dead*

This failure of linear continuity, temporarily disrupting the oeuvre before its next major development, is matched by what appears to be the willful shredding of narrative linearity within the *Texts*. Gone is the sense of trajectory with its increasingly frantic delivery that bound *The Unnamable* together. Instead, from page to page we find shards of scene and place, little suggestions of voyages that never go anywhere—"To set out from Duggan's door, on a spring morning of rain and shine, not knowing if you'll ever get to evening, what's wrong with that?" (STN, 89)—and that serve only to draw attention to the absence of any overall pattern. Finally, to put the effect beyond all doubt, Beckett broke up the book into thirteen pieces with no clear indication at all as to why one text should follow another.

There have been valiant efforts to restore narrative order to the *Texts*,[3] but like the effort to make a story of its author's oeuvre, the enterprise is a mistake. Hugh Kenner aptly described the *Texts* as having its own original integrity. After it, Kenner notes, "the Text, the short work with no real subject but its own queer cohesion, is a recurrent mode for Beckett's imagination to explore."[4] But the form Beckett developed specifically for the *Texts* was not *sui generis*. Rather, in composing the *Texts*, he exchanged the narrative genre of the quest for the broad nonnarrative genre of the meditative personal essay. The latter extends out of Montaigne's *Essais* and includes a rich romantic tradition of associative lyrical meditations ranging from Rousseau's *Rêveries d'un promeneur solitaire* to Coleridge's Conversation Poems. Much of the ambience and imagery of the *Texts* echoes that of the meditations of the English Graveyard

[New York: Grove, 1969], 209). The phrase "great creative period" is used in *Samuel Beckett: His Works and His Critics*, ed. Raymond Federman and John Fletcher (Berkeley: University of California Press, 1970), 63.

[3]The very lack of sequence has been a challenge to some. The most ingenious reading of the structure of this work is by Paul West, who proposed that its thirteen installments correspond to the thirteen last days Beckett spent in the womb before his birth on Good Friday, April 13. See West, "Deciphering a Beckett Fiction on His Birthday," *Parnassus* 7 (1983–84): 319–322.

[4]Hugh Kenner, *A Reader's Guide to Samuel Beckett* (London: Thames and Hudson, 1973), 119.

Poets and motivated, no doubt, Beckett's arch allusion to Edward Young's *Night Thoughts* in Text 8: "the hour of night's young thoughts" (STN, 115). Note, especially, Young's language of twilight liminality:

> This is creation's melancholy vault,
> The vale funereal, the sad cypress gloom;
> The land of apparitions, empty shades!
> All, all on earth is shadow, . . .
>   This is the bud of being, this dim dawn,
> The twilight of our day, the vestibule.
>   (Night I, 116–123)

One can match Young's language and vaguely iambic dying fall with any number of twilight passages from the *Texts:*

> I hear the curlews, that means close of day, fall of night, for that's the way with curlews, silent all day, then crying when the darkness gathers, that's the way with those wild creatures and so short-lived, compared with me. (STN, 76–77)

> Theirs all these voices, like a rattling of chains in my head, rattling to me that I have a head. That's where the court sits this evening, in the depths of that vaulty night, . . . (STN, 98)

> Those evenings then, but what is this evening made of, this evening now that never ends, in whose shadows I'm alone, that's where I am, where I was then, where I've always been, . . . (STN, 129–130)

Yet just as Beckett resists as he recollects his own work, so he resists as he recollects the literary tradition. The *Texts* not only carries on from its generic roots but, in doing so, starts afresh. By appropriating the romantic tradition of the associative, incondite meditation, Beckett accentuates his difference. In the romantic tradition, the quality of being formally unreined is grounded in the confidence that the individual mind can generate, through the free exercise of its own powers, texts that would be at once beautiful and wise, coherent and deep. The very looseness of the form in this tradition was a promise of higher connectedness; its obscurity, an intimation of higher meaning. But in Beckett's hands, the "looseness" of the text augments the anxiety of relatedness and the despair of meaning.

> When I think, no, that won't work, when come those who knew me,
> perhaps even know me still, by sight of course, or by smell, it's as
> though, it's as if, come on, I don't know, I shouldn't have begun.
> (STN, 127)

In this way, Beckett used the tradition to dismantle the structure of
thought it rested in, a romantic metaphysics that, in the middle of
his own century, was still thoroughly ingrained in Western cultural
mythology.

Everywhere in this work, Beckett stands the platonic structure
of Western thought on its head. The very transcendence that his
predecessors celebrated is, in these meditations, an inescapable
plague, floating this voice in a kind of no-place.

> The graveyard, yes, it's there I'd return, this evening it's there, borne
> by my words, if I could get out of here, that is to say if I could say,
> There's a way out there, there's a way out somewhere, to know ex-
> actly where would be a mere matter of time, and patience, and se-
> quency of thought, and felicity of expression. But the body, to get
> there with, where's the body? (STN, 121)

In such a context, the graveyard becomes a nostalgic locale where
the price of admission was a body. For Young, the graveyard was a
place one passed through, coming out on the other side refined of
one's material being. In Beckett's text, it seems instead a longed-for
point of reentry. Where those in the romantic tradition could even,
if their power served them, by-pass the graveyard and visit the transcendent realm, riding "the viewless wings of poesy," here in the
Texts all is already "borne by" words, and one can only hope to hit
by chance on that "felicity of expression" which would land one in
the brute materiality of the grave.

Such at least seem to be the predominating thematics. But one
must be careful how one reads them. Here, for example, is how the
passage above goes on to conclude Text 9:

> It's a minor point, a minor point. And I have no doubts, I'd get there
> somehow, to the way out, sooner or later, if I could say, There's a
> way out there, there's a way out somewhere, the rest would come,
> the other words, sooner or later, and the power to get there, and the

way to get there, and pass out, and see the beauties of the skies, and
see the stars again.

The swerve in the last two clauses is superbly unexpected, its special
impact prepared for by the succession of syntactical impedances that
lead up to it. But what do these two clauses indicate? A nostalgia for
life, not death? Is there conscious and self-deflating sentimentality
in this calculated tremolo, these near clichés—"beauties of the skies,
and see the stars again" (note that the next text begins: "Give up")?
What does "pass out" mean in the clause immediately preceding?
(Can it mean pass out of "here" where he is currently stuck if it
follows "to get there"?) Does it mean to pass on up out of the grave,
to move backward through death into life? This is a figure that Beckett has used before, yet in what nonliteral sense can we interpret it?
How does it fit?

All of which is to say that what is so difficult about *Texts for
Nothing,* what readers have found so frustrating about it, is also
what is rather wonderful about it: its capacity continually to sprout
something new in its words, something that at once fits and doesn't
fit, the "same old murmur" yet still unexpected:

> I stay here, sitting, if I'm sitting, often I feel sitting, sometimes stand-
> ing, it's one or the other, or lying down, there's another possibility,
> often I feel lying down, it's one of the three, or kneeling. (STN, 93)

To put this in other words, one can discuss the thematics of this
text, as I have just done, but what "remains when the thematics is
exhausted," to use Derrida's words, is the action in the language:
Beckett's signature. Looked at in this way, the *Texts,* far from being
detritus from *The Unnamable,* cobbled together in a pseudo-text, is
arguably Beckett's first full and thoroughgoing deployment of an
aesthetic of recommencement. The seeds of this aesthetic are scat-
tered everywhere in the work before 1950, but what makes it show
so clearly in the *Texts* is Beckett's deliberate abandonment of the
very practice that had worked so well in the trilogy and given it so
much of its power: its masterful deployment of the quest. To save
his art, he had to dispose of what was perhaps the single most effective weapon in his arsenal. Beckett must have felt the power of the
quest structure while he was writing the trilogy, just as his public

continues to celebrate its power. It is the resonance of that power which has given the trilogy much of its "legitimacy" in the pantheon of great prose fiction and thrown the *Texts* into the shade.

"It's the end that gives meaning to words" (STN, 111), says the voice in Text 8. Though the trilogy is technically endless and though it abounds in narrative subversion, it nonetheless defines a progression—a movement toward an end—which makes, in retrospect, an arrow of meaning. This arrow organizes our perception of its structure and gives the various parts a kind of belonging. The arrow is sustained even in *The Unnamable*, where Mahood gives way to Worm and Worm to a medley of pronouns, and where the rhythm of speech becomes increasingly frenetic as the "end" approaches. It is this sense of direction which is missing in the *Texts* and which gives it its radical newness. In this new departure, the *un*-quest or absolute of nonnarrative—that is, the twelve gaps between the texts—is as important as the texts themselves. The importance of these gaps is at once ontological and metaphysical, for they represent that absence out of which something keeps miraculously coming: "I'm the clerk, I'm the scribe, at the hearings of what cause I know not" (STN, 95). As here at the start of Text 5, the gaps give fresh emphasis to the way words erupt, ever the same, yet always with bizarre strokes of difference. There is no end to this, only new beginnings. "Tender mercies," as Mouth says in *Not I*, "new every morning" (CSPL, 221–222, 223).

And how, the voice asks, "are the intervals filled between these apparitions? Do my keepers snatch a little rest and sleep before setting about me fresh, how would that be?" (STN, 101). And what, Moran asks in *Molloy*, "was God doing with himself before creation?" (TN, 167). Augustine was asked the same question long ago and replied that God was busy preparing Hell for people who asked such questions. Augustine's joke papers over one of the great theological mysteries. Beckett's absurd hypothesis about the intervals between the texts restores attention to the same mystery. Is there anything in that unthinkable space out of which all things come? How does one even begin to think about beginning?

AND AGAIN

The next major prose text Beckett published was written almost a decade after the *Texts*. First composed in French, *How It Is* was published in 1961 as *Comment c'est* (which in English means "how it is"). As critics almost immediately noted, "comment c'est" is a close homophonic pun on either "commencer" ("to begin") or "commencez" ("begin").[5] Because Beckett had published scarcely any prose at all since the *Texts*, the pun has given powerful encouragement to those who have wanted to see in it a declaration by the author that his creative powers had been reborn. A comparison of manuscripts from before 1951 with those after shows that Beckett was truly struggling to get going again in the fifties. If the novels of the trilogy fairly flowed, the work that followed was a mass of revisions. This view of the matter was partially confirmed by Beckett himself in an interview with Israel Shenker in 1956 when he said that the work from 1946 to 1950 came to him very quickly, but that after that there was nothing but disintegration: "The very last thing I wrote—'Textes pour rien'—was an attempt to get out of the attitude of disintegration, but it failed."[6] The view was still further reinforced by the publication of two short prose texts in the interim between these two long ones, the first titled *From an Abandoned Work* (1956); the second, an advance segment of *How It Is*, titled "From an Unabandoned Work" (1960). Add to this the extraordinary syntactical innovation of the prose in *How It Is*, together with its brief unpunctuated strophes, and the almost perfect and unprece-

---

[5] Others almost as quickly noted, and also resonant, are *commençais, commençait,* and *comme on sait.*

[6] Quoted in Israel Shenker, "Moody Man of Letters," *New York Times,* May 6, 1956, sec. 2: 3. There is no doubting the intensity of Beckett's concern about the *Texts*. In two earlier letters to Barney Rosset, Beckett had described it as "the grisly afterbirth of *L'innommable*" (quoted in Enoch Brater, *The Drama in the Text: Beckett's Late Fiction* [New York: Oxford, 1994], 9, 177n). But to express disappointment in what he had achieved was the rule, rather than the exception, in Beckett's life. The decision to publish makes another statement.

dented symmetricality of the book's three-part structure ("before Pim, with Pim, after Pim"), and there is little cause for wonder that many (this writer included) have seen in it not only a major new departure but a turning point in Beckett's art.

There are, however, problems with this argument. One problem is that, if prose production was difficult for Beckett during the fifties, those years saw nonetheless the vigorous creation of significant dramatic work, including *Endgame* (Beckett's favorite among his plays), *Krapp's Last Tape,* two mimes, and his first works in the genre of the radio play, beginning with his longest and to many his finest, *All That Fall,* and including *Embers.*

Another important consideration is the timing of the Shenker interview referred to above. It caught Beckett right at the publication of the *Texts* (in 1956 in the volume, *Nouvelles et textes pour rien*). It caught him, in other words, at a point of apparent completion. These points could be hard on Beckett. He had no gift for endings, which may have been what prolonged the prose project of the late forties, first to two books and then to a trilogy. As Hamm says: "I hesitate . . . to end" (En, 3). We should acknowledge, then, how deeply inflected were his remarks to Shenker by this repetition of an old trauma. Moreover, though he was speaking gloomily of the *Texts* as the end of the line, they had been, as I have argued above, as radical a departure as anything that had come before them.

Finally, what needs special acknowledgment is how carefully Beckett appears to have bound his new departure of 1960 to that of 1950:

> how it was I quote before Pim with Pim after Pim how it is three
> parts I say it as I hear it

By setting out with a "quote"—that is, by implying that the voice that transmits the text is somehow separate from the voice that originates it—these opening lines connect directly with a central theme of *Texts for Nothing*: the bewildering multiplicity of the speaking subject ("who says this, saying it's me? Answer simply, someone answer simply" [STN, 91]). This is a riddle that moves like a ghost through almost everything Beckett wrote in the forties and is an integral feature of the larger mystery we have just addressed: Where, finally, do the words come from? How do they get put together in the way they do? More particularly, the opening lines of *How It Is* pick up the device of quotation from the very last words of the *Texts:* ". . . as soon now, when all will be ended, all said, it says, it murmurs." In context, these last four words of the *Texts* are an exotic grammatical turnabout, suggesting a quotational hall of mirrors. Beckett not only picks up this device in *How It Is* but adds an extra stitch at the end of his opening strophe by rephrasing "I quote" in these words: "I say it as I hear it" (to say it as one hears it is to quote). In doing so, Beckett exactly quotes his own words in Text 5: "the things one has to listen to, I say it as I hear it" (STN, 97).[7] Repeated in *How It Is,* the phrase is, as it were, the quote quoted. It remained for Beckett to take the last word of the *Texts,* "murmurs," and make it a seed-word quoted everywhere in *How It Is.* All of these deliberate strokes retroactively de-terminate *Texts for Nothing,* canceling that sense of an ending with which Beckett was trying hard to cope as he spoke with Israel Shenker.

From its first words, then, *How It Is* acknowledges the aesthetic of recommencement which Beckett had already developed with such compaction in *Texts.* Working together, these two projects carry out the wisdom of the pun: "commencer" is "comment c'est." Beginning again, he returns again. Inventing, he quotes.[8] As I argued above, it was the insistence of this insight that had led Beckett in the *Texts* to the strategic deployment of the gap between texts. These twelve gaps were in their turn yet another seed for *How It Is.* They

---

[7] The same point holds for the two French texts: "je le dis comme je l'entends" (Samuel Beckett, *Nouvelles et Textes pour rien* [Paris: Minuit, 1958], 163). This is not the only quotation of the *Texts* in *How It Is;* see Pilling, *Frescoes of the Skull,* 43.

[8] In the same way, *Texts for Nothing,* despite the brilliance of its departure from the trilogy, engaged frequently in alluding to it and the *Nouvelles,* often quite explicitly: as for example to *Molloy* and *Malone Dies* (STN, 92), to *Godot* (STN, 96), to "The Calmative" (STN, 79), and to "The End" (STN, 97). The best close analysis of Beckett's way of beginning by returning in *How It Is* is Victor Sage's "Innovation and Continuity in *How It Is,*" in *Beckett the Shape Changer,* ed. Katharine Worth (London: Routledge & Kegan Paul, 1975), 85–103.

grew into roughly 825 gaps, each of which, as John Pilling has pointed out, enabled a formal reenactment of the book's inception.[9] Setting out again, as he had a decade before in the *Texts,* Beckett bound his new work into yet another literary tradition, this time the epic, a form traditionally devoted to two subjects: *comment c'est* and *commencer,* how it is and how it all began. Just as the *Texts* alluded richly to the tradition of the personal meditation, so allusions to the epic tradition abound richly in *How It Is.* The circularity of this world, the sense of endless torment, the fragmentary "abandon hope" (HII, 46)—all suggest Dante's *Inferno.*[10] The reference to "life above in the light before I fell" (HII, 109) suggests the circumstance of Satan in *Paradise Lost,* as other falls above in the light (his wife's,

---

[9]Knowlson and Pilling, *Frescoes,* 63.

[10]As many critics have noted, there is language strongly resonant with *How It Is* in Canto 7 of the *Inferno,* where Dante depicts the punishment of the sullen and slothful. See Robinson, *The Long Sonata,* 216; Kenner, *Reader's Guide,* 138; Hutchings, " 'Shat into Grace,' or a Tale of a Turd: Why It Is How It Is in Samuel Beckett's *How It Is,*" *Papers on Language and Literature* 21 (Winter 1985): 69.

> che coi sospiri sui,
> L'auqua i fa brombolar stando là drento,
> Come vede per tuto i ochi tui.
> Piantai nel fango i grami dise a stento:
> Bruta vita, d'acidia nu impastai,
> Passà avemo là sora al sol, al vento;
> E in fango adesso semo qua impiantai.
> Nel gosso ghe vien rota sta canzon,
> Che drio man tuta no i pol dirla mai.
>   (7:118–126)

> with their gasps
> [They] send bubbles to the surface of this ooze
> As glancing roundabouts you may observe.
> Fixed in the slime they say: "Sullen we were
> In the sweet air cheered by the brightening sun
> Because of sulky vapors in our hearts;
> Now here in this black mud we curse our luck."
> This burden, though they cannot form in words,
> They gurgle in their gullets.

Dante Alighieri, *The Divine Comedy,* trans. Thomas G. Bergin (New York: Grossman, 1948), 24.

his father's) suggest that of Adam. These and many other echoes have been amply detailed in the literature on *How It Is.* Here I shall sketch the case that Beckett, in his reprocessing of the two epic subjects—how it is and how it began—abolishes the traditional structure and thematics of the former, subsuming the entire subject of "how it is" into an ontology of new beginnings.

How It Is

In the epic tradition, showing how it is has meant showing how things fit, how they work out. In the Bible and in epics coming out of the biblical tradition, this has also meant showing how the working out of things is just: justifying, as Milton described his task in *Paradise Lost,* "God's ways to man." It has meant showing how even pain and suffering have their place in the order of things, and how in the long run punishments fit crimes (as Dante sought to do with such exacting attention to detail in *The Divine Comedy*).

But in the world painstakingly elaborated by the epic bard of *How It Is*—"here where justice reigns" (HII, 134)—justice has been distilled to a final Newtonian essence as the perfection of order. The final object of "our justice" is to show that "we're regulated thus."

> to his eyes the spectacle on the one hand of a single one among us towards whom no one ever goes and on the other of a single other who never goes towards anyone it would be an injustice and that is above in the light (HII, 124)

In this recycling of the parable of the sheep (Matthew 18:12–13), every Pim becomes a Bom, every victim a victimizer. The entire problem of accounting for the presence of evil is resolved in the symmetry of an eye for an eye. Any minor disturbance in the system—as, for example, the problem of the distribution of sacks, on which so much of the book's late energy is expended—would bring the whole "caravan" to a halt, leaving its participants "frozen in injustice" (HII, 137).

Establishing the plausible exactitude of this symmetry is the epic challenge. In the third and last book of this epic, the drama becomes, increasingly, a drama of mathematics, as the creator strives against insuperable odds to work out in arithmetical terms the order he has been inspired to communicate. In desperation, he introduces radical changes at the eleventh hour in order to achieve some kind of fit:

> there he is then again last figures the inevitable number 777777 at the instant when he buries the opener in the arse of number 777778 and is rewarded by a feeble cry cut short as we have seen by the thump on skull who on being stimulated at the same instant and in the same way by number 777776 makes his own private moan which same fate
>
> something wrong there
>
> And who at the instant when clawed in the armpit by number 777776 he sings applies the same treatment to number 777778 with no less success
>
> so on and similarly all along the chain in both directions for all our other joys and sorrows all we extort and endure from one another from the one to the other inconceivable end of this immeasurable wallow (HII, 140–141)

"Something wrong there" is what prevails in the end. Proclaiming in the last pages that his construction is all wrong, this creator folds up and packs away the epic tradition and its dream of containment. Throughout, the scraps of memory from how it is "above in the light" have anticipated this failure of the tradition by repeatedly piercing the fabric of his construction in random incisions.

With the failure of his authorship comes the failure of the poet's authority. This failure of authority also goes to the heart of the epic mode. Of all the genres, the epic is the most authoritative. Anointed, visited in a dream inspired by the highest muse, the epic poet is chosen and, through that choice, granted the power to speak in the declarative and prophetic modes. For this reason, the reader is encouraged to see *through* what Milton considered an accommodation to our intelligence—the mere discourse and design of the epic itself—to the absolute truth of which it has been the chosen vehicle. In Beckett's update of the tradition, our gaze is drawn relentlessly instead to the vehicle itself. We are never allowed to forget its constructedness. Over and over, we are notified that there is "something wrong there," that things are not working out, that, finally, the whole thing is its own punishment, a terrible burden that its creator cannot wait to be rid of. It is indeed that punishment for the unbelieving, referred to in Augustine's cosmic joke and meted out in hyperspace: not an actual but a virtual Hell. Enduring it, we are taken a long way from Wordsworth, who at the conclusion of his own epic vision sang in triumph of

> The rapture of the Hallelujah sent
> From all that breathes and is, was chasten'd, stemm'd
> And balanced by a Reason which indeed
> Is reason; duty and pathetic truth;
> And God and Man divided, as they ought,
> Between them the great system of the world
> Where Man is sphered, and which God animates.
>   (Bk. XIII, lines 255–261)[11]

The abolition of justice and authority is part of the larger project of abolishing the deeply held Western proclivity to see "how it is" as design. This point brings us back to the subject of narrative, for narrative is the preeminent way of representing time as an entity with shape, of seeing history as design. Above, I argued that in the *Texts* Beckett for the first time freed himself fully in his prose work from the seductive power of narrative. In this regard, again, *How It Is* is not a turning point or brand-new beginning but a recommencement. Nothing so vividly manifests its status as postnarrative art than Beckett's travesty of the epic, world-girdling narrative that determines its structure. The function of this "narrative" is not to enlighten but to stupefy: "before Pim, with Pim, after Pim" or "the

---

[11] William Wordsworth, *The Prelude*, ed. Ernest de Selincourt (London: Oxford University Press, 1970), 236. Beckett may well have had Joyce's epic *Ulysses* in mind when he devised the fanfare of "yeses" in which the book culminates, affirming the completeness of its failure and playing off, as John Pilling suggests, against the "yeses" of Molly Bloom which punctuate Joyce's epic; see John Pilling, *Samuel Beckett* (London: Routledge, 1976), 45. Beckett made a similarly inverse allusion to Joyce's other epic when he wrote John Calder in 1960 that the project under construction was "work in regress" (cited in Frederik N. Smith, "Fiction as Composing Process: *How It Is*," in *Samuel Beckett: Humanistic Perspectives*, ed. Morris Beja et al. [Columbus: Ohio State University Press, 1983], 118).

journey the couple the abandon." On every page we are reminded of the whole structure. Like time in God's imagination, it is all a foregone conclusion. Always present in all its parts, it lacks the faintest vestige of narrative suspense. So if we are to look for what is interesting in this book, we must look elsewhere. As some early reviewers testily pointed out, there is hardly anything of interest in the impoverished world of Pim and Bom. The only "events" that surprise are those that come in at right angles to the text, fragments from "life above in the light" which pierce it like meteors: "I see a crocus in a pot in an area in a basement a saffron the sun creeps up the wall a hand keeps it in the sun this yellow flower with a string" (HII, 21). Like the fragments that litter *Texts for Nothing,* these "rags of life in the light" lack all semblance of that natural consecutiveness which is the life blood of narrative.

At the end of this text, when the voice packs up its construction, it does not eliminate everything. What goes is the order to which it aspired. Packing this structure away, it rejects not only the misrepresentation of design but the tyranny implicit in the artistic tradition that would command obeisance to design. In *How It Is,* this tyranny is vividly represented in Part Two by the hand that carves its words in the back of its victim. All of this is rejected. But the mud, the voice, the rush of words, and the curious and still unexplained being that lays claim to them remain: "only me in any case yes alone yes in the mud yes . . . with my voice yes my murmur yes" (HII, 146). The book winds up, in other words, where it began.

HOW IT BEGAN

The productivity of Beckett's aesthetic concentration, applied to what I have referred to as the wisdom of his pun on beginnings (*comment c'est* is *commencer*), does not stop where we left it above. Beyond the fused meanings that make up its content, this pun also bears freight as the trope for which it stands. "In the beginning was the pun," Beckett wrote in *Murphy,* over twenty years earlier. In doing so, he played on ancient wisdom that what is derives from the *logos* or, in the English biblical term, the Word of God: "In the beginning was the Word." To translate the biblical fiat into an all-generative pun was to invoke both the creative power of language and its problematic ambiguity, a semantic multiplicity that is with us in this text from its originating pun. Out of this slippery word of beginning comes the entire structure of *How It Is*. Yet thanks, too, to the excessiveness of language, the structure produced is as fragile as it is elaborate, subject increasingly, as we have noted, to the doubts of its "crawling creator" (C, 52). If the structure is corrupt, if perfecting it is absolutely the wrong way to proceed, the linguistic energy that both built it up and took it down again is no less worthy of awed attention.

In the very proclamation that his cosmic project is "all balls" (HII, 145), our discreator finishes off his handiwork with a pun as grand as the one with which it began, for the expression "all balls" procreates while it cancels. By binding negation with the male organs of generation (and perhaps the spheres of the universe), we are told that, like it or not, understand it or not, nothing ends. To end is, as Beckett wrote elsewhere, "to end yet again." That is, to begin. What is important in both of these puns is their relocation of the action. In place of narrative action and the traditional tyrannies of design, authority, and containment, we have here the action of linguistic productivity.

Beckett accentuated this view of things when he recycled the biblical metaphysics of origin even further by fusing the creativity of the word with that of matter, the "warmth of primeval mud" (HII, 11) in which the entire text is embedded. The repeated, unsettling image of "mud in the mouth" and the crawler's tongue "lolling" in the mud recycles both the mud out of which God made Adam and the Word by which God gave life to the mud. In similar fashion, Beckett's word producer gives life to Pim—"who but for me he would never Pim we're talking of Pim never be but for me anything but a dumb limp lump flat for ever in the mud but I'll quicken him you wait and see" (HII, 52)—indeed, gives life even to himself: "I hear me again murmur me in the mud and am again" (HII, 126).

The point to stress—to quote Estragon once again—is that "everything oozes." In this text, everything—imagery, mythology, language—is subject to the ooze of recyclement. The borderlessness of puns and the way they recycle meaning matches the recycling of everything from Christian mythology to food and to language: "suddenly we are eating sandwiches alternate bites I mine she hers and exchanging endearments my sweet girl I bite she swallows my sweet boy she bites I swallow" (HII, 30). Similarly the verbal background noise he refers to as "quaqua"—"the voice quaqua from which I get my life these scraps of life in me when the panting stops" (HII, 113)—is a kind of prearticulate verbal mud. If William Hutchings is right that "quaqua" is the latinate version of "caca,"[12] then here is yet another pun-abetted ooze of how things circulate. In this text, the concepts of expressing and excreting, like those of listening and eating, ooze each into each in a constancy of recyclement. This activity of recycling is also manifested in the abundance of repeated, yet subtly recontextualized, phrases that recur throughout the book ("I quote," "above in the light," "the panting stops," "no knowing," "vast tracts of time," "something wrong there"), a device that was to become a salient feature of Beckett's late signature. It even shows up in the punctilious way in which no proper name is allowed to stand on its own in this book. All identity is, as it were, oozing from one term to the next: Pim to Bom to Bem, Pam to Prim, Kram to Krim, Skom to Skum.

It is in the continual originating power of the language of this work, then—the volatility of its conceptual interchange—that the interesting action takes place. Throughout the epic construction of an entirely fraudulent world and the tedious narrative it seeks to contain, this action continues to happen, always present, always intruding to remind us how it really is: that is, how the imagistic and conceptual flow keeps starting in surprising new ways, over and over again.

Reading the Music of Origins

This discussion returns us to issues raised in the last three chapters: Is *How It Is* a poststructuralist manifestation of both language's in-

---

[12]Hutchings, " 'Shat into Grace,' " 87n.

determinacy (always gliding between signifieds) and language's dominion (making and unmaking worlds)? Is it a text in which the idea of extralinguistic agency and origination has evaporated? Can the questions of how things are and how they arose be accounted for in the processes of language? And is this a confirmation of the argument that all expression is alien matter, "falling" and "collapsing" upon itself? Is there any difference between the oozing of this text and the oozing that, I argued, triumphs in *Eleutheria*?

To answer these questions, we have first to answer the question How is this text read? To do this, we must look closely at a fragment of its verbal action. A strophe from late in Part Three will serve:

> and later much later these aeons my God when it stops again ten
> more fifteen more in me a murmur scarce a breath then from mouth
> to mud brief kiss brush of lips faint kiss (HII, 136)

Prose like this invites us to read it in three ways. And if we read with any attention, I would argue that all three ways of reading happen inevitably and with near simultaneity. To begin with, such prose asks to be normalized, which is perhaps just another way of saying that this prose is not entirely strange. Within the first few pages, we are given enough information about the circumstances of the speaker to know that this text is gasped out with no time for the niceties of discourse which ordinarily help a reader comprehend. Later, it is characterized explicitly as "unbroken no paragraphs no commas not a second for reflection" (HII, 70) and again as "little blurts of midget grammar" (HII, 76). That information, together with the local coherences in every passage, makes the impulse to turn this prose into comprehensible discourse irresistible. Mentally, we seek to finish a job we understand to be incomplete. We may not do so successfully—more often than not, we cut our losses and move on—but something like the following happens as we read:

> And later, much later
>   (these aeons, my God!),
> when it [the panting] stops again,
> [with] ten more, [or] fifteen more [words] in me,
>   a murmur,

> scarce a breath;
> then,
>   from mouth to mud [they go],
>   [a] brief kiss,
>   [a] brush of lips,
>   [a] faint kiss.

Worked out in this way, the strophe can be "understood" as one more late variation on the interchange of mud and word out of which the text arises. We also see in the first exclamation how the nutritive pauses, during which breath (inspiration) is recovered and the words (of the muse?) are heard, are aligned with the "aeons" out of which creation originally came. And in the last series of three phrases, we are reminded that the cycle of generation is powered by Eros ("brief kiss brush of lips faint kiss"). In this way, we "comprehend" this strophe. Most commentary on *How It Is* is based implicitly on this kind of normalization (just as I have repeatedly normalized passages to make points in the course of this chapter).[13]

But Beckett did not write this text as I have normalized it. Instead, he wrote:

and later much later these aeons my God when it stops again

So before normalization is achieved, and even after, there is a more fluid experience of the hesitation between possible normalizations. In the line just cited, the exclamation "my God" can apply to "these aeons" (as I have it above) or to "when it stops again" or even to "ten more fifteen more in me" in the line immediately following (my God, think of it, ten more words in me!). Similarly, "in me" can refer backward to "fifteen more" or forward to "a murmur": "[there are] fifteen more in me" or "in me [there is] a murmur." I feel reasonably confident about the normalization of the whole pas-

---

[13]Some critics have even added normalizing aids in their citations from *How It Is,* as for example Susan Brienza in her otherwise helpful reading: ' "if he talks to himself / no / thinks / believes in God / yes / every day / no" ' (Brienza, *Samuel Beckett's New Worlds* [Norman: University of Oklahoma Press, 1987], 98). Brienza contends that the dramatic action in Beckett's late work more than ever unfolds in the language.

sage I have provided above. Yet going back to the text as printed, I find it hard, even with this master-normalization in mind, to resist the subtle encroachment of these other normalizations—and not only these, but strange ones, too—abnormalizations like "murmur scarce," "mouth to mud brief," and "lips faint."

There are, then, these two kinds of reading that play off each other as the text proceeds, the one asserting control as the other entertains the relinquishment of control. But there is also a third reading that happens. It is harder to represent adequately, but the design below indicates roughly how it occurs:

> and later much later
> these aeons my God
> when it stops again ten
> more fifteen more in me a murmur
> scarce a breath then
> from mouth to mud
> brief kiss brush of lips faint kiss

Represented here is the way in which the sound effects become so insistent that they threaten to take over from the meaning. I have organized these lines roughly according to the domination of internal rhyming patterns. It is the fascination of unusual aural effects which generates this third reader-relationship, one that adds its resistent counterpoint to the play of normalization discussed above. Coming on a line like "brief kiss brush of lips faint kiss" one feels the desire to let go of sense altogether and simply to enjoy the sensory effect the contriver of this text has, once again, managed to achieve. As he notes elsewhere, "first the sound then the sense" (HII, 95); or to put it in context,

> so many words
> so many lost
> one every three
> two every five
> first the sound
> then the sense

To hear Swinburne here is appropriate. Like so much of Swinburne, like Poe, like Tennyson and Hopkins, Beckett writes a poetry in which sound seems to want to come into the ascendant, arrogating to itself the place traditionally held by meaning.

My stress, however, falls not on this last effect, but on the rich interplay of effects which comes about through the coexistence of the three modes of reading which the text demands. In this elegant interplay of meaning and sound lies the answer to the question left hanging above. If this text breeds in the fertile ooze of language, submitting to the rule of deferred meaning, the signs of artifice are nonetheless everywhere in abundance. Bringing to ruin the epic of containment and radiant design, Beckett concentrated attention on the wonders of origination. Combining the rhetorical strategies I have just enumerated, he trebled his capacity to surprise us with ever-new and striking inventions from the same old material. The counter tropes of reduction, negation, cancellation, and despair—always parts of the Beckett signature—invariably set off the vigor of that productivity. As Shira Wolosky argued in an essay on the *Texts,* Beckett's "gestures toward reduction inevitably give way to reproductive and inventive energy."[14] I think she is right. *Texts for Nothing* and *How It Is,* which critics have so often held widely apart from each other, can be seen as a joint project in which Beckett distilled this inventive productivity. Moreover, by abandoning narrative—the remaining structural implement of an art of containment—he was enabled to concentrate his power with full efficiency on an art of recommencement. The same move invites us as readers to turn our attention away from what lies ahead and to redirect it fully to the way in which this art unfolds. It is more than a little like music.

---

[14]Shira Wolosky, "The Negative Way Negated: Samuel Beckett's *Texts for Nothing,*" *New Literary History* 22 (Winter 1991): 227; Victor Sage said the same thing with the emphasis reversed when he wrote of *How It Is* that Beckett's "wit is a machine for making possibilities look like poverties" (Sage, "Innovation," 102).

Six

WRITING SCRIPTS

One is the victim of everything one writes.
—Samuel Beckett

As Beckett's art came together in the ten years between 1945 and 1955, so did his autographical investment in that art. It was an investment, I am arguing, of which he was aware and which required continual creative vigilance. And it was to a significant degree this vigilance that lay behind the exceptional strangeness of Beckett's work. As I argued in Chapter 2, his is a strangeness that has exceeded most attempts to give it some kind of twentieth-century "belonging." In this chapter, I apply this accounting of Beckett's strangeness to a feature of his development which is not so much strange as unusual in the development of an oeuvre: the almost regular alternation between prose fiction and drama which began in the mid-forties, when Beckett went from the composition of *Mercier et Camier* to that of *Eleutheria*. He took five similar steps in the decade that followed.[1]

Asked about the shift from fiction to drama, Beckett was charac-

---

[1]The six steps, coming in cycles of two, are these:

Fiction	May–Dec. 1946	*Nouvelles* and *Mercier et Camier*
Drama	Jan.–March 1947	*Eleutheria*
Fiction	Sept. 1947–July 1948	*Molloy* and *Malone meurt*
Drama	Oct. 1948–Jan. 1949	*En attendant Godot*
Fiction	1949–1951	*L'innommable* and *Texts pour rien*
Drama	1955–1956	*Fin de partie*

teristically noncommittal. "I didn't choose to write a play," he told
Israel Shenker. "It just happened like that."[2] At the very least,
though, the shift was the sign of a restless, curious, enterprising creativity. Beckett continued stepping back and forth across the genre
border and later ventured into mime, radio, film, and television as
well. If this experimentation was a sign of restless creativity, it at the
same time permitted an exponential augmentation of the resources
with which to reinvent his self-resistant art. Moreover, during those
first steps back and forth between his intense, increasingly claustro-
phobic prose fiction and his eminently stageable theater, Beckett
learned much about theatricality. For one thing, he got to know it
as a mode of tyranny not confined to staged or stageable scripts.
And for another, he got to know it not simply as an aspect of the
form and content of his craft but as an aspect of his own autographical relationship to that craft as well.

TYRANNY AND THEATRICALITY

There has been much interesting work since the mid-seventies on
the interpenetration of power and theatricality, beginning with the
first wave of renaissance new historicists who articulated a "poetics
of Elizabethan power" appropriate to the cultural anthropology of
an age in which power was uniquely "constituted in theatrical cele-
brations of royal glory and theatrical violence visited upon the ene-
mies of that glory."[3] In this they followed closely upon Foucault's
historicizing of power and theatricality.[4] In the years that followed,

[2]Israel Shenker, "Moody Man of Letters," New York Times, May 6, 1956, sect. 2: 3.
Beckett said the same thing to Paul-Louis Mignon in 1964: "Je n'envisageais pas une
carrière de dramaturge [I didn't envisage a career as dramatist]" (Mignon, "Le théâtre de
A jusqu'a Z: Samuel Beckett," L'avant-scène du théâtre 313 [June 15, 1964]: 8).

[3]Stephen Greenblatt, "Invisible Bullets: Renaissance Authority and Its Subversion,"
Glyph 8 (1981): 57.

[4]He discusses, for example, the public execution as a theater of terror which was in
turn the sustaining instrument of a specific constellation of power, knowledge, and technology prior to the eighteenth century; see Michel Foucault, Discipline and Punish: The

this interest in theater and the theatrical as an instrument of both the containment and disruption of power migrated with the new historicism into revisionist readings of the French Revolution and more broadly of romanticism itself.[5]

This feature of the historicist revival arises out of a root perception that theatricality and power are inevitably linked. Theater not only thrives on the agon, or conflict of power, but engages in its own form of tyranny. Theater is art applied to the human body and mind. It requires a director, and directors can be tyrants. The chain of command, moreover, extends through the performed play to the audience, who are much more nearly in the situation of captives than are, say, the readers of books.[6] "This indeed is the grand Privilege of a great Actor above a great Poet," noted Coleridge. "There is

---

Birth of the Prison, trans. Alan Sheridan (New York: Random, 1979). Another landmark historical text is Stephen Orgel's *The Illusion of Power: Political Theater in the English Renaissance* (Berkeley: University of California Press, 1975). The argument was widely developed in the early 1980s, together with interesting speculations on the role of theatricality in the construction of identity; see Jonathan Goldberg, *James I and the Politics of Literature: Jonson, Shakespeare, Donne, and Their Contemporaries* (Baltimore: Johns Hopkins University Press, 1983), esp. 113–209; Christopher Pye, "The Sovereign, the Theater, and the Kingdome of Darknesse: Hobbes and the Spectacle of Power," *Representations* 8 (Fall 1984): 85–106; and Robert Weimann, "History and the Issue of Authority in Representation: The Elizabethan Theater and the Reformation," *New Literary History* 17 (1986): 449–476.

[5]For work on the French Revolution see Marie-Hélène Huet, *Rehearsing the Revolution,* trans. Robert Hurley (Berkeley: University of California Press, 1982); Angelica Gooden, "The Dramatizing of Politics: Theatricality and the Revolutionary Assemblies," *Modern Language Studies* 22 (1984): 194–212; Mona Ozouf, *Festivals and the French Revolution,* trans. Alan Sheridan (Cambridge, Mass.: Harvard University Press, 1988). For an overview and searching revaluation of new work on theatricality and English romanticism, see Julie A. Carlson, *In the Theatre of Romanticism: Coleridge, Nationalism, Women* (Cambridge: Cambridge University Press, 1994). See also *The Performance of Power: Theatrical Discourse and Politics,* ed. Sue-Ellen Case and Janelle Reinelt (Iowa City: University of Iowa Press, 1991).

[6]A good example of reading founded in this sense of theatricality is Sheila Robillard's "Sam Shepard: Theatrical Power and American Dreams," *Modern Drama* 30 (1987): 58–71. Robillard argues that Shepard makes the coercive power of theatricality both his reflexive subject and a commentary on American culture, "where all speech is for the sake of its power to command attention and words are thus a tool of violent dominance" (67).

no time given to ask questions, or pass judgments. He takes us by storm."[7] It is this object/beholder relationship that has fascinated the new historicists and that also has led the art historian and theorist Michael Fried to identify the theatrical in visual art as a kind of bullying. This idea was put forcefully in "Art and Objecthood," his 1967 critique of "literalist" (minimalist) art. According to Fried, the theatricality of literalist objects is manifested in the way they take over the territory they inhabit, at once confronting, distancing, and isolating the beholder.[8] Indeed, in that early polemic, Fried goes so far as to oppose theatricality to genuine art.

At the least, then, autocratic control is implicit in the literal meaning of theatricality. This embeddedness of tyranny in almost all facets of the theatrical situation is summarized in Derrida's description of the "theological stage." At the same time, Derrida brings out another connotative thread that laces our usage of "theatricality." It implies

> an author-creator who, absent and from afar, is armed with a text and keeps watch over, assembles, regulates the time or the meaning of representation, letting this latter *represent* him as concerns what is called the content of his thoughts, his intentions, his ideas. He lets representation represent him through . . . interpretive slaves who faithfully execute the providential designs of the "master." Who moreover—and this is the ironic rule of the representative structure

---

[7]Samuel Taylor Coleridge, *Lectures 1808–19: On Literature,* vol. 1, ed. Reginald A. Foakes, vol. 5 in *The Collected Works of Samuel Taylor Coleridge,* Bollingen Series 75 (Princeton: Princeton University Press, 1986), 429.

[8]Michael Fried, "Art and Objecthood," *Artforum* 5 (June 1967): 11–23, repr. in *Minimal Art: A Critical Anthology,* ed. Gregory Battcock (New York: Dutton, 1968), 116–147. Since publishing that essay, Fried has elaborated his concept of theatricality through an extended analysis of French painting from the mid-eighteenth century to Edouard Manet. See Fried, *Absorption and Theatricality: Painting and Beholder in the Age of Diderot* (Berkeley: University of California Press, 1980); "The Beholder in Courbet: His Early Self-Portraits and Their Place in His Art," *Glyph* 4 (1978): 85–129; "Painter into Painting: On Courbet's *After Dinner at Ornans* and *Stonebreakers,*" *Critical Inquiry* 8 (Summer 1982): 619–649; "The Structure of Beholding in Courbet's *Burial at Ornans,*" *Critical Inquiry* 9 (June 1983): 635–683; and "Courbet's Metaphysics: A Reading of *The Quarry,*" *MLN* 99 (September 1984): 787–815.

which organizes all these relationships—creates nothing, has only the illusion of having created, because he only transcribes and makes available for reading a text whose nature is itself necessarily representative . . . . Finally, the theological stage comports a passive, seated public, a public of spectators, of consumers, of "enjoyers". . . .⁹

The additional element brought out here by Derrida is the nothingness that is cloaked in the theatrical transaction and that implicates the author-tyrant himself. Nothingness, in fact, is a common connotation of both the terms "theatrical" and "theatricality." What is theatrical is understood to be not real but only performed. It is mere "show." A theatrical person is someone who is acting while off stage, someone inauthentic, an actor. When we perceive theatricality, on or off stage, we perceive scriptedness.

In Foucault's account, a culture of theatricality and spectacle gave way in the nineteenth century to a culture of surveillance. But if such a shift occurred, it did not impede the production of vivid literary representations of theatricality, often thematically bonded with tyranny and nothingness.¹⁰ Indeed, in the great century for domestic fiction, composed, in the Foucauldian view, under the shadow of Bentham's Panopticon, the novels of Dickens could be described as an unremitting examination of theatricality.¹¹ Dickens is a good bridge figure to bring us back to Beckett, in part because he was a novelist Beckett most assuredly read and remembered and who probably had more influence on Beckett than has been ac-

⁹Jacques Derrida, "The Theater of Cruelty and the Closure of Representation," in *Writing and Difference,* trans. Alan Bass (Chicago: University of Chicago Press, 1978), 235.

¹⁰In fact, there is a long tradition here. One can draw a line from Shakespeare's *Richard III* to Jarry's *Ubu Roi,* Mann's *Mario and the Magician,* and Genet's *The Balcony.* An especially powerful development of the trinity of associations I am concerned with can be found in the 1981 Hungarian film *Mephisto,* directed by Istvan Szabo. See also Frantisek Deak, "Kaloprosopia, the Art of Personality: The Theatricalization of Discourse in Avant-Garde Theatre," *Performing Arts Journal* 13 (May 1991): 6–21.

¹¹With an emphasis quite different from my own, Joseph Litvak reappraises the Foucauldian "society of surveillance"; see Litvak, *Caught in the Act: Theatricality in the Nineteenth-Century English Novel* (Berkeley: University of California Press, 1992).

knowledged.[12] Of his many treatments of theatricality, perhaps his most compressed was Rigaud, the impotent, inconsequential, really disappointing "villain" of *Little Dorrit*. Rigaud, with his "theatrical air," is a pure succession of performances, including that of the stage villain complete with a cape, who appears under several aliases (Blandois, Lagnier) and is always identifying himself in dramatic cadences:

> "Call me five-and-thirty years of age. I have seen the world. I have lived here and there, and lived like a gentleman everywhere. I have been treated and respected as a gentleman universally."

> "I am sensitive and brave. I do not advance it as a merit to be sensitive and brave, but it is my character."[13]

With an efficiency of dispatch which made this figure almost purely emblematic, Dickens bonded Rigaud's theatricality with both qualities we have been discussing. On the one hand, he suggests a complete absence of inner being. Rigaud is a concentrated presentation of human nothingness in a novel that was written out of a preoccupation with the words "nothing" and "nobody." He is a shadow villain, whose machinations come to nothing and who is himself erased in the gratuitous implosion of Mrs. Clemmans's house. On the other hand, he is obsessed with being the master. "I am proud," he says. "I say nothing in defence of pride, but I am proud. It is also my character to govern. I can't submit; I must govern."[14] To seal this association, Rigaud is paired with the diminutive, completely submissive John-Baptist Cavalletto, who does the bidding of his master in all things.

One could make a good case that Rigaud and John-Baptist were somewhere in Beckett's mind when he developed Pozzo and Lucky. Like Pozzo, Rigaud throws his menial scraps of his food. His mode of command could serve as a template for Pozzo: "Get up, pig!"

---

[12]But see Victor Sage's detailed alignment of the two authors in "Dickens and Beckett: Two Uses of Materialism," *Journal of Beckett Studies* 2 (Summer 1977): 15–39.

[13]Charles Dickens, *Little Dorrit* (Harmondsworth: Penguin, 1967), 47, 49–50.

[14]Ibid., 49.

"Sing the refrain, pig!"[15] But most striking is the tight cluster of associations—theatricality, tyranny, and nothingness—shared by both Pozzo and Rigaud. If theatricality and tyranny are obvious traits of Pozzo, the third of these qualities is accentuated in his role as well. Of all the parts in *Godot,* Pozzo's, in its abrupt movement from one voice to another, is the one that appears to be most completely a collage of fragmentary roles plastered over nothingness.

Ah yes! The night. (*He raises his head.*) But be a little more attentive, for pity's sake, otherwise we'll never get anywhere. (*He looks at the sky.*) Look! (*All look at the sky except Lucky who is dozing off again. Pozzo jerks the rope.*) Will you look at the sky, pig! (*Lucky looks at the sky.*) Good, that's enough. (*They stop looking at the sky.*) What is there so extraordinary about it? Qua sky. It is pale and luminous like any sky at this hour of the day. (*Pause.*) In these latitudes. (*Pause.*) When the weather is fine. (*Lyrical.*) An hour ago *(he looks at his watch, prosaic)* roughly *(lyrical)* after having poured forth even since *(he hesitates, prosaic)* say ten o'clock in the morning *(lyrical)* tirelessly torrents of red and white light it begins to lose its effulgence, to grow pale *(gesture of the two hands lapsing by stages)* pale, ever a little paler, a little paler until *(dramatic pause, ample gesture of the two hands flung wide apart)* pppfff! finished! it comes to rest. But—*(hand raised in admonition)*—but behind this veil of gentleness and peace night is charging *(vibrantly)* and will burst upon us *(snaps his fingers)* pop! like that! *(his inspiration leaves him)* just when we least expect it. *(Silence. Gloomily.)* That's how it is on this bitch of an earth. (WG, 25)

The comparative vividness of Pozzo's many voices and the abruptness with which they give way to one another intimate an almost perfect absence of depth. What he is is what we see and hear. As in the case of Rigaud, this purity of theatrical "show" is set off more sharply still by the presence of a diminished other, Lucky, who com-

---

[15]Ibid., 41 and 820, respectively. The national indeterminacy of this duo is a quality also echoed in the parts of *Godot.* John-Baptist Cavalletto has an Italian surname and an English given name. As to his own extraction, Rigaud says: "I own no particular country. My father was Swiss—Canton de Vaud. My mother was French by blood, English by birth. I myself was born in Belgium. I am a citizen of the world" (ibid., 48).

bines in his role Pozzo's antitypes: little power (certainly no power to tyrannize); little capacity or inclination for theater (in spite of continual demands that he perform); and, diminished as he may be, distinct evidence of something more than nothing. This last strikes the audience with great impact when, in his climactic monologue, he escapes the control of his master. He is finally more of a mystery than Pozzo in giving evidence of an earnestness and internal drive that cannot be accounted for as either theatrical performance or the will to tyrannize.

Lucky's escape (such as it may be) from his master's control belongs to the same paradigm as the commonest plot in Dickens. John-Baptist and Rigaud are themselves a compressed and heightened version of that plot: a quiet, diminished figure, a waif, an orphan, an almost nothing, under the absolute authority of some voluble performer, usually a parent or step-parent, with an exacting script for the waif which the waif at the key moment of the plot escapes (as John-Baptist, true to form, escapes Rigaud). This is also the plot of Beckett's 1982 play, *Catastrophe*. A theatrical director, who is also a *theatrical* director, exercises despotic authority (squared, as it were, by the mediation of an obedient assistant) over one of Beckett's closest approaches to characterological zero, the protagonist P. This is a protagonist who notably cannot and does not act, but is instead acted upon by actors, tyrannized by theater. So the escape in this plot is all the more striking when, after the script ends and the applause begins—in supratheatrical time and space—P raises his head. The ingenuity of this sequence features, not the nothingness, but the somethingness of this event. However obscure its origins, there is real drive implicated in this slight movement of P's head, and it echoes the much more spectacular, if much less deliberate, escape of Lucky from his theatrical director.

In both Dickens and Beckett, then, theatricality is a condition linking tyranny and nothingness. Put in psychological terms (terms that may, in the final analysis, work more persuasively than philosophical or linguistic terms), nothingness in this context is a felt impoverishment of being. The impoverished figure seeks to restore the illusion of being through the forcible impoverishment of others, that is, through tyranny. It is in Beckett's tyrants that Adorno's "historical disintegration of the subject as a unity" is most patently manifest.[16] The tyranny of characters such as Hamm and Pozzo—two of Beckett's most desperate people—is a protest against this felt dissolution. In performance, as I argued in Chapter 2, the discontinuities of these characters are bound together by the persistent singularity of the actors who give them voice and embodiment. This is an important aspect of their total effect. But it is an aspect lost on the characters themselves. These are entities who cannot conceive of being except as it is constructed in the received discursive universe. In other words, they are characters upon whom poststructuralist insight weighs most heavily. In direct proportion to the threat of nothingness, then, does theatricality come into play, tyrannically appropriating the attention of others ("Good. Is everybody ready? Is everybody looking at me?" [WG, 20]). In this way, theatricality not only mediates nothingness and tyranny but is their combined expression: performance overlaid on nothingness which seeks to elude even as it gives clear evidence of that nothingness. The flamboyant Pozzo is as empty as the flamboyant Director of Catastrophe, as tyrannical and as evanescent. Two of Beckett's most vivid creations, they are the gist of that sentiment Beckett insists on: "Nothing is more real than nothing."

But does this inevitable inherence of tyranny in theater, echoed as it is by Beckett's own thematic linking of theatricality, tyranny, and nothingness, have anything to do with why he should turn to theater in the first place and why he returned to it repeatedly throughout his career? Why, particularly, should Beckett, late in 1948, emerge from a year's sustained engagement with what was already his longest masterwork of prose fiction to make theater? What were the motives and effects of this sudden immersion in the theatrical on the author, a man consistently described by those who knew him as a gentle, generous man of peace?

The question is especially pertinent when one considers that

---

[16]Theodor W. Adorno, "Towards an Understanding of Endgame," in Twentieth-Century Interpretations of "Endgame," ed. B. G. Chevigny, trans. Samuel M. Weber (Englewood Cliffs, N.J.: Prentice-Hall, 1969), 92.

Beckett tried harder than most playwrights to exert control over the production of his scripts. For all the evidence that can be marshaled to include Beckett among those who, like Artaud or the performance artists, seek ways to avoid the repression (tyranny) of conventional theater, his author-itarianism points in a different direction. There is nothing spontaneous abut his art, no approach to festival or to what Josette Féral described as the "authorless, actorless, and directorless *infratheatricality*" of performance.[17] Beckett's directorial reputation was for exactitude: the precise realization of his will on stage. One should keep in mind, moreover, what Beckett did to his actors. He tied ropes around their necks and crammed them in urns—urns that were too short for them to stand in and too narrow to sit in. He tied them to rockers. He buried them in sand under hot blinding lights. He gave them impossible scripts to read at breakneck speed. If this is not torture, it bears a strong resemblance to it. Once, in an address to Irish students, Peter O'Toole gave a scathing indictment of Beckett's cruelty to actors.[18] If one still needs to be convinced, one can listen to Billie Whitelaw describe the experience of being completely bound with straps and braces for a performance of *Not I*. At one point, she broke into tears and fled to her dressing room. "Oh, Billie!" Beckett cried, "What have I done to you!"[19]

Why *did* he do it? Why did Beckett turn to theater in October of 1948 when he took a breather from *Malone Dies* to write *Godot?* And why did he keep on writing plays? Dickens could treat the theatrical thematically in his novels all his professional life. Why couldn't Beckett stay in his room, without leaving it to become contaminated, as it were, by theater? Did the gratifications of theatrical tyranny

[17]Josette Féral, "Performance and Theatricality: The Subject Demystified," *Modern Drama* 25 (March 1982): 170–181. Two other helpful efforts to go beyond any strict opposition of theatricality and performance are Régis Durand's "The Anxiety of Performance," *New Literary History* 12 (Autumn 1980): 167–176, and Mária Brewer's "Performing Theory," *Theatre Journal* 37 (March 1985): 13–30.

[18]From a conversation with Declan Kiberd.

[19]Taped conversation with Billie Whitelaw, November 1984. This tape is available in the Learning Resources archives at the University of California, Santa Barbara.

prove to be irresistible? Despite his keen conscience, his generosity of spirit, and the array of nontyrannical satisfactions open to anyone who writes for the stage, was Beckett not just a little bit of a sadist, as incapable as any existentially impoverished being of doing without a socially legitimated vehicle of tyranny when he is lucky enough to have one? To answer these questions, we need more fully to account for what the turn to theater meant to a writer as deeply immersed in prose fiction as Beckett was in 1948. At the same time, we should keep Dickens in mind as a specular comparison or control for Beckett. Dickens loved the theater and enjoyed acting, but his lifetime specialty remained the long three-decker Victorian novel. There were good autographical reasons for his doing so.

AUTOGRAPHY AND SELF-SCRIPTING

The question brings us to the theoretical issue of what the differences are between prose fiction and drama, particularly in regard to the relations of the author to the artistic mode. If we go back to Dickens with this question in mind, we notice an interesting thing: that though, with certain qualifications, he remained a novelist throughout his life, he read from his novels, in public, at every opportunity.[20] They were in this regard scripts for the dramatic rendering of the author himself. Their status as authorial scripts accounts in part for the distinctive and predominating narrative voice that Dickens sustained almost everywhere in his oeuvre. For many years in this century, readers have been warned by formalists, structuralists, and poststructuralists alike not to associate this narrative voice

[20]Early in his career, between 1836 and 1838, Dickens wrote four pieces for the stage. These were not great successes, but the stage versions of his novels, which he encouraged and at times had a hand in, were often very successful, opening sometimes before the prose version had finished appearing serially in print. If there is a main theme, though, in Dickens's personal relation to theater, it is his love of performing. He had a private theater built at Tavistock House (his home in London), where he frequently performed for his guests. See F. Dubrez Fawcett, *Dickens the Dramatist: On Stage, Screen, and Radio* (London: W. H. Allen, 1952).

with the author, who (if a real entity in the nondiscursive universe) was unknowable and irrelevant. For the New Critic, voice was simply an element in autonomous texts. Yet in the work of Dickens this narrative presence carries over from text to text, and Dickens gave his own audible voice to it from public lecterns. However autonomous his novels were as prose fiction, collectively they became a script for what one could call authorial theater.[21]

Of course, it is a long way from Dickens—reading in public, publishing serially, hearing month by month from a responsive audience, inviting his readers in so many ways to find in his narrative voice a dramatic rendering of the author himself—to Beckett, writing alone in his room with no audience and to most appearances no desire for one. But what the example of Dickens shows is the script condition of prose narrative. If Dickens exploited it more than most novelists, and Beckett sought to avoid it more than most, its trace is unavoidable. In a reversal of the creative sequence, any author— Austen, Hardy, Hemingway, Woolf, Beckett—becomes scripted by the texts he or she writes. More than by any other agency, authors are what can be inferred from their texts, because readers, eventually, will transgress all formalist cautions. It follows, then, that even in the space of one's own prose text theatricality is at work. And, true to form, such theatricality is also a mode of tyranny, insofar as the authorial script imprisons the author. Fiction is tyranny brought upon oneself, not simply through the readership of others but through one's own agency as both maker and inevitable reader of one's own text. Depending on one's autographical needs, one can find such bondage intolerable. It persists beyond the reading and worse, as Derrida would point out, it is an enforced servitude to illusion.[22]

---

[21]For an account of Dickens as a public reader, Charles Kent's eyewitness reports are an invaluable resource; see Kent, *Charles Dickens as a Reader* (London: Chapman and Hall, 1872). See also Raymund Fitzsimons, *Garish Lights: The Public Reading Tours of Charles Dickens* (Philadelphia: Lippincott, 1970), and Philip Collins, ed., *Charles Dickens: The Public Readings* (London: Oxford University Press, 1975).

[22]One could plausibly argue that the situation of *any* reading, despite its tight, comparatively unencumbered circle of text and mind, contains all the elements of the "theological

So the third part of the theatrical triangle we found in Dickens and Beckett—nothingness—is also present in the reflexive theater of autographical reading. The authorial tyranny of prose fiction is tyranny in the service of the not-me masquerading as me. It is tyranny that comes out of, as it accentuates, nothingess. In this regard, the New Critics were right: Dickens's fictional persona is not Dickens, but a stand-in. However assiduously the author may have cultivated the illusion that Dickens is really Dickens, the narrative situation is fundamentally theatrical, a performance out of nothing. We can, of course, still read the Dickensian persona, and the denial it represents, as an autographical trace or symptom. We can see, that is, its polish and its measured cadences as signs of the author's considerable need for theatrical self-displacement. So it is possible to suggest as an ancillary hypothesis that the reason the theater-loving Dickens remained a novelist was the special personal theatrical function of prose fiction, a function very difficult to achieve if one writes for the theater, for in theater it is the actors who do the performing.

Beckett, whose relations to his texts would appear to be more ambivalent than those of Dickens were to their author, must have found himself in an increasingly Dickensian situation in 1948. Two years before in the *Nouvelles* he had found a narrative voice:

> I don't know when I died. It always seemed to me I died old, about ninety years old, and what years, and that my body bore it out, from head to foot. But this evening, alone in my icy bed, I have the feeling I'll be older than the day, the night, when the sky with all its lights fell upon me, the same I had so often gazed on since my first stumblings on the distant earth. ("The Calmative," STN, 27)

It was a rich, flexible voice, brilliant in its many registers, yet consistent enough to be instantly recognizable. And from the summer of

---

stage" as described by Derrida. So it is possible to say that what theater in its staged condition does is make vivid the tyranny inherent in all textual encounters. Put in another way, the repressive character of writing and representation, so frequently referred to in contemporary theory, is in fact their theatricality. What often masks this condition is the fictivity of art and our corresponding willingness to dwell in its constructedness. As readers (or beholders) of fiction, we play the game, willingly allowing ourselves to be taken prisoner, because we know we will be set free. In reading a book, one's illusion of being free to come and go is, of course, even greater than it is in viewing a play.

1947 to the fall of 1948, Beckett had sustained basically the same voice over the course of two long texts: *Molloy* and *Malone Dies.*

> I have only to open my eyes to have them begin again, the sky and smoke of mankind. My sight and hearing are very bad, on the vast main no light but reflected gleams. All my senses are trained full on me, me. Dark and silent and stale, I am no prey for them. I am far from the sounds of blood and breath, immured. (*Malone Dies,* TN, 186)

In effect, what was happening was that these texts were becoming, collectively, a script.

This is, in fact, a central theme of *Malone Dies*: the inevitability of the script character of fiction. Malone's plan is to abandon the script, to play, to inhabit a stranger and in this way to avoid the fate of "the wretches famed in fable, crushed beneath the weight of their wish to come true" (TN, 194). But his pathetic tales of Sapo and MacMann are permeated everywhere in this text by the unmistakable voice—witty, mordant, earnest, and seductive—that threatens to stand for the author. The mirror inset of the theatrical function of prose texts is Moll's letters to MacMann, both in their language ("Sweetheart, Not one day goes by that I do not give thanks to God, on my bended knees, for having found you, before I die. . . . Ah would we had met but seventy years ago!") and in the representation of their transmission:

> While he read Moll held a little aloof, with downcast eyes, saying to herself, Now he's at the part where, and a little later, Now he's at the part where, and so remained until the rustle of the sheet going back into the envelope announced that he had finished. Then she turned eagerly towards him, in time to see him raise the letter to his lips or press it against his heart, another reminiscence of the fourth form. Then he gave it back to her and she put it under his pillow with the others there already, arranged in chronological order and tied together by a favour. (TN, 260–261)

All the elements of the personal exploitation of textual theater are foregrounded here: performer, script, and audience. Moll aligns herself with her audience as he reads ("Now he's at the part where, and a little later, Now he's at the part where") becoming through his agency the romantic part conveyed by her awful diction and then maintaining her textual being in a neat bundle under the head of her necessary perceiver. No wonder Malone killed her. But no wonder, too, that Malone, for all his superiority to Moll, for all his quality of being in his way fun to be around, had to be killed off as well, literally, on the last page, by the being whom he threatened to displace.

The next move was to *Godot*. There may be several good reasons for this move, but one of them, I am arguing, is that dramatic scripts displace personal scripts. The turn to theater offered the possibility of detheatricalizing the self. Where Dickens, in spite of his love of theater, chose to stay in the authorial theater of prose fiction, Beckett sought to elude it. As an autographer, Dickens welcomed the familiar repetition of the script he created and his audience loved. The autographer Beckett, shy of nothing so much as an audience, feared the embrace of such happy recognition. What theater offered was the possibility of escaping the bondage of script by imposing it on others. To put this another way, if theater is a temptation to tyranny over others, it is a release from the tyranny of prose over oneself. The opportunity of divesting personal scripts may provide one explanation for why, tyrant though he had been in monitoring the production of his plays, Beckett was quite liberal in allowing the free adaptation of his prose pieces to the stage.

The question now is the reverse of the one asked above: Why, given the personal advantages of writing for the stage, did Beckett not stay in the theater? There is, after all, the impressive example of Shakespeare, who stayed in the theater and went on to become our literary culture's best-known unscripted personage. To answer the question, we must come back to my leading hypothesis that, whatever else Beckett's art may be, it is also conscious autography. The problem, then, is exactly that of The Unnamable: to remain under erasure is as intolerable as to be misrepresented. The impossible object is the particular force for which those false signifiers "Samuel Beckett" stand. For this reason, I believe, even as he was erasing the slate in *Godot*, the sly character Beckett had come to be in the trilogy winks at the reader behind, as it were, the audience's back. These winks occur in those moments in *Godot* which can be appreciated only in the stage directions ("Vladimir uses his intelligence," Pozzo "puts on his glasses and looks at the two likes"). At these points, the text becomes authorial script again. Beckett's autographical intention is pursued, then, in two kinds of textual act, not one. They are the acts of scripting and then of unscripting the self, acts that, from a distance, appear to succeed each other in Beckett's alternation from the theater of prose to that of the stage, but that can already be seen faintly to coexist in *Godot*. As these acts were brought closer and closer together, they led to an increasing hybridization of Beckett's art, an art that draws on, as it often confounds, prose fiction and drama.[23] Such works as *Not I*, in which only the lips of the staged displacement are visible, or *A Piece of Monologue*, in which a paragraphless block of prose (much of it a kind of stage-directionese) is delivered by a "Speaker," or *Ohio Impromptu*, in which the staged action is the reading of a prose text, are liminal works. By negotiating the competing constraints of the text and the stage, they seek to elude those constraints altogether, to evade all modes of theatrical tyranny in the interests of an austere autography.

This vital autographical function of his art is a significant factor, then, behind those six steps Beckett took between 1946 and 1956, at the outset of this exploratory process. Beckett told Paul-Louis Mignon of the relief he felt when he turned from *Malone meurt* to write *Godot*. After more than a year of steady work on *Molloy* and *Malone meurt*, turning to the theater was like coming out of the dark into a game with clear rules to which one had no choice but to submit.[24] ("Now it is a game. I am going to play" [*Malone Dies*, TN, 180].) The experience had a major impact on the evolving character of Beckett's synthetic, highly rhythmical, postnarrative art. But in ret-

---

[23]This hybridity of Beckett's later fiction is a main theme in Enoch Brater, *The Drama in the Text: Beckett's Late Fiction* (New York: Oxford University Press, 1994).

[24]"Le travail du romancier est dur; on s'avance dans le noir. Au théâtre, on entre dans un jeu, avec ses règles, et on ne peut pas ne pas s'y soumettre [A novelist's work is hard; one advances in the dark. In the theater, one enters into a game, with its rules, and one can not not submit oneself to them]" (quoted in Paul-Louis Mignon, "Le théâtre de A jusqu'a Z," 8).

rospect it must also have given him a deeper conviction of the inescapability of the tyranny of theater—that is, the constraint of the human by the externality of form—in all the forms of art available to him.

The persistence of this conviction is registered in the exaggerated theatricality of *Catastrophe* (1982): its parody of Aristotelian tragic form complete with characters, rising action, and catastrophe. In a masterstroke of compression, Beckett at once foregrounded and fused the tyrannies of theater and state in this play. Much of the early response to *Catastrophe* was blurred by a debate as to whether its focus is political or aesthetic. But fully to appreciate this play, one cannot respond to it either as an attack on political tyranny which exploits the metaphor of theatrical production or as a reflexive meditation on theater which exploits a political occasion. The aesthetic and the political are two faces of a single meaning in *Catastrophe*, and they merge in the insight that the political will that seeks to constrain human life to an imagined social order, imprisoning or eliminating those uncontrollable elements threatening that order, is rooted with the aesthetic will that seeks to dominate the human through formal representation.

What keeps this interpretation from trivializing the political force of this play—from trivializing the meaning of political tyranny and the suffering of Václav Havel, to whom the play is dedicated—is knowing that aesthetic tyranny involves something more than just some abstract concept of "the human." In Beckett's case, it was more than abstract. There was a particular human life at stake in this aesthetic tyranny, and my argument is that this life—the life on the block, as it were—was his own. As it was quickly noticed, the fibrous degeneration Beckett suffered from (Dupuytren's Contracture) turned his hands into claws much like those of P, the mute protagonist standing on the block in *Catastrophe*.[25] P is a diminished

---

[25]Rosette Lamont, "New Beckett Plays: A Darkly Brilliant Evening," *Other Stages* (June 16, 1983): 3; Alfred Simon, "Du théâtre de l'écriture à l'écriture de la scène," *Revue d'esthétique*, n.s. (1986): 83; Enoch Brater, *Beyond Minimalism: Beckett's Late Style in the Theater* (New York: Oxford University Press, 1987), 146.

signifier of B, and he raises his head, somewhere, on the outskirts of his own art.

The idea that Beckett's first need as an artist was autographical and that it pursued its end in a continual play with the coercive theatricality of texts, on stage and off, makes more sense the more one pays attention to his originality. In its turn, the perspective throws into relief other features of Beckett's difference from his contemporaries. In *Speech and Phenomena,* for a final example, Derrida wrote that "hearing oneself speak is not the inwardness of an inside that is closed in upon itself; it is the irreducible openness in the inside; it is the eye and the world within speech. *Phenomenological reduction is a scene, a theater stage.*"[26] Though rarely expressed with such metaphorical verve, the basic idea here has almost become a commonplace. If P and, before him, Lucky do not (cannot) refute the proposition, they constitute a protest. Resisting theatricality, displacing their masters, they suggest at the very least that the returns on the subject of being are not yet in.

---

[26]Jacques Derrida, *Speech and Phenomena,* trans. David B. Allison (Evanston, Ill.: Northwestern University Press, 1973), 86.

SEVEN

POLITICAL BECKETT

Christ, what a planet!
—*All That Fall*

I argued at the conclusion to the last chapter that, for Beckett, political and artistic tyranny are rooted together. As autography, Beckett's oeuvre became a complex lifetime effort to use the tyranny of art against itself in the interest of original design: in the interest, that is, of the constant and constantly changing register of Beckett's own persistent singularity. But stated as such, this argument does not necessarily invalidate Georg Lukács's criticism that Beckett's art is so attenuated that it denies any possibility of a just and humane society, and, a fortiori, any role his art might play in the achievement of such an end. "For people who want to change our globe so that it may become habitable," wrote Werner Hecht, "Beckett's theatre is uninteresting."[1] In these and kindred readings, Beckett is an instrument of the political status quo. The common early representations of Beckett as an "apolitical" writer only strengthened this view. Beckett and his creations are "caught in the viscous substance of arrested history because of their refusal to intervene into history." At best, they serve as "an appropriate warning." At worst, they serve to "le-

---

[1]Georg Lukács, *The Meaning of Contemporary Realism*, trans. John Mander and Necke Mander (London: Merlin Press, 1962); Werner Hecht, "Brecht 'und' Beckett," *Theater der Zeit* 14 (1966): 30 (cited in Darko Suvin, "Beckett's Purgatory of the Individual; or The 3 Laws of Thermodynamics," *Tulane Drama Review* 11 [Summer 1967]: 23).

gitimize the deceptive means by which domination is maintained in a social order, whether it be capitalist or socialist."[2] Such criticisms may appear flat-footed, but the question still remains: how does the autographical Beckett inflect our view of the a/political Beckett? The most vigorous and most frequently cited counterargument to Lukács's criticism is that of Theodor Adorno. Yet Adorno, far from rescuing Beckett for epic representation and realist exegesis, takes the very formal qualities that disturbed Lukács and makes of them Beckett's great strength. Instead of seeing in them "an abstract, subjectivist ontology," Adorno finds a paradoxical art beyond meaning and representation for which understanding "can only be understanding why it cannot be understood."[3] As pessimistic as a Marxian theorist ever gets, despairing of change arising from the working class, Adorno could never indicate a clear path out of the new "collectivist" world order of consumer capitalism. In a series of personal meditations (*Minima Moralia*) published on the eve of *En attendant Godot*, Adorno argued that the only recourse is to denounce the lie of "free and honest exchange" which undergirds this new world.[4] In Beckett, he found a writer who not only undertook this task, but pursued it as it needed to be pursued, root and branch. Beckett heroically refuses to accept the common agreements about language and meaning which had blinded existentialists and socialist realists alike. Abandoning Western individualism "like an outmoded bunker," Beckett puts on display its illusory character. His is an art in which "everything seems to be a sign of something inward" and yet

---

[2]Suvin, "Beckett's Purgatory," 27; Jack Zipes, "Beckett in Germany/Germany in Beckett," *New German Critique* 26 (1982): 157. With regard to Beckett's statement that he joined the Resistance only because of what was happening to his friends, Bair writes that "he was being consistent in his apolitical behavior" (Deirdre Bair, *Samuel Beckett: A Biography* [New York: Harcourt, Brace, Jovanovich, 1978], 308).

[3]Theodor W. Adorno, "Towards an Understanding of *Endgame*," in *Twentieth-Century Interpretations of Endgame*, ed. B. G. Chevigny, trans. Samuel M. Weber (Englewood Cliffs, N.J.: Prentice-Hall, 1969), 83, 88, 84; 1st pub., 1961.

[4]Theodor Adorno, *Minima Moralia: Reflections from Damaged Life*, trans. E. F. N. Jephcott (London: New Left Books, 1974), 44.

at the same time an art in which "the implicit referent no longer exists."[5]

But if meaning itself is at risk, is not the issue of intervention in history highly, if not terminally, problematic? And if there is no chartable course out of the mess we are in, can a work or reading predicated on that view even be considered political or politically engaged? "You're on earth," as Hamm says. "There's no cure for that!" (En, 53, 68). The question is a narrative question: Is there an achievable history other than the one that seems to be writing itself? Lukács demands of a novelist only that this question be kept open. And Adorno, for all his differences with Lukács, keeps it open as well. Without defining its shape or the stages of its realization, Adorno remained passionately committed to the idea of utopia. It is the possibility of utopia that gives political instrumentality to the "inescapable" authenticity of Franz Kafka and Beckett.[6] The paradox is that their art can enable utopia only by denying it:

> Like theory, art cannot concretize Utopia, not even negatively. The new as a cryptogram is the image of demise. Art is able to utter the unutterable, which is Utopia, through the medium of the absolute negativity of the world, whose image is a composite of all that is stigmatized as ugly and repulsive in modern art. While firmly reject-ing the appearance of reconciliation, art none the less holds fast to the idea of reconciliation in an antagonistic world. Thus, art is the true consciousness of an epoch in which Utopia—the belief that this

---

[5]Ibid., 90, 91. Such art, Adorno wrote toward the end of his life, "ends up taking a stand that ceases to be one . . . . The determinate negation of content becomes its principle of form. What is more, it negates content as such" (T. W. Adorno, *Aesthetic Theory*, trans. C. Lenhardt, ed. Gretel Adorno and Rolf Tiedemann [London: Routledge & Kegan Paul, 1984], 354).

[6]"Kafka's prose and Beckett's plays, or the truly monstrous novel *The Unnameable* [*sic*], have an effect by comparison with which officially committed works look like pantomime. Kafka and Beckett arouse the fear which existentialism merely talks about. By dismantling appearance, they explode from within the art which committed proclamation subjugates from without, and hence only in appearance. The inescapability of their work compels the change of attitude which committed works merely demand" (Theodor Adorno, "Commitment," in *The Essential Frankfort School Reader*, ed. Andrew Arato and Eike Gebhardt [New York: Continuum, 1990], 314–315).

earth here, now and immediately could, in virtue of the present potential of the forces of production, become a paradise—is as real a
possibility as total catastrophic destruction.[7]

The argument between Lukács and Adorno set the framework for
much of the early political discussion of Beckett. Given the extremity
of Adorno's defense, it is understandable that Beckett—such easy
prey for political critique, so stubborn a challenge for political endorsement—has been read most often in nonpolitical modes. Yet
Beckett's works are loaded with political resonances. *Catastrophe*
and *What Where* are vivid evocations of fascist control. *Play, Rough
for Radio II,* and other plays are built on the model of interrogation.
Jacques Moran is the quintessence of bourgeois complacency; Pozzo
and Hamm are overlords (landed gentry, bourgeois magnates);
Lucky and Clov are members of the exploited and disposable under-
class; Winnie is a prisoner of bourgeois fetishes; Krapp, a prisoner
of technology. So insistent are these features that Brecht could plan
a production of *Godot* in which Estragon would be cast as a worker,
Vladimir as an intellectual, and Pozzo as a landowner.[8] It seems
undeniable that, however one determines the relationship of Beckett's art to history and to the social distribution of power, he intended these political resonances to be felt.

Less noticed, yet even more to the point, is Beckett's rich reinvention of the most politicized of all literary forms, the utopia.[9] In pur-
suing this project, Beckett gave prominence to the very concept
(utopia) that for Adorno was the necessary (if absent) enabler of
authentic modern art. After his abandonment of narrative, Beckett
assiduously developed a series of utopian fictions in the twelve years
between 1954 and 1966.

Utopia

In H. G. Wells's 1894 evolutionary dystopia, *The Time Machine,* the
Time Traveller leaps to the year 802,701 and finds there a pale, atten-

---

[7]Adorno, *Aesthetic Theory,* 48.

[8]Suvin, "Beckett's Purgatory," 34.

[9]In reference to the broad literary tradition discussed in this chapter, the terms "utopia" and "utopian" encompass "dystopia" and "dystopian."

uated vestige of the human species. The Eloi are sweet, diminutive creatures with uncomplicated brains. Their beauty is so uniform that the difference of sexes is almost indeterminate. On his first full day among the Eloi, the Time Traveller rescues one of them from drowning, and from then on, his "little woman, as I believe it was," accompanies him everywhere during his eight-day sojourn, holding his hand by day and sleeping with him by night. "She was exactly like a child. She wanted to be with me always."[10]

The smallness, passivity, unquestioning devotion, and sexual indeterminacy of the Traveller's friend are closely matched by the narrator of Beckett's short prose narrative of 1966, *Assez*, which he translated into English as *Enough* in 1967. The text could well be the Eloi's account of her travels, hand-in-hand, with a grotesquely aged and bent version of the Time Traveller, someone whose elevated discourse she barely understands. "I did all he desired," she writes. "I desired it too. For him. Whenever he desired something so did I" (CSPR, 139).

There are other parallels between these two texts. In *The Time Machine,* the world of the future is described as a "weedless garden," strewn everywhere with "delicate and wonderful flowers."[11] In *Enough,* the narrator and her companion walk through a world carpeted everywhere with flowers in a climate "eternally mild. As if the earth had come to rest in spring" (CSPR, 143). These flowers are foregrounded throughout both texts and in both participate in closely parallel ending lines, similarly overlaid with the theme of companionship and the mood of nostalgia:

And I have by me, for my comfort, two strange flowers—shrivelled now, and brown and flat and brittle—to witness that even when mind and strength had gone, gratitude and a mutual tenderness still lived on in the heart of man.[12]

[10]H. G. Wells, *The Time Machine,* in *The Time Machine / The War of the Worlds,* ed. F. D. McConnell (New York: Oxford University Press, 1977), 54, 55.

[11]Ibid., 36.

[12]Ibid., 104.

Now I'll wipe out everything but the flowers. No more rain. No more
mounds. Nothing but the two of us dragging through the flowers.
Enough my old breasts feel his old hand. (CSPR, 144)

These parallels indicate how deeply passages of Beckett's childhood reading sank into his mind. Throughout his work one can find
remnants of Dickens, Kingsley, Wells, and other nineteenth- and
early-twentieth-century novelists whom Beckett must have read
when he was a boy. But if the reprocessing of these fragments was
largely unconscious, what was quite conscious was Beckett's deployment of the utopian tradition. In *The Time Machine,* the flowers
themselves are Wells's own highly conscious reworking of the floral
world of William Morris's *News from Nowhere* (1890). And Morris,
in his turn, had traded on a rich tradition of utopian garden imagery.[13] Beckett also uses flowers as an explicit utopian marker in a
passage referring to the world before it was entirely floral: "He mur-
mured of things that for him were no more and for me could not
have been. The wind in the overground stems. The shade and shelter
of the forests" (CSPR, 144).

Beckett's development of the utopian literary tradition has gone
largely unnoticed, despite the clear evidence of its presence in this
text and in others he wrote from the mid-1950s. No doubt this development has been screened by the assumption of an apolitical
Beckett as well as by those qualities that have encouraged this apolitical encoding—his difficulty, his intense inwardness, his roots in the
high modernist aesthetics of Joyce and Proust. These traits are remote from the popular and inevitably politicized features of nine-
teenth- and twentieth-century Anglo-American utopian fiction. The
genre in many ways typifies what Adorno found so repugnant in
socialist realism. Published in the wake of Bulwer-Lytton's *The Coming Race* (1871) and Edward Bellamy's *Looking Backward* (1887),
these novels were devoted to assessing, often with wearying doctrinal
commentary, the future consequences of social transformation.

---

[13]See John Dickson Hunt, "Gardens in Utopia: Utopia in the Garden," in *Between
Dream and Nature: Essays on Utopia and Dystopia,* ed. D. Baker-Smith and C. C. Barfoot,
DQR Studies in Literature, ser. 2, vol. 61 (Amsterdam: Rodopi, 1987), 114–123.

Given the way Beckett has been critically packaged and the modernist strangeness of his texturing, to yoke his work with such novels as
these would seem aesthetically dissonant.

Yet with *Endgame*, which Beckett began late in 1955, Beckett not
only deploys a dys/utopian framework but invites us to see it as
such. Like the final pages of *The Time Machine* and like *Enough*,
Endgame is a vision of the last days of life on the planet. Situated in
a bunker-like structure, the play takes place in what appears to be
the last remaining vestige of lighted space in a depopulated world,
variously described as "gray" (En, 31), "corpsed" (En, 30), and finally "extinguished" (En, 81). Like Wells, too, Beckett milked the
devolutionary motif, continually reminding us of the things that are
no more: forests (as also in *Enough*), bicycles, coffins, Turkish Delight.[14]

In the ten years after *Endgame* (written 1955–56), Beckett wrote
a number of utopian fictions. In addition to *Enough* (written 1965),
the series includes *How It Is* (1958–60), *All Strange Away* (1963–65),
Imagination Dead Imagine (1963–65), *Ping* (1965–67), *Lessness*
(c. 1967), and *The Lost Ones* (1965–70). Other works, written during
this period, take a coloration from this project. In *Happy Days*
(1961), "the last human kind" are a faint memory, while the fixed
light of the sun suggests an earth that has come to rest just as it has
in the far distant future of *The Time Machine* (or again in *Enough*,
where it seems the "earth has come to rest in the spring"). Winnie's
sensation of being "sucked up" may well indicate the closer proxim-
ity, and hence stronger gravitational pull, of the sun on a planet that
is closing in on its final end. In *Rough for Theatre I* (written c. 1956–
57), the only green left on the earth is "a little moss" and the earth
seems to "have got stuck, one sunless day, in the heart of winter, in
the grey of evening" (CSPL, 72). This context also gives a more than
simply practical accounting for *Krapp*'s setting in "a late evening in
the future." And already, in *Godot*, the emptied, unfruitful, and

---

[14]Barely noticeable is Hamm's waking remark: "What Dreams! Those trees!" (En, 3).
But in a swerve that marks the difference half a century can make, Hamm later barks at
Clov to kill a flea for fear that "humanity might start from there all over again" (En, 33).

barely populated landscape suggests a world left over after global calamity.

Beckett not only developed the genre but foregrounded the pre-eminent nineteenth-century concern out of which utopia had its rebirth: the nature and consequences of social engineering. As utopia gave way to dystopia, the buoyant optimism of Victorian texts such as *News from Nowhere* and *Looking Backward* was succeeded by the anxiety of texts such as Aldous Huxley's *Brave New World,* Yevgeni Zamyatin's *We,* George Orwell's *1984,* and John Updike's *The Poorhouse Fair,* in which the hubris of technocratic social reconstruction turned to nightmare. In this context, Beckett's *How It Is* is a striking distillation of the rugged social critiques of Huxley and Orwell. Devoted to the construction of an entire planet in which "justice" prevails in the form of absolute symmetry, *How It Is* gives rare expression to the fear of deadly conformity which has so absorbed twentieth-century dystopian texts:

> at the instant I reach Pim another reaches Bem we are regulated thus our justice wills it thus fifty thousand couples again at the same instant the same everywhere with the same space between them it's mathematical it's our justice in this muck where all is identical our ways and way of faring right leg right arm push pull. (HII, 112)

The suffocation that comes with this tyranny of abstract order is foreshadowed in the "bottling" of progenitors in *Endgame* and redeveloped in the urn burial inquisition of *Play.* Beckett continued to distill the form in the sixties, entombing single or paired individuals in *All Strange Away, Imagination Dead Imagine,* and *Ping,* and canning an entire population in *The Lost Ones.* Unquestionably, this is a literature of protest. But in what way, and to what extent, can this protest be focused on political or social instrumentalities? If one does so focus it, is one exceeding or ignoring the text in any way? More specifically, does such a focus accommodate the two principal formal innovations that Beckett worked into the utopian tradition?

BREAKING THE HISTORICAL FRAME

The first innovation is Beckett's dismantling of the conventional device by which the two worlds—the present world and the utopian one—are linked. In *The Time Machine*, for example, the machine itself is the vehicle by which the worlds are connected. By means of the machine, we are allowed to locate the Eloi in space and time, establishing their empirical relationship to ourselves. In *The Coming Race*, the link is established by means of a fissure in a mine through which the narrator passes from our world to the long-buried society of the Vril-ya. In *Looking Backward*, the link is established by means of a 113-year trance. Even in twentieth-century dystopias that begin *in situ*, the relation of the fictional setting to our own is established clearly. Within the first three pages of *Brave New World*, we learn that the action takes place in London in the year 632 AF (After Ford). In *1984*, the temporal coordinate is the title itself. By these devices, the reader can apply the alien narrative to the present world, familiarizing the unfamiliar and canceling the effect of "hesitation" attributed by Tzvetan Todorov to the fantastic.[15] This cancellation is a necessary part of the rhetoric of this strain of utopian fiction. Without the cancellation of the fantastic, the historical and political agenda of these texts would be undermined.

In *Endgame*, the utopian frame is manifestly breached. On the one hand, the world appears to have come to its end through the implacable march of entropy or some other agency of extinction. On the other hand, our contemporary world—the world of sugar plums and boating excursions on Lake Como—is well within the memory of the players. In this way, Beckett makes terminally indeterminate the temporal relation of the fictive world to our own. He further aggravates the uncertainty of temporal distance by including a corrupt version of another conventional linking device: that of referring during the course of the narrative to historical events that take place somewhere in the interval between utopian and real-world time. Morris, for example, does this in *News from Nowhere* when he refers to "the great clearing of houses in 1955."[16] In *Endgame*, Hamm seems to do this through his account of a man who

[15]Tzvetan Todorov, *The Fantastic: A Structural Approach to a Literary Genre*, trans. Richard Howard (Ithaca, N.Y.: Cornell University Press, 1975).

[16]William Morris, *News from Nowhere* (London: Longmans, Green, 1908), 16.

may have, at some earlier time, come crawling toward him, "pale, wonderfully pale and thin," his face "black with mingled dirt and tears":

> It's my little one, he said. Tsstss, a little one, that's bad. My little boy, he said, as if the sex mattered. Where did he come from? He named the hole. A good half-day, on horse. What are you insinuating? That the place is still inhabited? No no, not a soul, except himself and the child—assuming he existed. Good. I enquired about the situation at Kov, beyond the gulf. Not a sinner. Good. (En, 52)

The passage suggests an intermediate historical stage in the deterioration of the planet. The reference to "the situation at Kov, beyond the gulf" imitates the retrospect of historic sieges common to science fiction. One imagines a final outpost of survivors in the Siberian town of Kov, slowly dying on the shores of the Arctic Ocean. Yet, in context, Hamm's story is a highly conscious set piece, a ritualized performance, which he refers to as "my story." Delivered with exaggerated artifice, it tells of a manifestly incredible meteorological coincidence: a Christmas day on which it was "zero by the thermometer," "fifty by the heliometer," "a hundred by the anemometer," and "zero by the hygrometer." We never learn whether or not there is any historical truth to it, much less whether or not the child involved was Clov, as many critics have presumed.

Moreover, what dominates our attention in this dystopic setting is the inassimilable strangeness of the figures on stage: Hamm on his throne and his parents in their trash bins. What absorbs attention is what Robbe-Grillet calls the "presence" of figures on the stage and their disconnection from past and future.[17] Here, as everywhere in his theater, Beckett capitalizes on the phenomenology of the stage to create worlds that are at once present and remote, viscerally immediate and bizarrely alien. In this context, the late-nineteenth-century utopian revival, with its careful linking of past and future, was a genre waiting for Beckett's disconnecting pen.

---

[17]Alain Robbe-Grillet, "Samuel Beckett, or 'Presence' in the Theatre," in *Samuel Beckett*, ed. Martin Esslin (Englewood Cliffs, N.J.: Prentice-Hall, 1965), 108–116.

In the next decade, Beckett continued to draw on the utopian tradition to construct the otherness of worlds nowhere "on earth."[18] In each of these works, Beckett breaks the utopian frame as he does in *Endgame,* severing those links to our own world which have traditionally given utopia its rhetorical force.[19] In *How It Is,* as in *Endgame,* Beckett includes teasing references to another world, perhaps our own. "Life above in the light" appears to be the place of normality where people don't crawl in the mud, where they have dogs, fall in love, commit suicide. But the references to this other life are so tenuous, and its place in space and time so indeterminate, as to deny any solid ground for reading *How It Is* as a historical extrapolation. The same can be said even more emphatically of *Imagination Dead Imagine* and *The Lost Ones.* The former begins as if in the aftermath of the death of a planet, perhaps ours:

> No trace anywhere of life, you say, pah, no difficulty there, imagination not dead yet, yes, dead, good, imagination dead imagine. Islands, waters, azure, verdure, one glimpse and vanished, endlessly, omit. Till all white in the whiteness the rotunda. (CSPR, 145)

What appears in the rotunda are two bodies—barely breathing and murmuring "Ah." At the end they are abandoned, "a white speck lost in whiteness," never to be found again, as the voice of the text, following the sci-fi topos of the search for life on other planets, voyages in quest of "better elsewhere." In *The Lost Ones,* the disconnection of worlds is still more emphatic. With its opening sentence, the reader is constrained to focus entirely on the gratuitous presence of a world: "Abode where lost bodies roam each searching for its lost one" (CSPR, 159)—not, "There is an abode" or "Imagine an abode," but simply "Abode."

By deploying the utopian generic structure, Beckett trades on expectations he then breaks. Breaking frame, he creates what Erving

---

[18]Samuel Beckett, *All Strange Away,* passim (CSPR, 117–128).

[19]The concept of frames and framing, as well as that of breaking frame, is adapted loosely from the sociologist Erving Goffman's *Frame Analysis: An Essay on the Organization of Experience* (New York: Harper and Row, 1974; rpt., Boston: Northeastern University Press, 1986).

Goffman has called a "negative experience"—"a violation of the realm of being that [the artistic mode tries] to establish."[20] In this regard, Beckett's use of the utopian literary tradition is in keeping with what I called in Chapter 2 his late-modernist procedure. It was a delicate challenge. Beckett always had to be on guard that he not reach the point where the disruption of artistic expectations became the norm. He had to avoid creating an ambiance in which the shock and discomfort Goffman attributed to the "negative experience" were softened by familiarity. Beckett capitalized on utopia in part because it came equipped with a powerful set of expectations which he could thwart with precision. For the same reason, he abandoned the genre after a decade's experimentation, thereby avoiding the familiarity of repetition.

But the care with which, in this aesthetic process, he provoked the sense of historical disconnection created its own implicit thematics. As we have already noted, Beckett's transition to the static plane of *Godot* was a major step in releasing his work from narrative sequencing. The two acts of *Godot* accentuate the absence of story by the small differences that disrupt their similarity. Swallowed in that absence is the important political idea of a plausible historical order of events. "Have you not done tormenting me with your accursed time!" cries Pozzo. "It's abominable! When! When! One day, is that not enough for you, one day he went dumb, one day I went blind, one day we'll go deaf, one day we were born, one day we shall die, the same day, the same second, is that not enough for you?" (WG, 57). "Yesterday!" cries Hamm. "What does that mean? Yesterday!" To which Clov answers, "That means that bloody awful day, long ago, before this bloody awful day" (En, 43–44).

Without question, Beckett wants us to feel the weight of political injustice, the outrage of tyranny, the stifling inhumanity of engineered lives, the bitter residue of a system of self-interest. Yet, at the same time, he communicates a vision of history as, at once, blind and catastrophic—wholly beyond the reach of narrative control. And he does this not simply in his thematics (always the prey of

[20]Ibid., 403.

allegorical renegotiation) but in the experience of the form itself. In pointedly adopting the highly politicized form of the utopia, Beckett pointedly withdraws from it any hope of the historical mechanism of utopian reform. By so doing, he undermines the one essential element that enabled Adorno's affirmative political reading. We can, of course, postulate another world with another kind of history, unendorsed by Beckett, and situate Beckett's work within it. And we can further imagine Beckett's work performing a vital function within such a world. But it would appear from the evidence that we do so without Beckett's authority. Indeed, in his explicit engagement with utopia, Beckett appears almost to speak directly to Adorno, to cry out, "Use your head, can't you, use your head, you're on earth, there's no cure for that!"

Most positive political readings of Beckett have required the extratextual supplement of a world context in which improved social conditions and ways to achieve them are plausible. If this is clearly the case with Adorno, it is more subtly so with the political interpreters who have come after deconstruction. Having abandoned utopian modes for more chastened, improvisatory, situational modes, such critics as Steven Connor and David Lloyd train their attention on exposing and contesting the myriad agencies of cultural hegemony.[21] Committed not to utopia but rather to a more equita-

---

[21]Steven Connor, *Samuel Beckett: Repetition, Theory and Text* (Oxford: Blackwell, 1988); David Lloyd, "Writing in the Shit," in *Anomalous States: Irish Writing and the Post-Colonial Moment* (Durham, N.C.: Duke University Press, 1993), 41–58. For Connor, Beckett's work enacts a wide-ranging disarticulation of the hegemony enforced through culture's naked repetitions. At the same time, he sees in the "Beckett industry" the seductive power of cultural agencies to rearticulate hegemony, making of Beckett himself a supporting cultural monolith. Lloyd, in a study focused on the case of Ireland, addresses the cultural politics of identity. His concern is with the way in which nationalism reinstates the conditions of colonialism by requiring in its turn a monologic culture. In that context, Beckett's oeuvre "stands as the most exhaustive dismantling we have of the logic of identity that at every level structures and maintains the post-colonial moment" (56). Another reading that has something of the same post-Adorno restraint is Jan Bruck's "Beckett, Benjamin and the Modern Crisis in Communication," *New German Critique* 26 (1982): 159–171. Of the growing number of recent political readings of Beckett, three interesting departures are: Thomas Cousineau, "*Waiting for Godot* and Politics," *Coriolan: Théâtre et politique*, Travaux de l'université de Toulouse-Le Mirail, ser. B, vol. 5 (1984):

ble human arrangement in which voices are heard rather than silenced, both Connor and Lloyd present Beckett as an artist who
exposes the normalizing control of language and culture while he
demonstrates the power of art to open up gaps in the seemingly
smooth surface of those same entities.

Carefully as they step, however, intent as they are to avoid the
occlusion (silencing, marginalization) of others, such readings generally engage in their own form of occlusion. The problem stems
from the urgency both Connor and Lloyd feel to exorcise or decons-
truct terms of the subject like "author" (Connor) or "identity"
(Lloyd), as did Adorno before them regarding the term "individual."
Like other post-Enlightenment terms of the subject, these terms are
embedded in the cultural status quo they serve and encrusted with
normative functions. Yet in concentrating on the process of occlusion which these terms enable, criticism finesses the complex problematic of individually specific force. This jettisoning of terms for
the subject has left in their place, at best, the existential/postmodern
"void" or "*néant*" or "nothing," terms that have become in their
turn occluding reifications of intellectual culture. What is missing,
and no doubt impossible, is a term that identifies the topic (the place
of attention) while, at the same time, it acknowledges unknowing.
One of Beckett's most promising terms for this double intent was
"The Unnamable." In a doomed effort to preserve his term from
accreting a false knowledge (which, by the nature of naming, it already had), Beckett refrained from using it anywhere within the
novel to which it gave its name. But if the effort failed, the intensity
of Beckett's focus remained, casting a nimbus over all his representations and giving his work its special reflexivity.

REFLEXIVE WORLDS

Reflexivity was the second major innovation that Beckett applied to
the utopian tradition. In the process, he continued to elaborate the

161–167; Jon Erickson, "Self-objectification and Preservation in Beckett's *Krapp's Last Tape*," in *The World of Samuel Beckett*, ed. Joseph H. Smith, Psychiatry and the Humanities 12 (Baltimore: Johns Hopkins University Press, 1991), 189; Christian Prigent, "A Descent of Clowns," *Journal of Beckett Studies*, n.s. 3, no. 1 (1993), 15–17.

imbrication of tyranny and creativity. He never lets us forget that these fabricated worlds are worlds at the disposal of their fabricator. Social engineering, so constant a theme in utopian fiction, is fused with the aesthetic engineering of the text; revulsion against the one brings on the destruction of the other: "all these calculations yes explanations yes the whole story from beginning to end yes completely false yes" (HII, 144). The genre of the utopia gave Beckett both focus and impact in his alignment of the artistic and tyrannical cravings for order. In *All Strange Away,* the artistic project is a planet in the shape of a prison cell.

> Imagine eyes burnt ashen blue and lashes gone, lifetime of unseeing glaring, jammed open, one lightning wince per minute on earth, try that. Have him say, no sound. No way in, none out, he's not here. Tighten it round him, three foot square, five high, no stool, no sitting, no kneeling, no lying, just room to stand and revolve, . . . (CSPR, 118)

Here, as elsewhere, the voice both gives shape to the text and acts upon its human content. All these texts anticipate the artist/tyrant of *Catastrophe* and all grow out of the dominating figure of Beckett's first full experiment with utopia. Ham actor and impresario, Hamm squeezes the life out of his supporting cast and may, for all we know, have squeezed the life out of the planet.

Ironically, it is Clov who expresses the *reductio* of the utopian ideal: "I love order. It's my dream. A world where all would be silent and still and each thing in its last place, under the last dust" (En, 57). This is a world with no surprises, a world with "all strange away." As a political statement, it would be a caricature were it not for the extraordinary implication that tyranny is rooted in the imagination. The creating of art, like the making of worlds, is a matter of cramming, jamming, wedging, bending, poking. Nothing is sacred in this process. The muse/beloved herself, "lovely beyond words," is broken down into her four erogenous zones and distributed on to the four walls of a cubic cell: "Imagine him kissing, caressing, licking, sucking, fucking and buggering all this stuff" (*All Strange Away,* CSPR, 119).

There is a further twist to Beckett's reflexivity in these utopian fictions, and it further complicates the issue of agency. It is most consistently apparent in Beckett's use of the imperative mood ("Imagine him kissing . . ."). Who directs attention? Who looks? Who gives orders? Who takes them? The echo of the divine grammar of "fiat lux" is surely intentional, but the self-relationship of a creator at once above and imminent within his works is much less assured. Throughout the cluster of planetary constructions, agency is distributed in a grammar of imagining which includes not just ordering and carrying out but also reacting to a sometimes intransigent imagined:

> Light flows, eyes close, stay closed till it ebbs, no, can't do that, eyes stay open, all right, look at that later. Black bag over his head, no good, all the rest still in light, front, sides, back, between the legs. Black shroud, . . . (*All Strange Away*, CSPR, 118)

Any assessment of these texts as utopia must accommodate not simply the imagery of tyrannical containment but these complexities of their enactment. It may now be clear how the concerns I am raising here complement those raised by Beckett's other innovation of the genre: his breaking of the historical frame. On both fronts, historical agency and personal agency, he complicates our sense of the cause of utopian tyranny. The specular reflection of the problem of personal agency can be found, as can that of historical agency, in the story Hamm delivers with such fanfare in *Endgame*.

As we noted above, it is impossible to determine if the "facts" of Hamm's story occupy the same ontological space as that of the play (so that in reference to the play they are "true") or are parts of a fiction performed within that space (so that in reference to the play they are "untrue"). Early in the play, Hamm asks Clov, "Do you remember your father?" (En, 38), a question providing a kind of preparatory ballast for the story's factuality. Yet Hamm preserves the option of bringing on "other characters" (En, 54), and the story's ending seems at the mercy of his creative energy:

CLOV: Will it not soon be the end?
HAMM: I'm afraid it will.
CLOV: Pah! You'll make up another.
HAMM: I don't know.

(*Pause.*)
   I feel rather drained.
(*Pause.*)
   The prolonged creative effort.
          (En, 61)

A story that is and is not a "chronicle" (En, 58) and in which Hamm and Clov are and are not players, Hamm's narration is at once the record of something that actually took its course and the coming into being of something that takes shape at the bidding of its creator. But the story is more than a specular reflection or *mise en abyme,* because the play that contains the story is at the same time implicated in it, insofar as the story tells a history of which the play is a part. The fate of the world on stage is somehow tethered to the creative effort of Hamm. Maintained in a life parallel to that of the play, recurring at several points and entering Hamm's final soliloquy, the story is called on to finish the play: "reckoning closed and story ended" (En, 83). If the mysteries of the story and its telling are, on the one hand, a specular reflection of the situation that contains them, they belong to, on the other, a narrative action that contains all the rest. This perception is reinforced in other details that directly relate to the power of Hamm.

One of the things which stands out in the story's thematics, for example, is the close accord between the extinction of life on earth and Hamm's desire for that extinction: ". . . not a soul, except himself and the child—assuming he existed. Good. I enquired about the situation at Kov, beyond the gulf. Not a sinner. Good." There is more than a faint suggestion in this sequence that what happens in this world, including its extinction, is in some way governed by Hamm. If such were the case, it would be as if a chess game could be conducted from within, by one of the pieces on the board. This possibility is, in fact, suggested by the play's setting. Matching the reduction of life in the world outside, the setting on stage is that of a one-sided chess game reduced to three pieces—a king (Hamm) and two pawns (his parents in ashcans). Hamm's opening words, "Me . . . to play" (En, 2), suggest that he is at once piece and player. In Keeping with a destructive bent that comes closer and closer to being visited directly upon himself, he expends moves pointlessly, ordering himself moved about in a circle and commanding the elimination of his pawns by having them "bottled." As the play nears its end, Hamm's reflexive authority becomes more pronounced: "An aside, ape! Did you never hear an aside before? (*Pause.*). I'm warming up for my last soliloquy" (En, 77–78). When the last soliloquy arrives, Hamm takes over the stage directions, correcting his lines when the need arises:

Raise hat.
(*He raises his toque.*)
Peace to our . . . arses.
(*Pause.*).
And put on again.
(*He puts on his toque.*)
Deuce.
(*Pause. He takes off his glasses.*)
Wipe.
(*He takes out his handkerchief and, without unfolding it, wipes his glasses.*)
And put on again.
(*He puts on his glasses, puts back the handkerchief in his pocket.*)
We're coming. A few more squirms like that and I'll call.
(*Pause.*)
A little poetry.
(*Pause.*)
You prayed—
(*Pause. He corrects himself.*)
You CRIED for night; it comes—
(*Pause. He corrects himself.*)
It FALLS: now cry in darkness.
(En, 82–83)[22]

Like the "devised deviser devising it all" in *Company* ("fabling of one fabling"), Hamm is both in and out of the play. He travels, as it were, on both sides of a Möbius strip. In this regard, he is a stage

[22]Beckett experimented with this effect in *Eleutheria* when he had Henri Krap call for the curtain at the end of Act I (El, 67/64).

version of the supradiegetic voice that speaks without warning through the narrators of the trilogy: "What a rabble in my head, what a gallery of moribunds. Murphy, Watt, Yerk, Mercier and all the others" (*Molloy*, TN, 137). If this uncertainty destabilizes received notions of authorship and the origins of art, it at the same time keeps our attention closely attuned to the question of where this play is coming from.[23] If Beckett's art works to undo the power implicit in the notion of "unity of intention, grounded in the figure of the author," as Connor suggests,[24] it works at the same time to sustain a strong feeling of wonderment about textual origination. This aspect of Beckett's dealing with the question of the "subject" is as important as that which he dismantles. Finally, Hamm provides a model for what must have been Beckett's feeling of "Möbic" relation to his art: victim and victimizer, created and creating, locked inside his works and traveling from one to another.

TRAVELING THROUGH THE DEAD ZONE

As the reflexive concentration of his utopian fictions increased, Beckett further adapted the first innovation we discussed above—the disruption of historical causality—to the representation of his complex relations to his works over time. When Beckett set the utopian series in motion, he created a sequence of abodes in the now familiar process of recollection by invention, establishing in each work the mark of persistence by the mark of difference. It is probably the

---

[23]In his dramatic work, Beckett introduced the "Möbius effect" in his first play, when he had the Prompter in *Eleutheria* quit in disgust because the players were not following their lines. As the Prompter leaves, the Glazier calls for the script, which comes sailing back through the air. The sequence creates an exquisite, if momentary, unease: the perception that the play contains the script that contains the play. Lucien Dällenbach's concept of "réduplication aporistique" also describes this effect. One of three modes of *mise en abyme*, it occurs when a fragment of a work is presumed to include the work that includes it ("fragment censé inclure l'oeuvre qui l'inclut") (Dällenbach, *Le récit spéculaire: Essai sur la mise en abyme* [Paris: Seuil, 1977], 51).

[24]Connor, *Samuel Beckett*, 188.

case that Beckett intended (or discovered) in that strange locution "imagination dead imagine" a formula for the succession of works. In this reading of these three words, the break between works is marked by "dead" and the persistence in difference marked by the way the verb "imagine" both recalls and reinvents the noun "imagination." The verb also signifies in its active voice and present tense that new work is now under way. As if to hold this sequencing of works up to view, Beckett incorporated the principle of the world-separating gap or break—the "dead" zone—into both *Imagination Dead Imagine* and its earlier companion piece, *All Strange Away*. In effect, he recreated within the microcosm of the individual work the persistence through stoppage which characterizes the oeuvre.

In *All Strange Away*, the break comes after three pages devoted to the male figure, Emmo (with Emma on the walls):

> Then lost and all the remaining field for hours of time on earth. Imagination dead imagine to lodge a second in that glare a dying common house or dying window fly, then fall the five feet to the dust and die or die and fall. No, no image, no fly here, no life or dying here but his, a speck of dirt. Or hers since sex not seen so far, say Emma standing, turning, sitting, . . . (CSPR, 120)

The text, revived, continues with renewed imagining, but it now features Emma in the cell (with Emmo on the walls). In *Imagination Dead Imagine*, the break occurs halfway through the text between one sentence and another: ". . . enduring tumult. Rediscovered miraculously after what absence in perfect voids it is no longer quite the same, . . ." (CSPR, 146). Having first adapted by subversion the historical connectedness of traditional utopia, Beckett adapted his adaptation. The historical break became the dead space between imaginings, its function that of the twelve breaks in the *Texts for Nothing* and the 825 breaks in *How It Is*. As such, the breaks arouse not only feelings of destruction, failure, and loss, but the astonishment of renewal ("rediscovered miraculously"). The term "renewal" is a good one because it encompasses both continuation and difference. If the ground base in this series is a dystopian compound of reduction, constraint, cruelty, despair, and the dispersion of self, the counterpoint is the irrepressible return of new beginnings: "tender mercies," as the Mouth in *Not I* would say, "new every morning" (CSPL, 221–222).

From beginning to end, Beckett's art is one long protest. It is written out of a horror of human wretchedness and a yearning that this wretchedness be lessened. But the overriding sense in Beckett is not that there is something wrong with society or with the means of production or with the distribution of goods and privileges or with the hegemony of social control, but that there is something massively wrong with the entire arrangement, from birth to death. Beckett's social protest is always shadowed by his metaphysical bafflement. To downplay the weight in his work of the contradictions inherent in life, including the dominion of death, is also to reduce the enigma of individually distinct consciousness and something of its *frisson.*

Beckett's redirection of the manifestly political genre of the utopia throws his priorities into sharp relief. I have tried in this chapter to sketch the components of this redirection and to indicate how powerfully Beckett's political and historical representations are dominated by the enigmas of death and personal agency. In the utopian sequence, we can see once again how important it is to keep in mind the specific enigma of Beckett's own poetic agency. It is only by seeing his oeuvre as a continuing autographical project that one can gather the immediacy and the urgency of Beckett's complex vision.[25] One can also see something of its poignancy, for if Beckett

---

[25]In *All Strange Away,* Beckett compresses this complexity into six words of one sentence which contain, back to back, the two titles of the companion pieces he wrote in 1963–65: ". . . imagination dead imagine all strange away" (CSPR, 121). As always in Beckett's late prose, the syntax bristles with semantic possibilities. In the mind of this reader, two stand out. (1) "Imagination dead. Imagine all strange away." In other words, abolish all strangeness ("Jolly and Draeger gone, never were"). This is the evacuating imagination, Hamm's ruthless desire to extinguish everything. (2) "Imagination Dead. Imagine. All strange away." In this reading, the death of the imagination is followed by its birth and, with it, the rallying cry: "All strange away!" Here strangeness is not evacuated but endorsed. (And indeed, the strangeness of this text does not let up.) Together, these two readings encompass the symbiotic relationship of creation and tyranny which shows up everywhere in Beckett's mature art and which gives it so much of its vigor.

in his utopias conceived of writing as writing through a series of deaths—playing the game of imagination dead imagine—he wrote at the same time under the shadow of a death that to all appearances is absolute. "No, life ends and no, there is nothing elsewhere" (*Imagination Dead Imagine,* CSPR, 147). In his own case, and that of those he loved, Beckett's work was no proof against death. It was a fact he anticipated long before the end, though it never kept him from testing the resources of his art.

EIGHT

SUPERNATURAL BECKETT

The grave unites . . .
—Alexander Pope

Beckett's great poem about death is *A Piece of Monologue*. Begun early in 1977 under the working title "Gone," it was put in its final form in 1979 when the actor David Warrilow asked Beckett for a play on the subject of death.[1] The poem culminates a long artistic engagement with death which began with Beckett's first published short story, "Assumption" (1929). Before 1950, death in Beckett is generally a matter of dying (by assumption, by accident, by medical malpractice, by being boiled alive, by explosion, by drowning, by suicide, by murder, by decrepitude). After 1950, death is increasingly a matter of mourning. Whether this shift was catalyzed by the death of Beckett's mother, May Beckett, on August 25, 1950, one can only speculate.[2] Certainly a pivotal work in this chronology is *Krapp's Last Tape* (1958), in which dying is imminent and mourning pervasive. I argued in Chapter 4 that *Krapp* represents a self-conscious

---

[1] The seed for *A Piece of Monologue* appears to have been sown in a manuscript titled "The Voice VERBATIM," which Beckett wrote in January 1977. See Charles Krance, "Beckett's *Encores*: Textual Genesis as *Still-Life Performance*," *Essays-in-Theatre* 8 (May 1990): 122–123.

[2] The most extended, and in some ways the sanest, commentary on death in Beckett's work is Christopher Ricks's *Beckett's Dying Words* (Oxford: Oxford University Press, 1993).

consolidation of craft by which Beckett inscribes dying and mourning with the dense, highly wrought music that was his live signature.
A work of obsessive mourning, *A Piece of Monologue* displays an
even tighter symbiosis of intense feeling and intensely rhythmical
musicality. As in *Krapp,* time's arrow in the later play is both inexorably straight and made to dance in circles. But the kind of music
Beckett makes in *Monologue* involves a logistical complexity that far
exceeds anything in *Krapp.* This combination of lyrical simplicity
and mind-resisting inventive excess is a standard feature of the later
work. Barely more than a staged, single-voiced lyric, *A Piece of
Monologue* is at once so intricate and so compact that it seems to
bend understanding. As I hope to show, these two qualities—the
play's focus on death and the logistical complexity of its music—are
related. If we can grasp that relationship, we can understand an additional facet of Beckett's autographical investment in his art.

THE ART OF THE LYRIC

Taken strictly as lyrical art, *A Piece of Monologue* can be situated
within the traditional modes of loss (the monody, the threnody, the
elegy, the lament). In that context, it is marked by its austere dedica-
tion to its mood. If it lacks the diversity and the consolatory gestures
of philosophical transcendence which often characterize works in
the elegiac tradition, it has in exchange a heightened intensity of
focus, as if Beckett had gone back to the purer forms of the expression of grief (the dirge, the coronach). In the modern period, it is
difficult to find anything quite so unrelieved. Swinburne, for example, whose constriction of emotional range can come close to Beckett's, still trades on the conventional language of relief:

> Content thee, howsoe'er, whose days are done;
> There lies not any troublous thing before,
> Nor sight nor sound to war against thee more,
> For whom all winds are quiet as the sun,
> All waters as the shore.

There is no similar perspectival movement outward in *A Piece of
Monologue.* Its confinement is infernal. Beckett's monodist, in a brief

gesture at an entr'acte, struggles to escape the intensity of focus to which he is condemned ("Move on to other matters. Try to move on. To other matters"), only to be drawn almost immediately back again into his obsessive circling when he stumbles on the key word "gone": "Or gone the will to move again. Gone. Faint cry in his ear" (CSPL, 268). At the end, he concedes: "Never were other matters. Never two matters. Never but the one matter. The dead and the gone. The dying and the going" (CSPL, 269).

This confinement of the narrative, together with the manner of its staging, makes the play a black-and-white object of great density. Throughout, Beckett accentuates the exclusivity of "dying and going" by extracting all color from the staging and almost all reference to color from the monologue, leaving only the mordant shades: black, white, and grey. Photographs have been ripped from the wall and torn to pieces, leaving "grey void[s]" for the father and mother, and a "grey blot" for the family. The vision of burial which recurs three times is a masterfully compressed evocation of bereavement: "Grey light. Rain pelting. Umbrellas round a grave. Seen from above. Streaming black canopies. Black ditch beneath. Rain bubbling in the black mud. Empty for the moment. That place beneath" (CSPL, 268).

The oxymoron on which the monologue opens—"Birth was the death of him"—establishes this austere confinement of focus at the start. Instead of extending meaning outward as would a paradox in the Joycean mode, it seeks some point of absolute compression in the "one matter" that is the play's subject. "Birth" (that begins the play) and "Gone" (that ends it) are fused by the action of the play into the single word "Begone," a word that both binds and subordinates the word "be" to the word "gone." If one hears the word "begin" in this word as well, it is equally subordinated.[3] The many echoes of this melding of opposites into one entity ("Born dead of night," "Dying on") and related puns such as "Waiting on the rip

---

[3] See Jane Alison Hale, *The Broken Window: Beckett's Dramatic Perspective* (West Lafayette, Ind.: Purdue University Press, 1987), 127–128; and Enoch Brater, *Beyond Minimalism: Beckett's Late Style in the Theater* (New York: Oxford University Press, 1987), 116.

word" (in which the "untimely ripped" of Macduff's birth is blended with "Rest In Peace") are equally governed by the same gravitational pull. In its bare narrativizations, the birth scene itself is presented as an expiration in which the first breath marks not the beginning but the end of life: "Fade. Gone. Cry. Snuffed with breath of nostrils" (CSPL, 269).[4] Even the word "matter" subordinates "mater" (both mother and the benignity of mother earth) to the dark side of the pun, imaged by the "black mud" of the cemetery.

This certainly is original art, yet in this aspect of its originality— its extraordinary focus and intensity—*A Piece of Monologue* is, as I noted above, readily compatible with the ancient lyrical tradition of the lament. Where the play departs from the tradition—and departs radically—is in the management of its dramatic and narrative material. Though one can to a certain degree thematize Beckett's innovations, making them conform to larger elegiac purposes, there is an excess of invention in this text (as in almost all of Beckett's postwar texts) which will not permit normalization in this way. This monologue in particular is at one and the same time so delicately multiple and so densely compacted that hardly two commentaries fail to conflict on one or more details of its literal content.

STRANGE LOOPS

The dramatic situation is this. A man stands in "faint diffuse light" by a lamp in a room with a pallet bed and delivers a monologue in the third person. And the narrative situation (what we learn from

---

[4]Commenting on the first phrasing of this event, "stifled by nasal," Beckett told the Fletchers that it describes "the nasal consonant in 'gone.' " See Beryl S. and John Fletcher, *A Student's Guide to the Plays of Samuel Beckett* (London: Faber, 1985), 244. In the context of the birth night, however, this phrase and the later "Snuffed with breath of nostrils" must also refer literally to the onset of regular breathing once the baby's first cry has ceased. Connotatively, the phrasing makes this stillness of peaceful nose breathing a death that follows upon the last sound from the old life in the womb, the birth cry, or, in this inversion of our normal way of viewing it, an agonized death cry. Of course, the sentiment expressed by all cries in this work is "gone."

the monologue) is this. A man arises at nightfall as he has countless nights before, goes to the window, then gropes his way to a lamp which he lights in a process using three successive matches; then he turns to the eastern wall of his room (stage front) from which photographs of loved ones have long ago been (untimely) ripped, and there he waits until the first word ("Birth") of the monologue takes shape in his mouth. This is the same monologue that we ourselves have been hearing.

With the word "Birth," the narrative setting shifts to the night of his birth. "That first night" is very like the night just described, with a few salient exceptions. It takes place in a room like the one we see, though it contains a brass bed, not a pallet. This, by inference, is the bed in which he was born. As in the night just described, the action begins with a gaze out the western window, long after the sun has "sunk behind the larches." The gazer (again, by inference) is the speaker himself, as if transported to the scene of his birth. The scene continues on to the lighting of a lamp, though this time by someone else and not with three matches but with a lighted "spill," and continues as does the present night through the dying of the lamp and the restoration of darkness. With the fading of the lamp comes the birth cry.

In other words, the sequence of acts in the present night—starting with the gaze out the window at nightfall and culminating in the first word ("Birth") of the monologue—acts as a kind of fuse which delivers up a vision of the night of birth. But this vision in its turn delivers up a second, that of the funeral cited above, which is described in such general terms that it could be that of any of the speaker's "loved ones," as well as his own.[5] Moreover, the mono-

---

[5]Linda Ben-Zvi reads the funeral scene as the increasingly undeniable "approaching death of the speaker" (11–14) in a play that focuses "less on a replaying of the past than on the experience of the present and future" (12). Kristin Morrison reads the play as the speaker's last night, representing his effort "to evade something which he is coming to understand very well: the imminence of his own death" (354). See Ben-Zvi, "The Schismatic Self in 'A Piece of Monologue,'" *Journal of Beckett Studies* 7 (Spring 1982): 7–17, and Morrison, "The Rip Word in *A Piece of Monologue*," *Modern Drama* (September 1982): 349–354. In my own view, Beckett probably repeated the funeral scene three times because that number corresponded with the three individuals who have been specified as

logue we hear continues with two more repetitions of this complex triple loop: (1) the actions in the present night, including the monologue that begins by recapitulating them, leading to the nearly identical visions of (2) the night of birth, followed by (3) the funeral.

Here, then, is how the monologue is structured by its interconnected loops of narrative time (punctuated with brief interludes in which the speaker observes himself speaking):

Overture (lines 1–13:[6] "Birth was the death of him" to "Wick turned low.") This section encapsulates an overview of life "from funeral to funeral." It moves from birth to death to birth, concluding with the first few details in the description of the night of birth.

First Sequence (lines 13–108)

THIS NIGHT (13–80: "And now. This night" to "Birth.") This is a sequence of nightly actions, bringing us to the moment in which the first word of the monologue is uttered. This is the longest sustained piece of consecutive narrative in the play. There are two quick recapitulations of the action so far at lines 27 and 61, respectively. The concluding word, "Birth," comes at almost exactly the midpoint of the play.

THE BIRTH NIGHT (80–97: "Then slow fade up of a faint form" to "Thirty thousand nights.") This section is a fuller version of the night introduced in the overture. The key differences from the present night—the hands lighting the lamp with a "spill" and the "Glimmer of brass bedrail"—are introduced, but the birth cry is muffled with the general statement "Birth the death of him."

The Speaker at the Moment (97–99): "Stands at edge of lamplight staring beyond" to "Again and again gone.") In

---

gone or going: father, mother, speaker. One should also keep in mind that the speaker anticipates his death in the first lines of the monologue, and elsewhere he yearningly seeks the "blest dark." As for the future, it is indistinguishable from the past and the present, each being comprised of just the "one matter."

[6]Numbers refer to lines of prose in *A Piece of Monologue* as it is printed in *The Collected Shorter Plays* (New York: Grove, 1984), 263–269.

all particulars, the words in these interludes describe the
speaker as we see him, standing and speaking.

THE FUNERAL (99–105: "Till dark slowly parts again" to "Then
Fade.") As the accompanying version of the birth night omit-
ted the birth cry, this first rendering of the funeral omits men-
tion of the coffin.

The Speaker at the Moment (105–108: "Dark whole again"
to "Making do with his mouth.")

Second Sequence (lines 108–124)

THIS NIGHT (108–111: Lights lamp as described" to "Birth.")
Very brief.

THE BIRTH NIGHT (111–115: "Parts the dark" to "A cry. Stifled
by nasal.") The birth cry is now included.

THE FUNERAL (115–117: "Dark parts" to "Gone.") As the accompanying rendering of the birth night introduces the birth cry,
this version of the funeral now introduces a "Coffin out of
frame."

The Speaker at the moment (117–124: "Move on to other
matters" to "Then parted by cry as before.") This is the
gesture of escape in which the speaker seeks other matters
only to be drawn back by the inevitable resonances of his
own words.

Third Sequence (lines 124–164)

THIS NIGHT (124–131: "Where is he now?" to "Of lips on
tongue.")

THE BIRTH NIGHT (132–141: "Fade up in outer dark of window"
to "Again and again gone.") Here the brass bed is noted twice
in a countdown toward birth which closely echoes the countdown to the beginning of the play: "Brass bedrail catching
light. Thirty seconds. To swell the two and a half billion odd.
Fade. Gone. Cry. Snuffed with breath of nostrils."

THE FUNERAL (141–146: "Till whose grave?" to "Gone.") Com-
plementing the accompanying version of the birth scene, the
coffin now is "on its way," again following the same countdown: "Thirty seconds. Fade. Gone."

The Speaker at the Moment (146–164: "Stands there staring
beyond" to "Alone gone.") As the speaker comments gen-

erally on the "ghost" character of what he consorts with
night after night, and as he waits "on the rip word," his
self-description now coincides with the conclusion we are
at the moment experiencing. He carefully monitors the fading of the light during the last thirty seconds.

As a design that accentuates the inescapability of loss, this complex structure can be seen as serving a fundamentally lyrical intention. A version of the dramatic monologue, it suggests through its
relentless circularity a grief with no exit in a victim whose entire
being is constituted by the experience of loss. But to stress the lyrical
intention of traditional art, however fiercely original its expression,
as a full accounting of this design is to normalize a text that is bent
on resisting any generic normalization. At the heart of this resistance
is the ungraspable relation between the monologue itself and the
narrative action it recounts. Seen as drama, this is a piece in which
the entire dramatic action is the monologue, a character "Making
do with his mouth" (CSPL, 268). Seen as narrative, the utterance of
this monologue is itself a piece of the narrative action it relates,
action that both precedes the monologue and continues after it. The
dramatic universe, in other words, contains the narrative universe,
and the narrative universe contains the dramatic universe.

This problem of ontogeny is complicated further by the different
realities within the narrative (the strange loops)[7] and the problem of
knowing when, where, and how these different realities come into
being. At all three points in the monologue when these additional
sets of double loops begin, they are initiated not by the completion
of the monologue but by the utterance of its first word, "Birth":

[First double loop] Birth. Then slow fade up of a faint form. Out of
the dark. A Window.

[7] The term "strange loop" is taken with considerable license from Douglas Hofstadter's
Gödel, Escher, Bach: An Eternal Golden Braid (New York: Basic Books, 1979). Hofstadter
devised the idea of a strange loop to explain the relation between the determinate bio/
neurological processes and the "higher" activities of our brains (thought, hope, agency,
consciousness). But the term seems tailored precisely for the kind of loops I am describing, and because I hope to show that they, too, bear on the mystery of self-consciousness,
I feel comfortable with my appropriation.

[Second double loop] Birth. Parts the dark. Slowly the window.

[Third double loop] Birth. Parts lips and thrusts tongue between them. Tip of tongue. Feel soft touch of tongue on lips. Of lips on tongue. Fade up in outer dark of window.

If the vision of the past arises with the first word of the monologue, then this action in the past is in some sense happening as the monologue continues, even while the words in the monologue are treating of other things (lighting the lamp with matches, staring at the eastern wall, and so on).

In other words, if we attend closely to the sequencing of events, then the demands on our imagination are daunting. During the interludes in which the speaker reflects on himself as he is at the moment, he is described as at the same time being in the action and hearing himself speak: "Stands staring beyond half hearing what he's saying" (CSPL, 268). This layering of one state on another reinforces what seems inevitably to be the case: that we are asked to imagine all the levels of action—the action of the present night, the action of the night long past, the action of witnessing the funeral, the action of voicing the monologue—as coexisting. We are asked to do this even as the temporal distinctness of these actions is emphasized. Both the "birth" of the monologue and the emergence of the vision of the past are located very precisely in the action of "This night," and "This night" is kept historically separated from "That first night." This synchronicity of normally incompatible time and space is, among other things, a travesty of divine omniscience, that is, of the capacity to see all things in an eternal present commonly attributed to God. As such, it chimes with other divine travesties: the discreating word "Begone" and the creative goal, not of light, but of "Blest dark" (let there be night). But these are serious travesties in a play so constructed as to strain our mortal incapacity.

We have referred to the "Möbius strip" effect of Beckett's reflexivity in *Company, Endgame,* and *All Strange Away* (Chapters 1 and 7). Beckett's strange loops represent a similar connectivity of mutually exclusive worlds and, as such, a similar challenge to human understanding. Though they are more common to Beckett's late theater, an early loop occurred when he superimposed the second act of *Godot* on the first, burdening us with a confluence of two different orders of time. *Play* shifts midway from one world to another, or at least from one level of consciousness to another, then loops back and forth again when the play is repeated. The relations of the narrative loops in such plays as *Embers* and *Footfalls* have challenged Beckett's ablest interpreters. Why does he do this? Or to ask it again: Why should Beckett take a text that is so powerfully effective as lyrical art in its own right and then overlay it with such an insistent challenge to our capacity fully to grasp what it is we are watching?

INCANTATION

The answer, I think, is that Beckett is doing magic. Ruby Cohn has noted how the repetitive pacing of May in *Footfalls* calls to mind the biblical description of the Devil who walks "up and down" and "to and fro in the earth." With this coloration of its principal action, *Footfalls* becomes a ritualistic effort of conjuring.[8] Such a reading fits the ambiance of gothic settings and arcane practices which pervades the later drama of Beckett: its repetitive formulas and ritual acts, disembodied voices and sounds, ghostly visitations, prayers, strange rites carried on in the dark of night. In *Embers*, Henry calls up sounds and ghost presences through the power of his words. In *Not I*, a mouth seeks other magic words, ringing changes on its rush of verbiage, hoping to "hit on it in the end." In . . . *but the clouds* . . . , the face of the dead beloved is conjured through nightly ritual. In *Ohio Impromptu*, a sacred text is read aloud, the reading periodically interrupted with raps on the table. These works, as well as *Play, Eh Joe, That Time, Ghost Trio, Nacht und Träume*, can all be seen as works of sorcery, clothed with the trappings of the dark craft.

From this perspective, *Monologue*'s nightly repetition of acts in precisely the same order—gazing out the western window, lighting the lamp with the magical three matches, turning to the eastern

[8]Ruby Cohn, *Just Play: Beckett's Theater* (Princeton: Princeton University Press, 1980), 136.

wall, waiting until the arrival of the word that brings in its wake the monologue—can be seen as a rite of conjuring which brings on the visions of birth and death. To see the play in this light is, in effect, to "normalize" it through conventions of the abnormal. It "explains" how the speaker can be present at his birth (as was Scrooge at his funeral) and how (as a hovering spirit) he can have the strangely elevated take on the umbrellas in the cemetery.

If this is an accurate reading, then it is also the case that the incantation is something to which the initiate is condemned, night after night (as is the case with so many of the rituals in Beckett). Moreover, though visions arise, achieving the final object of incantation is always in doubt. Because if the incantation is done right, such is the hope, the speaker will at last have done "revolving it all" and jump through death to a birth that is not, once again, a death in birth's clothing. In the infinitesimal fourth act of *Footfalls*, the possibility that such a jump has occurred is suggested by May's non-reappearance. This construction would make the repetitions in *A Piece of Monologue* a form of *reculer pour mieux sauter*, backing up in order to jump further forward. The speaker backs up to launch himself. At the end, he waits "on the rip word," which, as Rosemary Pountney reads it, is resignedly accepted as the start of the next inevitable repetition.[9] But there is always the faint hope that the incantation will finally succeed and that birth really will be birth this time.

Seeing the text as a representation of conjuring gives a special license to its complex unreadability. Our minds bent in the effort to grasp a fusion of stasis and motion, past and present, word and action, we are put through a cognitive warp, feeling in our synapses the exquisite failure of generic expectations without which magic does not happen. I would also argue, however, that magic for Beckett was more than a mode of normalization by abnormality, or a means by which he gave a special depth and complexity of effect to his lyrical enterprise. His work was closer to real sorcery than that.

---

[9]Rosemary Pountney, *Theatre of Shadows: Samuel Beckett's Drama, 1956–1976* (Gerrard's Cross: Colin Smythe, 1988), 217.

The Reflexive Loop

One of the stranger loops the young Beckett came across in the reading of his early twenties took shape suddenly, about fifty pages into *The Captive,* the sixth published volume of Proust's *Remembrance of Things Past.* "Then she would find her tongue and say: 'My _____' or 'My darling _____' followed by my Christian name, which, if we give the narrator the same name as the author of this book, would be 'My Marcel,' or 'My darling Marcel.' "[10] In a single light stroke, Marcel Proust dares us to read his novel autobiographically, a work for which, after reading five volumes, we have by now comfortably established a novelistic mindset. The stroke is coy. It is not asserted, but suggested in passing as a possibility.

Seventy pages further on, Proust does it once again, this time in a letter from Albertine addressed to "Mon chéri et cher Marcel" and which concludes, " 'My darling dear Marcel . . . . The ideas you get into your head! What a Marcel! What a Marcel! Always and ever your Albertine.' "[11] There is no explicit narratorial optioning at this point, as there was in the first instance, but the name is still archly packaged. It appears in a text within the text (a letter composed, moreover, by an inveterate liar), and it is qualified in such a way as to underscore the problematical character of this business of naming: "What a Marcel," indeed. What kind of a Marcel is this? How is he constituted? Why should Proust want to thread his way into his work in this manner, suggesting some interconnection between the loop of fictive narrative and that of a life lived in what is usually called the real world? And how in turn might this glimpse of the

---

[10]Marcel Proust, *The Captive,* in *Remembrance of Things Past,* vol. 3, trans. C. K. Scott Moncrieff and Terence Kilmartin (New York: Vintage, 1982), 69. "Elle retrouvait la parole, elle disait: 'Mon' ou 'Mon chéri' suivis l'un ou l'autre de mon nom de baptême, ce qui en donnant au narrateur le même prénom qu'à l'auteur de ce livre eût fait: 'Mon Marcel,' 'Mon chéri Marcel' " (Proust, *La prisonnière,* in *A la recherche du temps perdu,* vol. 3 [Paris: Robert Laffont, 1987], 72).

[11]Proust, *The Captive,* 153–154. "Quelles idées vous faites-vous donc? Quel Marcel! Quel Marcel! Toute à vous, ton Albertine" (*La prisonnière,* 133).

autobiographical loop relate to the reflexivity of the conclusion of *Remembrance of Things Past,* in which the long novel we have just been reading looks forward to what appears to be its birth, that is, to the birth of a novel by Marcel Proust?

This "barely suggested, seemingly accidental semihomonymy of the narrator-hero and the signatory"[12] has been a crux throughout the criticism of *Remembrance of Things Past.* Here, too, the desire to normalize and have done with it has often been strong. Gérard Genette, in his landmark structuralist reading of the novel, made the aesthetic motive dominate by excluding autobiography and by reading Proust's use of his first name as a symbolic representation of "the difficult experience of relating to oneself."[13] Though Beckett did not directly take up the crux of Proust's use of his name in his own 1931 reading of *Remembrance of Things Past,* he put his emphasis quite differently from Genette's. For Beckett, Proust was a late romantic artist of the "inexplicable," one moreover who engaged in the "perpetual exfoliation of personality" (P, 13). As such, Beckett's Proust would have counted on the sudden loss of bearings created by the intrusion of the author's given name. The coy maneuvre of Proust's narrator compounds the alignment of being with mystery and elusiveness. By the same act, being is connected with what Beckett called "the magic of literature" (P, 63), and set against the consecutive orderings of experience which constitute the accessible modes of biography and autobiography. In the same spirit, Beckett

---

[12]Gérard Genette, *Narrative Discourse: An Essay in Method,* trans. Jane E. Lewin (Ithaca: Cornell University Press, 1980), 249.

[13]Ibid. "Naming the hero Marcel," Genette writes in a footnote, "is obviously not identifying him with Proust; but this partial and fragile coincidence is highly symbolic" (ibid., 249n). In a riposte, David R. Ellison argues, "I do not believe much is gained or solved if we affirm, with Genette and Germaine Brée, that the first-person narration in the *Recherche* is the result of a conscious aesthetic choice rather than the sign of confession or 'confidence directe.' This hypothesis amounts to isolating the text in the realm of an abstract, self-sufficient fictional space where existential force is simply replaced by the free play of forms. What Genette, Brée, and many other readers of Proust note in passing rather than examine deeply is the *perversity* of saying *je* when one may or may not, may and may not 'mean what one says' " (Ellison, *The Reading of Proust* [Baltimore: Johns Hopkins University Press, 1984], 139).

warned with regard to these comfortable and comforting modes that "there is no allusion in this book to the legendary life and death of Marcel Proust" (P, Foreword).

Nicholas Zurbrugg has written at length on the richly creative divergence of Beckett from Proust,[14] but in this instance it would seem that a Proustian seed was sown that grew and blossomed after the war. At a number of points in his later drama Beckett appears to engage in an autobiographical dare much like Proust's. In *Not I*, the subject is "coming up to seventy," as was the author. In *Catastrophe*, as I noted in Chapter 5, P is pointedly given "clawlike" hands, "crippled," as Beckett's were, by "fibrous degeneration." In writing *Footfalls*, after considering the names Emily and Mary, Beckett settled on his mother's name, May. And in his own version of Proust's foregrounding of the name Marcel, Beckett gives the name May an insistence through pauses and repetition: "May—the child's given name—May: Not enough. The mother: What do you mean, May, not enough, what can you possibly mean, May, not enough? May: I mean, Mother, that I must hear the feet . . ." (CSPL, 241).[15] Then, in the play's third "act," the name May reappears anagrammatically as Amy, and again a pause is introduced to draw attention to the name: "and fixing Amy—the daughter's given name, as the reader will remember—raising her head and fixing Amy full in the eye" (CSPL, 243).

These are very delicate touches, but they suggest that the fiction of which they are a part is porous and that in some way a filament from the fictive realm can circle out into another kind of reality. It is something like this effect, I believe, which Beckett sought in the reflexivity that has characterized his drama ever since Spectateur jumped on stage in *Eleutheria* or Estragon looked out into the auditorium and described the "inspiring prospects" (WG, 10) or Clov trained his eyeglass on the audience in *Endgame*. Here we can turn again to *A Piece of Monologue* and note (as many have) how, in the

---

[14]Nicholas Zurbrugg, *Beckett and Proust* (Gerrard's Cross: Colin Smythe, 1988).

[15]I am tempted to see in the repetitions of May's name in *Footfalls* a very personal incantation: "May . . . May . . . May . . . May . . . May: I mean, Mother, ..."

middle of the piece as the speaker approaches the word "Birth," he not only adopts the phraseology of stage directions but describes with precision the onset (or birth) of the very performance we are observing:

> Still as the lamp by his side. Gown and socks white to take faint light.
> Once white. Hair white to take faint light. Foot of pallet just visible
> edge of frame. Once white to take faint light. Stands there staring
> beyond. Nothing. Empty dark. Till first word always the same. Night
> after night the same. Birth. (CSPL, 267)

Similarly, with the conclusion (or death) of the performance, he notes "the light going now. Beginning to go." In these instances and others in which he describes the action as it unfolds, the speaker is at once on stage and off.

In a play that carefully aligns scenes of birth and death (moving by three successive increments to the full birth cry as the coffin moves by similar increments into the earth), Beckett aligns as well the birth and death of speech, and the birth and death of the performance we are observing. This final alignment creates an opening into the nonfictive world, an opening which Beckett, through the speaker, exploits carefully. The dark stillness "beyond" the eastern wall which he is presumed to face is where we sit when the play is performed:

> Nothing stirring. Faintly stirring. Thirty thousand nights of ghosts
> beyond. Beyond that black beyond. Ghost light. Ghost nights. Ghost
> rooms. Ghost graves. Ghost . . . he all but said ghost loved ones.
> Waiting on the rip word. Stands there staring beyond at the black veil
> lips quivering to half-heard words. (CSPL, 269)

By words such as these, the monologue becomes a play seeking to exceed itself. It appropriates the audience. And in our turn, participants in what Genette might call the dramatic paratext,[16] we become ghosts, both in the play and out of it, both ourselves and something else.

---

[16]For a full development of the theory of the paratext see Gérard Genette, *Seuils* (Paris: Seuil, 1987).

Beckett's drama thrives on effects of liminality like this. My argument is that, in an oeuvre that has been devoted to nothing so much as the apprehension of the force from which it originates, these liminal spaces (if the phrase works) are where the magic transaction has a chance of happening.[17] They may also have been for Beckett key elements in an art "devised for company." The latter phrase comes from *Company,* which appeared the year after *A Piece of Monologue* (C, 8). On the face of it, the phrase has a bitter, solipsistic cast, as if it were constructed out of Hamm's lines in *Endgame:* "Then babble, babble, words, like the solitary child who turns himself into children, two, three, so as to be together, and whisper together, in the dark" (En, 70). As if to reinforce this bitter solipsism, *Company* ends with the single word "Alone," just as *A Piece of Monologue* ends with the two words "Alone gone."

Yet, given the fact that Beckett wrote all his life for audiences, and given a reflexive looping that doesn't let us ever forget this fact, these emphatic concluding assertions, like his use of the third person, take on the quality of what I have called elsewhere "radical displacement"—a denial so strenuous it denies the denial.[18] Just as "begone" contains "be" in embryo, "alone" is almost "all one." The point is that nothing is settled in Beckett. When his words are at their most emphatic ("Not I!"), we cannot help but see glimmers of the counterstatement. So, too, this simple lyric is immensely complex. Its dogged singularities want to turn into weddings, not only of concepts (like birth and death) but of entities (like actors and audiences, ghosts and a playwright). Even at their most funereal, these weddings take place. This alchemy was not simply a matter of form and thematics for Beckett. Stages and texts were alembics, and art a kind of conjuring. How desperately pursued, or if at all joyful, he alone knew.

---

[17]For a parallel argument on the linguistic space created by Beckett's bilingualism, see Ann Beer, "Beckett's 'Autography' and the Company of Languages," *Southern Review* 27 (Autumn 1991): 771–791.

[18]H. Porter Abbott, "A Poetics of Radical Displacement: Samuel Beckett Coming Up to Seventy," *Texas Studies in Literature and Language* 17 (Spring 1975): 219–238.

NINE

THE READER IN THE AUTOGRAPH

All the world knows me in my book,
and my book in me.

—Montaigne

Beckett has not always been kind to his audience. In *Murphy,* the narrator refers to the reader as the "gentle skimmer" (M, 84). Vladimir calls us "that bog" (WG, 10). Such defensive mockery accords with Beckett's frequent representation of the perceiving eye as a threatening eye ("like say without hesitation hell gaping they part and the black eye appears" [*All Strange Away,* CSPR, 124]). Beckett's only film is devoted to "the agony of perceivedness" (*Film,* CSPL, 165). Yet Beckett worked energetically on *Film,* as he did on *Murphy* and *Godot* and all his projects, fully aware that the object of all this effort was to send something out into the world, something bearing his name, to be perceived by thousands. Camera-shy, publicity-shy, furtive, a mole in a molehill, Beckett nonetheless, and by his own choice, has lived among us for years as a virtual presence, "whole body like gone" (*Not I,* CSPL, 222). Concentrating on the tight weave of his thematics and formal innovation, I have sought to show in this book some of the things Beckett's virtual presence in his art has meant. It remains to address more directly the role we play in Beckett's autography.

Since *Krapp's Last Tape,* Beckett has, with few exceptions, included a perceiver in his dramatis personae: Krapp himself, Willie in *Happy Days,* the spotlight in *Play,* Joe in *Eh Joe,* Auditor in *Not I,* Listener in *That Time,* May in *Footfalls,* F in *Ghost Trio,* M in . . .

but the clouds . . . , the Dreamer in *Nacht und Träume*.[1] In *A Piece of Monologue*, Beckett approached the literal ground of what is figured in these listeners. When the monologuist locates us in the gray realm into which he stares, he indicates that in some ghostly way we have been on stage with him all along, for "thirty thousand nights," in performance after performance, play after play. Two years later, Beckett capitalized on an opportunity that seemed tailor-made for staging his audience. It was a conference devoted to his work, and he gave it a play that staged his audience. He staged them not as theatergoers, as he had when Spectateur climbed into the playing space of *Eleutheria*, but as a reader and a listener. In this way, *Ohio Impromptu* not only brought the perceiver into the action but achieved an intricate meshing of the two major generic strands of Beckett's career: his prose and his drama. By the same stroke, Beckett stood on its head one of the major topoi of the nineteenth-century novel. If we start this chapter with a brief look at this convention, we will gain a historical frame that will help set in relief what Beckett was doing when he brought us, as novel readers, on stage.

A LITERARY CONVENTION TURNS INSIDE OUT

The topos is the scene of an evening at the theater. From Balzac to Proust, novelists brought their readers to a theater and there directed attention not so much to what is happening on stage as to what is happening in the audience. As an occasion for mapping social relations, the device had great utility. The theater scene exceeded most novelistic venues (weddings, funerals, banquets, balls, salons, Sunday promenades) in its capacity to gather representative types into a single place, sufficiently compact to be commanded by the eye. In the theatrical space of the nineteenth-century audience, one

---

[1] For more on Beckett's staged perceivers, see Bernard Beckerman, "Beckett and the Art of Listening," and Katherine Worth, "Beckett's Auditors: *Not I* to *Ohio Impromptu*," both in *Beckett at 80/Beckett in Context*, ed. Enoch Brater (New York: Oxford University Press, 1986), 149–192.

could observe both the comparative elevation of these types and the chemistry of their interchange. In Balzac's *Père Goriot,* when Eugène de Rastignac escorts Mme de Beauséant to *Les italiens,* the reader can join him in observing the sociology of love and money as the Count d'Ajuda Pinto momentarily abandons the box of the wealthy Rochefides for that of his old lover. At the same time, the reader can observe the obscure Rastignac insert himself into the devolving drama of a banker's wife and the Count de Marsay.

The device worked well in rendering a society for which identity was conceived in terms of visual spectacle—in theatrical terms of place, role, costume, and convention—while the value of the device was proportionally heightened when the nature and meaning of those terms were placed under exceptional pressure, as they were throughout the nineteenth century. It was the fluidity and loopholes and general slippage of the social terms of place, role, and convention which gave the keenest fascination to what was going on in the theater audience. For the readership, a great deal was at stake in this slippage. It is not surprising, then, that the finest and most elaborate example of this device—the twenty-five pages Proust devotes to an evening at the Opéra which open the third volume of *Remembrance of Things Past*—appeared in a work devoted to the waning years of the society that made it possible.

Proust's brilliant scene anticipates and counterbalances the chaotic postwar milieu that Marcel observes many years later in the Guermantes' drawing room during the closing pages of his epic. In his autobiography, Sartre drew on the same topological tradition to express his own understanding of the gulf between pre- and postwar social self-awareness when he juxtaposed two theater audiences: that of nineteenth-century drama and that of twentieth-century cinema. Where the nineteenth-century bourgeois turned from the stage to see what he could take to be a coherent and reassuring image of society, the twentieth-century moviegoer awoke from the film to a world without form:

> Where was I? In a school? In an official building? Not the slightest ornament: rows of flap-seats beneath which could be seen their springs, walls smeared with ochre, a floor strewn with cigarette stubs

and gobs of spit. Confused murmurs filled the hall, language was reinvented, ...

The social hierarchy of the theatre had given my grandfather and late father, who were accustomed to second balconies, a taste for ceremonial. When many people are together, they must be separated by rites; otherwise, they slaughter each other. The movies proved the opposite. This mingled audience seemed united by a catastrophe rather than a festivity.[2]

Here Sartre anticipates the conclusion of Thomas Pynchon's *Gravity's Rainbow*, in which humanity is figured as an agglutinated mass of moviegoers, chanting in darkness with death only nanoseconds away.[3]

This late modern disarticulation of the theater audience is central to Beckett's effects. Dougald McMillan and Martha Fehsenfeld contend that when Beckett, in *Eleutheria*, swept the Kraps' bourgeois drawing room "into the pit," he swept with it what remained of the nineteenth-century theater, clearing the stage for *Godot*.[4] With the antics of the incorrigible Spectateur and his assistant, Tchoutchi, Beckett disposed of the old audience as well. Since *Eleutheria*, formal indeterminacy of the audience has become a common notation in Beckett, as when Vladimir identifies the audience as "that bog" or when Clov peers at it through a telescope: "I see . . . a multitude . . . in transports . . . of joy. (*Pause.*) That's what I call a magnifier" (E, 29). The disintegration of the audience which Beckett built into his theater is matched in his prose by gray, indeterminate observers

---

[2]Jean-Paul Sartre, *The Words*, trans. Bernard Frechtman (New York: George Braziller, 1964), 120–121.

[3]By stressing at the same time the magical power of film—"the delirium of a wall" (77)—Sartre also anticipates Jean Baudrillard's theory of the postmodern condition, epitomized by the final depthlessness of Americans for whom nothing is real save what is rendered on a screen. See Baudrillard, *Simulations*, trans. Paul Foss, Paul Patton, and Philip Beitchman (New York: Semiotext(e), 1983); *America*, trans. Christina Turner (New York: Verso, 1989).

[4]Dougald McMillan and Martha Fehsenfeld, *Beckett in the Theatre: The Author as Practical Playwright and Director* (London: Calder, 1988), 17.

such as the anonymous readers of Molloy's manuscript or the inscrutable Kram of *How It Is*.

If Beckett was ever troubled by the formal disintegration of the audience, he also depended on it. The remnant of the old coherent audience is the canned applause of *Catastrophe*. Exactly the same every night, it is displaced by the tentative, confused response of the real audience which follows after the applause dies away. In 1952, before his theater debut, Beckett told Roger Blin that the ideal audience for *En attendant Godot* would probably be an empty house.[5] There is more than hyperbole in this comment. Beckett's work requires emptiness in the theater in the sense that it requires an openness to the unexpected. When the audience of the American premier of *Godot* left the theater in droves in Miami, they registered in their way the success of Alan Schneider's direction. The audience that week was a recrudescence of nineteenth-century socially structured self-awareness and it was driven from the modern theater.

The process begun in 1947 when Beckett swept the nineteenth-century theater into the pit achieved its consummation in *Ohio Impromptu*. In this short play, Beckett displaced not simply nineteenth-century theater but theater itself, replacing it with the reading of a book. In the context of the novelistic topos we began with, *Ohio Impromptu*—a play that features a table, a hat, a book, a Reader, and a Listener—provides the most interesting variation on Beckett's late plays of listening. Point for point, the situation in *Ohio Impromptu* is an absolute inversion of the nineteenth-century device of *theatrum theatri*. Where the latter was a prose-narrative presentation of the arena of staged performance, the former is a staged presentation of the arena of prose narrative. But it gets more complicated than that.

WRITING FOR COMPANY

To begin with, Beckett's anxiety about his perceivers is patent. Hostility may not be too strong a word. Written on request for a confer-

---

[5]Alec Reid, *All I Can Manage, More Than I Could* (Dublin: Dolmen Press, 1968), 50.

ence of scholars, *Ohio Impromptu* consists entirely of two ancient white-haired men, "As alike in appearance as possible" (CSPL, 285), poring over a text.[6] Given the topicality (unique for Beckett) of the play's title, together with such fine details as Listener's requests to stop and go back over small critical points, and the precise textual reference to "Page forty, paragraph four" (CSPL, 286),[7] it is hard to overlook the caricature of the audience for which it was composed— scholars who spend their professional lives poring over texts and reading them to one another. From this perspective, the repeated phrase "the unspoken words" suggests the object of the entire interpretive enterprise: those words that, when spoken, would release the meaning of the text. Were the words shown to be permanently out of reach, one might presume the scholars would go on to other texts. Such a presumption would make the play's concluding line (repeated for emphasis) a supplication from an author more than usually beleaguered by interpretation: "Nothing is left to tell" (CSPL, 288).

Pierre Astier writes that one of the departures of this impromptu from the impromptu tradition is that "Beckett does not seem to defend anything or attack anyone" in it.[8] But surely there is an acid touch in these details, as well as in the final description of these two sounders of textual depths: "Buried in who knows what profounds of mind" (CSPL, 286). Much earlier, Beckett had had hard words for exegetes:

The only line is to refuse to be involved in exegesis of any kind. And to insist on the extreme simplicity of dramatic situation and issue. If

---

[6]*Ohio Impromptu* was written on request for the symposium "Samuel Beckett: Humanistic Perspectives," which took place May 7–9, 1981, at the Ohio State University under the sponsorship of the College of Humanities. It was first performed on May 9, directed by Alan Schneider, with David Warrilow as Reader and Rand Mitchell as Listener.

[7]In one of the holograph versions, there is an additional reference: "See appendix 4"; see Samuel Beckett, "Transcription of the *Ohio Impromptu* Holograph," in *Samuel Beckett: Humanistic Perspectives,* ed. Morris Beja et al. (Columbus: Ohio State University Press, 1983), 194.

[8]Pierre Astier, "Beckett's *Ohio Impromptu:* A View from the Isle of Swans," *Modern Drama* 25 (1982): 332.

that's not enough for them, and it obviously isn't, it's plenty for us, and we have no elucidations to make of mysteries that are all of their making. My work is a matter of fundamental sounds (no joke intended) made as fully as possible, and I accept responsibility for nothing else. If people want to have headaches among the overtones, let them. And provide their own aspirin. Hamm as stated, and Clov as stated, together as stated, nec tecum nec sine te, in such a place, and in such a world, that's all I can manage, more than I could. (D, 109)

The person to whom these words were written was Alan Schneider, the same man who, twenty-three years later, directed the first performance of *Ohio Impromptu* at the conference in Columbus. After the performance, Schneider fielded questions from the audience and in his answers attended tenaciously to the play's empirical reality—to details of staging, costuming, props, and pacing—all the while astutely dodging invitations to engage in more transcendent modes of critique.

But to send up professors is to bring down pretty easy prey. Moreover, simplicity in Beckett is always the sign of its opposite— or, more accurately, itself and its opposite. For one thing, the scholars on stage are reading not just any tale but a tale in which they are the participants. The distance of satire is breached with the coalescence of a moving threnody of loss and a tableau of two dusty scholars poring over an ancient text. Beckett's capacity to bond incongruities of this sort contributes to the aesthetic charge of much of his work. Such strange unions revive awareness by a process of making strange. The effect falls within the general conceptual framework of "defamiliarization" but also within that extreme form of defamiliarization which I have called "radical displacement"—an incongruity managed in such a way that it is an apparent denial of the aesthetic object.[9] By virtue of the resistance set initially in place by the appar-

[9]Two of Viktor Shklovsky's important essays on defamiliarization *(ostranenie)*—"Art as Technique" and "Sterne's *Tristram Shandy*: Stylistic Commentary"—can be found in English in *Russian Formalist Criticism: Four Essays,* trans. Lee T. Lemon and Marion J. Reis (Lincoln: University of Nebraska Press, 1965), 3–57. Shklovsky's fullest attempt to integrate the concept with his other ideas (*O teorii prozy,* 1925) has been made available

ent denial, the full effect, when it happens, does so with penetrating force.

As a threnody on the subject of love lost, *Ohio Impromptu* compares favorably with *Krapp's Last Tape* and *Enough*. In all three, the furnishings or veneer of the work make it appear to be anything but a love story; yet, when the full impact of the work is felt, the resistance these furnishings provide can be seen in retrospect as an indispensable part of that effect. The vestige of slapstick in *Krapp*, for example, which Beckett has retained through all his tinkering with the play and which has proved such a challenge in a work of such lyrical depth, at once frames and bonds with that depth. Similarly, the extraterrestrial *bizarrerie* of *Enough* plays a vital part in our reacquaintance with the memory of love. In *Ohio Impromptu*, as we watch, the power of the play enlarges with the growing likelihood that the dusty scholar is the passionate lover. Nor is it just any dusty scholar, but a refracted caricature of scholars like those in the audience who read the same old stories over and over again, looking and looking for what has not yet been seen. It is just here, in such unlikely breasts, that one finds such pain.[10]

There is a further twist to this staging of the audience in *Ohio*

in English as *Theory of Prose*, trans. Benjamin Sher (Elmwood Park, Ill.: Dalkey Archive, 1990). Related to Shklovsky's *ostranenie* is Berthold Brecht's *Verfremdung*, though I think the latter concept on the whole less useful for discussions of Beckett. For a treatment of radical displacement, see H. Porter Abbott, "A Poetics of Radical Displacement: Samuel Beckett Coming Up to Seventy," *Texas Studies in Literature and Language* 17 (Spring 1975): 219–238.

[10]It is important to stress that the material of resistance (all this equipage that suggests two scholars in a cell) is not simply instrumental in producing an effect "other" than this material—serving, in other words, primarily as a framing device. Rather, the final effect is synthesized, and in that sense inseparable from this material. Not only do we become reacquainted with an ancient emotion, but we see—through the agency of this material—how the emotion itself is strange. For this reason, I think, the irascibility and impatience that Alvin Epstein and Alan Mandell introduced into their versions of Reader, and that augmented the surface strangeness of the play, were viable. They contributed shades of the boring, the aggravating, and the predictable to the play's complex structuring of grief—qualities commonly screened out in the representation of that emotion. For a different slant on this performance, see Jonathan Kalb, *Beckett in Performance* (Cambridge: Cambridge University Press, 1989), 48–62.

Impromptu: the author of the play was himself a scholar. So if there is an edge of contempt in Beckett's offering, it is that finely honed contempt that only a fellow scholar can have. "I might have been a professor," says the narrator of *From an Abandoned Work.* "A very fair scholar I was too, no thought, but a great memory" (CSPR, 131).[11] According to Professor Rudmose-Brown, his mentor at Trinity, Beckett was destined to be not just any professor but a "great professor."[12] The star pupil of his class in Romance languages, Beckett had by the time he was twenty-five earned his master of arts, published a monograph on Marcel Proust, and actually begun a career as a lecturer in French at Trinity. Moreover, like many of the great modernists, Beckett was a scholar who (despite his protestations of ignorance and bafflement) continued to wear his learning in almost everything he wrote.

But if, in his mature work, scholarship provides one of the many dimensions of Beckett's style, in *Ohio Impromptu* it signifies the effort of scrutiny—the constant seeking of the truth in texts. The scholar is the epitome of the reader/listener. The scholar also embodies the isolated, often rarefied artistic receptivity that recurs in modernist texts. The condition was forecast by Dostoevsky's Underground Man, a figure of comparable ambivalence, at once admirable and ridiculous, whose "disease of lucidity" confines him to the hermetic cell of his imaginings and sets him off against the "man of action" who accepts his role on the world stage and plays it with verve. The Underground Man suffers from terminal exegesis, the endless reading and rereading of his life story with no hope of crossing over into a reassuring world of fixed, unassailable meaning.

The shadings of the scholar which characterize the identical players in *Ohio Impromptu* situate them in this tradition while they reit-

---

[11]The full quote reads: "Fortunately my father died when I was a boy, otherwise I might have been a professor, he had set his heart on it. A very fair scholar I was too, no thought, but a great memory." In the actual chronology of events, Beckett quit his post at Trinity on December 15, 1931, and his father died on June 26, 1933.

[12]Deirdre Bair, *Samuel Beckett: A Biography* (New York: Harcourt, Brace, Jovanovich, 1978), 137.

erate a predominating Beckett figure: the one who knows he will never know yet never ceases to want to know. A presence for decades in what is commonly called Beckett's "prose fiction," by 1981, this obsessive reader/writer of texts had transgressed the boundaries of his genre and crowded his way out into what we commonly call Beckett's "theater." In *Ohio Impromptu,* he took over the entire theatrical space. The dramatic action is the reading of a book. In the process, Beckett has bonded with an audience of scholars—scholars, moreover, who are devoted specifically to what he, Beckett, writes—and with gentle mockery inscribed his own urgent inquiry in their image.[13] Out of a simple play devoted to a simple story, Beckett creates a complex experience in which both author and audience are at once inside and outside the art, participants and observers.

This complexity is mirrored in the action of the play and at the same time augmented. The book being read is an autobiography in the third person. It is Listener's story, but in a strange loop like those of *A Piece of Monologue* it includes within Listener's story the reading of Listener's story. "One night as he sat trembling head in hands from head to foot a man appeared to him and said, I have been sent by—and here he named the dear name—to comfort you. Then drawing a worn volume from the pocket of his long black coat he sat and read till dawn." Not only does the book include the reading of the story but it extends beyond the end of its own reading: "Till the night came at last when having closed the book and dawn at hand he did not disappear but sat on without a word" (CSPL, 287).

I have been using the terms "Möbius strip" and "strange loop" during the latter part of this book to try to get at the way in which universes are made to cohabit in Beckett's work. The level of the complexity we have got to in our discussion of *Ohio Impromptu* is quite extraordinary. Beckett has put both audience and author at once inside and outside the play. He has figured them (audience and

---

[13]Pierre Astier suggests that the hat on the table is all of Beckett's hats and the book all the books thought out under that hat: "All the texts filling the book would thus constitute a writer's lifework, a whole *oeuvre* representing in this case, I think, that of Beckett himself in the form of a make-believe compilation of all his writings so far" (Astier, "Beckett's *Ohio Impromptu,*" 338).

author) in the play as both the reader and the read. And he has them (audience and author) both read and inhabit yet another narratricidal event: a self-negating narrative in which time both is and is not—a tale about ending in which the ending is swallowed in the telling. The playwright/novelist does all this in a play that is entirely devoted to reading and with a tragic intensity that is leavened throughout by amusement and mockery, both broad and subtle.

At the heart of this array of merged contradictions is Beckett's effort to bring his audience into every facet of his autographical endeavor. Through the mediation of a tale that is absorbed into its telling, the audience is brought onstage to interlock with Beckett. The staged reading of an autobiography in the third person of a passionate man is at the same time a text by Beckett read by scholars passionate on the subject of Beckett. So closely compacted are they that it is impossible to distinguish the reader from the listener.

READING FOR THE SIGNATURE

Beckett made an unusually personal false start in writing *Ohio Impromptu*. By good fortune (or by design), a holograph fragment was included on the back of one of the manuscript pages that Beckett donated to the conference organizers. They in turn included it (with Beckett's permission) in the volume that came out of the conference. So immediate and personal are these few lines that they are conceivably the inspiration for the word "impromptu" that wound up in the title.

> I am out on leave. Thrown out on leave.
> Back to time, they said, for 24 hours.
> Oh my God, I said, not that.
> Slip [into] on this shroud, they said, lest you catch your death of cold
>   again.
> Certainly not, I said.
> This cap, they said, for your [death's-head] skull.
> Definitely not, I said.
> The New World outlet, they said, in the State of Ohio. We cannot be
>   more precise. *Pause.*

> Proceed straight to [Lima] the nearest campus, they said, and address
> them.
> [Address] whom? I said.
> The students, they said, and professors.
> Oh my God, I said, not that.
> Do not overstay your leave, they said, if you do not wish it to be
> extended.
> *Pause.*
> What am I to say? I said.
> Be yourself, they said, [you're (   )] stay yourself.
> Myself? I said. What are you insinuating?
> [Yourself before, they said.]
> *Pause.*
> [And after.]
> [*Pause.*]
> [Not during? I said.][14]

Considering its title, one of the odd things about the final version of *Ohio Impromptu* is how deliberately programmed it seems. In the words of Linda Ben-Zvi, "there is nothing impromptu about the piece."[15] By contrast, Beckett appears in this false start to have picked up his pen to write with Professor Gontarski's request still ringing in his ears. The whole sequence of composition, then, from false start to finish, would appear to support Gontarski's argument in *The Intent of Undoing*: that Beckett starts with personal material, which he then proceeds to "undo" as he hammers out the finished art. Perhaps, too, there is additional support for that argument in Beckett's delightful question: "Myself? . . . What are you insinuating?" In other words, are you insinuating that I am ever myself in my public presentations? Do you presume to know me from my art?

But this question is not necessarily a rhetorical one. And even if it were rhetorical we would have no way, finally, of determining its implied answer, for it could just as easily be reformulated as "Am I ever *not* myself?" This interpretation would accord with one of the

[14]Beckett, "Transcription of the *Ohio Impromptu* Holograph," 191–192. Words in brackets were deleted by Beckett.

[15]Linda Ben-Zvi, *Samuel Beckett* (Boston: Twayne, 1986), 176.

ways to read *Not I,* according to which Mouth's futility of denial is understood to carry over reflexively to the author (of course it's her; of course it's Beckett). This interpretation also receives support from one conceivable reading of the "unreadable" question that concludes the false start in brackets (the false start of the false start):

[Yourself before, they said.]
Pause.
[And after.]
[*Pause.*]
[Not during? I said.]

This final question is as delicate as the one that precedes it. Its implied suppositions are equally indeterminate. But in context. "Not during?" seems most to be an amused protest: Am I only the idea of myself gathered from the past or projected into the future, but not myself in the present? Am I only myself before or after the performance, not during?

"During" also resonates with the word "impromptu." Yet, as noted above, one of Beckett's many wry pleasantries in this work was to submit as an impromptu a play that was as stiff as a board. In the third act of *Eleutheria,* the prompter quits in disgust because the players are not following their parts. In this play, all the lines are read from a book. Moreover, the two players involved have read the same text many times before. There is, in fact, only one point in the entire play when we hear a word that is not written in the book Reader reads. This is the word "Yes," and it comes in the following passage:

In this extremity his old terror of night laid hold on him again. After so long a lapse that as if never been. [*Pause. Looks closer.*] Yes, after so long a lapse that as if never been. Now with redoubled force . . . .
(CSPL, 286)

The word has become a crux of sorts, and most who write on the play have something to say about it.[16] But in the context of the

---

[16]Kathleen O'Gorman writes that the word "Yes" indicates "a 'metanarrative' which to some extent calls into question the embedded narrative"; Kristin Morrison contrasts the

evolution of this play from the immediate, spontaneous, highly personal sketch with which Beckett began to the methodical, mordant recitation of a written text with which he concluded, this "Yes" is the last vestige of the impromptu. It is a faint trace of that susceptibility to free improvisation—the sudden appearance of the unanticipated—which one associates with the word Beckett chose to keep in the title.

This small but significant disturbance of the play's glacial finish is especially important to bear in mind when one turns to the sentence that provokes Reader's "Yes": "After so long a lapse that as if never been." The impromptu quality of "Yes" reinforces the suggestion that, even after Reader's many readings, these written words have a capacity to startle, to cause scrutiny (*"Looks closer"*), to generate perhaps new thought. A further indication that this possibility was on Beckett's mind originally is an additional "Hm" in the holograph manuscript after the second repetition of the curious sentence.[17] The elimination of the "Hm" is in keeping with Beckett's austere subtlety, but the vestige of free play which remains tells us that reading—even the most ritualistic—is never merely repetition and can always spring surprises. This emphasis gains plausibility (and importance) when one looks at the distinctive peculiarity of the strange sentence in question. Not only does the sentence depart from all other sentences in the play, but the character of its perversity—above all, its syntactical parsimony—makes it quintessential late-Beckett prose.

---

repetition brought on by Reader's "Yes" with the six "significant" repetitions requested by Listener, making "Yes" primarily the verification of a "syntactically awkward" line; Pierre Astier ventures that the "Yes" may simply have been occasioned by the "discovery in the text of such an unexpected and perfect alexandrine." See O'Gorman, "The Speech Act in Beckett's *Ohio Impromptu*," in '*Make Sense Who May': Essays on Samuel Beckett's Later Works*, Irish Literary Studies 30, ed. Robin J. Davis and Lance St. J. Butler (Gerrard's Cross: Colin Smythe, 1988), 115; Morrison, *Canters and Chronicles: The Use of Narrative in the Plays of Samuel Beckett and Harold Pinter* (Chicago: University of Chicago Press, 1983), 121–122; and Astier, "Beckett's *Ohio Impromptu*," 334.

[17]Beckett, "Transcription of the *Ohio Impromptu* Holograph," 193. In his later French version of the play, Beckett maintained the effect: "Si longtemps après que comme si jamais été. (*Un temps. Il regarde de plus pres.*) Oui, si longtemps après que comme si jamais été" (*Impromptu d'Ohio* [Paris: Minuit, 1982], 63).

In effect, the sentence is Beckett's signature. I like to picture Beckett signing it with a wry smile, knowing who is in the audience ("Scholars, take note. Who is it murders syntax in this way?"). For a moment, we see two Beckett scholars, at the end of their days, still having a hard time with the master's prose. But this is serious fun and it echoes the fun Beckett had when he asked in the false start: "Myself? . . . What are you insinuating?" What *can* be insinuated, when Reader hesitates over the words he reads, is what both is and is not—for want of a better term—Beckett. It is not the autobiographical Beckett, the narratable self in retrospect ("Yourself before"). But it *is* Beckett as he signs himself.

Moreover, there is action in this signature, action that depends on us to happen. It is action that is set in motion by our own collaborative engagement with Beckett's syntactic defamiliarization. It is, in short, Beckett "During," and by this sly wink he notifies us of his presence. The reader who reads in the right way can make Beckett happen. All the terms of our analysis of Beckett's prose effects in Chapter 5 apply in microcosm to this sentence. English has not been abolished, but it works at a distance, beckoning the reader—"[It laid hold on him] after so long a lapse [of time] that [it was] as if [it had] never been." At the same time, the reader hears a set of sounds in a rhythmical order that seems to want to have nothing to do with English. The rich counterpoint of the two is that fusion of words and music which Beckett realized twenty years earlier in *Cascando*.[18]

In a passage of *The Captive* in which Proust/Marcel argues for the inevitably autographical character of great art, he proposes an interesting embellishment on *symboliste* theory:

And, just as certain creatures are the last surviving testimony to a form of life which nature has discarded, I wondered whether music might not be the unique example of what might have been—if the invention of language, the formation of words, the analysis of ideas had not intervened—the means of communication between souls. It

[18]For reinforcement in this reading of *Cascando*, see William Kraft, "Beckett and Music: A Composer's View," forthcoming in *Beckett and Music*, ed. Mary Bryden (Reading, England: Beckett International Foundation, 1996).

is like a possibility that has come to nothing; humanity has developed along other lines, those of spoken and written language.[19]

In context, Marcel is commenting on the individually specific "strange music" that such exceptional artists as Vinteuil invariably pull out of themselves, a music that is nowhere more indelibly their own than when they seek to go farthest afield.[20] One of the wonders of Beckett's career is just how far afield he succeeded in going to remain himself. In the texture of his late prose alone, he invariably pushed against the limits of conventional discourse in such unexpected new ways that, in keeping with Proust's paradox, it was impossible to mistake who was doing the pushing.

[1970] So true it is that when in the cylinder what little is possible is not so it is merely no longer so and in the least less the all of nothing if this notion is maintained. (*The Lost Ones,* CSPR, 167)

[1974] Sepulchral skull is this then its last state all set for always litter and dwarfs ruins and little body grey cloudless sky glutted dust verge upon verge hell air not a breath? (*For to End Yet Again,* CSPR, 181)

[1981] Simply savour in advance with in mind the grisly cupboard its conceivable contents. (ISIS, 41)

[1983] First on back to unsay dim can go. (WH, 27)

[1988] Rest then before again from not long to so long that perhaps never again and then again faint from deep within oh how and here that missing word again it were to end where never till then. (SS, 25)

In addition, the music Beckett listened for and reinvented in his prose was matched by his development of an increasingly musical structuring of his drama. If, at the center of this play, Beckett has lodged a signature piece of the kind of music he had been achieving in his prose, he in turn absorbed that piece into the larger music of

[19]Marcel Proust, *The Captive,* in *Remembrance of Things Past,* vol. 3, trans. C. K. Scott Moncrieff and Terence Kilmartin (New York: Vintage, 1982), 260.

[20]"And it was precisely when he was striving with all his might to create something new that one recognized, beneath the apparent differences, the profound similarities and deliberate resemblances that existed in the body of a work" (Proust, *The Captive,* 257).

the play of which it is a part. The play is broken by six double knocks by Listener, each of which calls for Reader to go back and repeat the phrase immediately preceding. The phrase marked by "Yes" takes part in a seventh repetition. It falls in the middle of the play between the third and fourth double knocks. Whereas the pattern of the six other repetitions is Phrase-Knock-Phrase-Knock, here at the center of the play we have Phrase-Yes-Phrase. Moreover, like the play's strange time-defying loops of narrative and narration, this symmetrical rhythm is a continuous override of the forward thrust of narrative, arresting it, turning it back on itself.

Just as the "Yes" phrase is a complex music made up of sound and sense, it is in turn part of an overarching structural counterpoint of sound, sight, and sense. In other words, just as the terms of the analysis of Beckett's prose in Chapter 5 apply to the phrase, so the terms of the analysis of *Krapp's Last Tape* in Chapter 4 apply to the orchestration of the dramatic context. A tragic tale, unalleviated by any sign that the separation it tells of is anything but absolute, is made to dance to strange rhythms. The combined effect is to give this "Yes" an additional resonance. Just as *Krapp*, featuring a failed novel and a farewell to the whole business of art, was cherished and nourished by its author, so *Ohio Impromptu*, featuring a worn book that is put away for the last time, is a gift for an occasion dedicated to the continuing rediscovery of the author's work. In this regard, *Ohio Impromptu*, like all of Beckett's mature work, draws our attention to the autographical trace. In the oeuvre's long conversation with itself, the persistent singularity of Beckett's own kind of strangeness is music on the Proustian model and carries with it the same mystery of origins.

In this chapter, I have also tried to show how Beckett, by inverting the novelistic device of the theater evening, not only staged the entire range of his audience (book readers, theater listeners) but indicated where the action was. In *Ohio Impromptu*, the abandoned one (or bereaved one—we never know for sure) in Reader's book is described as pausing at the "downstream extremity of the Isle of Swans," to "dwell on the receding stream. How in joyous eddies its two arms conflowed and flowed united on" (CSPL, 285–286). In context, the image expresses what the subject yearns for most, and what the play relentlessly denies right up to its reiterated final line: "Nothing is left to tell." Yet this play about the inevitability of separation is itself a compound of unions and confluences, of which the most salient is the confluence of Beckett and his audience. It is we who bring out the autographical trace by our willingness to engage Beckett's array of structural defamiliarizations. Beckett "During" includes us. The paradox of his singularity is that it is a company project. We bring him into being by the collaborative effort of our intelligence as it in turn is catalyzed by his exact notations.

Beckett never let up in his presentation of the agony of perceivedness. If it is an accident that *Godot* was finished in the same year (1949) that Jacques Lacan delivered his lecture on The Mirror Stage, the conjunction of the two is nonetheless expressive.[21] Lacan's short essay has become an encapsulation of the twentieth-century anxiety of self-displacement. In this lecture and numerous supplements, Lacan elaborates a condition of perpetual exile and yearning in a world of signs. *Godot* gives embodiment to a combination very much like it. But, then, Beckett never let us forget any of the outrages of life, including the ancient fact that we, and all those we love, are sentenced to death without cause or consolation. It would be a corruption of his intentions to slight the power of this protest of human distress. In turning his work in such a way that we can see it as autography, I do not mean in any way to diminish the dark honesty of his vision, only to give an enlarged awareness of what drove his art.

In the present intellectual climate, we tend to look away from the individually specific, to see art as artifact rather than as achievement, to keep as resolutely as we can to questions of the functions and symptomatology of art in its social, cultural, or linguistic context. This book has been written not as an opposition but as a counter-

---

[21]Jacques Lacan, "The Mirror Stage as Formative of the Function of the I as revealed in Psychoanalytic Experience," *Ecrits: A Selection*, trans. Alan Sheridan (New York: Norton, 1977), 1–7. Lacan's lecture was delivered on July 17, 1949, at the 16th International Congress of Psychoanalysis in Zurich. *Godot* was begun October 9, 1948, and completed January 29, 1949.

weight. My argument has been that there is an excess in Beckett's art which was enormously important for him. If he insisted that we feel the full weight of the desperation he depicts, he inscribed it everywhere with the music of this excess. It is an old truism that, when it is done well, art pleases even when the material distresses most. The twist of my argument is that an important part of the pleasure is an autographical pleasure: for Beckett and for us reading Beckett. To see Beckett's art as a life project, a project in which an exacting craftsman made and remade his art and, in that process, was enabled to observe the trace of distinctive originating power which somehow belonged uniquely to him is to grasp a key aspect of its intensity, its urgency, and its excitement. It is also to appreciate that metaphysical openendedness the acknowledgment of which is a necessary condition of any truly skeptical vision. Even as Beckett's voices inveigh against the sin of generation, his work flaunts the mystery of it. If this valuation of the importance of inventive force in art is itself culture-specific, I cannot see that such cultural specificity necessarily reduces the possibility of significance *sub specie aeternitatis*. It may be that we have hit upon something in our fetish of originality, in not being able to get enough of it, and in wanting to celebrate it when it happens.

ABBREVIATIONS

C   *Company.* New York: Grove, 1980.

CSPL   *Collected Shorter Plays of Samuel Beckett.* New York: Grove, 1984.

CSPR   *Collected Shorter Prose, 1945–1980.* London: Calder, 1984.

D   *Disjecta: Miscellaneous Writings and a Dramatic Fragment.* Ed. Ruby Cohn. London: Calder, 1983.

El   *Eleutheria.* Paris: Editions de Minuit, 1995. *Eleuthéria.* Trans. Michael Brodsky. New York: Foxrock, 1995.

En   *Endgame.* New York: Grove, 1958.

HD   *Happy Days.* New York: Grove, 1961.

HII   *How It Is.* New York: Grove, 1964.

ISIS   *Ill Seen Ill Said.* New York: Grove, 1981.

M   *Murphy.* New York: Grove, 1957.

P   *Proust.* New York: Grove, n.d. [1931].

SS   *Stirrings Still.* New York: North Star Line, 1988.

STN   *Stories and Texts for Nothing.* New York: Grove, 1967.

TN   *Three Novels by Samuel Beckett: Molloy, Malone Dies, The Unnamable.* New York: Grove, 1965.

WG   *Waiting for Godot.* New York: Grove, 1954.

WH   *Worstward Ho.* New York: Grove, 1983.

CHRONOLOGY

From 1946 on, Beckett composed in both French and English, commonly translating his own texts. The following is a chronology giving the years of composition of the principal texts cited in this book, together with their dates of first publication in both languages.

1946   The *Nouvelles*: "La Fin," "L'expulsé," "Le calmant," and "Premier amour." With the novel *Mercier et Camier* (also written in 1946), these short stories were Beckett's first extended works in French. The first three were included in *Nouvelles et textes pour rien* (Minuit, 1955). "La fin" and "L'expulsé" were translated by Richard Seaver and Beckett as "The End" and "The Expelled." "Le calmant" was translated by Beckett as "The Calmative." They appeared in *Stories and Texts for Nothing* (Grove, 1967), cited here as STN.

1947   *Eleutheria* (French). Beckett's first complete play, it was withheld by Beckett during his lifetime and not published until 1995 (Minuit). A translation by Michael Brodsky was published later in 1995 as *Eleuthéria* (Foxrock).

1947–50 The trilogy: *Molloy* (1947), *Malone meurt* (1947–48), and *L'innommable* (1949–50). The first two novels were published in 1951, the third in 1953 (Minuit). *Molloy* was translated into English by Patrick Bowles and Beckett, the other two by Beckett alone (as *Malone Dies* and *The Unnamable*). They were published by Olympia Press in 1955, 1956, and 1958, respectively. Citations are taken from the 1965 Grove combined edition, *Three Novels* (TN).

1948–49 *En attendant Godot.* Written in the interval between *Ma-*

lone meurt and *L'innommable,* this play was published in 1952 (Minuit) and first performed in 1953 (Paris). Beckett's English translation, *Waiting for Godot,* was published in 1954 (Grove).

1950–51   *Textes pour rien.* Thirteen short texts, they are included in the volume *Nouvelles et textes pour rien* (Minuit 1955). Beckett's English translation, *Texts for Nothing,* appeared in the 1967 Grove volume, *Stories and Texts for Nothing* (cited here as STN).

1955–56   *Fin de partie.* First performed in Beckett's English translation as *Endgame* in 1958 (London), this play was published in French in 1957 (Minuit) and in English in 1958 (Grove).

1956   *All that Fall.* Beckett's first radio play was broadcast in 1956 (BBC) and published in 1957 (Grove). Robert Pinget's translation, *Tous ceux qui tombent,* was also published in 1957 (Minuit). Citations are from CSPL.

1958   *Krapp's Last Tape.* First performed (London) and published (Evergreen Review) in 1958, this play was translated into French by Pierre Leyris and Beckett as *La dernière bande* (Minuit 1960). Citations are from CSPL.

1958–60   *Comment c'est.* Published in 1961 (Minuit), this novel was translated into English by Beckett as *How It Is* (both Calder and Grove 1964).

1960–61   *Happy Days.* Published in 1961 (Grove), this play was first performed in 1962 (New York). Beckett's French translation, *Oh les beaux jours,* was published in 1963 (minuit).

1961–62   *Cascando.* A radio play in French with music by Marcel Mihalovici, it was first broadcast (ORTF) and published (*L'VII*) in 1963. Beckett's English translation, also titled *Cascando,* was published in 1964 (*Evergreen Review*). Citations are from CSPL.

1963–65   *All Strange Away* and the closely related piece, *Imagination morte imaginez*. Both are short prose texts. The latter was published both in French (Minuit) and in Beckett's English translation, *Imagination Dead Imagine* (Calder), in 1965. *All Strange Away* was revised and eventually published in 1976 (Gotham Book Mart). Citations for both are from CSPR.

1965   *Assez*. Published in 1966 (Minuit), this short prose text was translated into English by Beckett as *Enough* (Calder 1967). Citations are from CSPR.

1965–70   *Le dépeupleur*. Segments of this prose text were published in 1967 and 1968, but the complete work was not published until 1970 (Minuit). Beckett's English translation, *The Lost Ones*, was published in 1972 (Calder). Citations are from CSPR.

1972   *Not I*. First performed in 1972 (New York), this play was published in 1973 (Faber). Beckett's French translation, *Pas moi*, was published in 1975 (Minuit). Citations are from CSPL.

1975   *Footfalls*. First performed in 1976 (London), this play was published in the same year (Grove). Beckett's French translation, *Pas*, was published in 1977 (Minuit). Citations are from CSPL.

1977–79   *A Piece of Monologue*. First performed in 1979 (New York), this play was published in the same year (*Kenyon Review*). Beckett's translation, *Solo*, was published in 1982 (Minuit). Citations are from CSPL.

1977–79   *Company*. Published in English (by both Calder and Grove) in 1980, this prose text was translated into French by Beckett as *Compagnie* (Minuit 1980).

1980   *Ohio Impromptu*. First performed in 1981 (Columbus, Ohio), this play was published in the same year (Grove). Beckett's French translation, *Impromptu d'Ohio*, was published in 1982 (Minuit). Citations are from CSPL.

1982   *Catastrophe* (French). This play was first performed in
            1982 (Avignon) and published in the same year (Minuit).
            Beckett's English translation, also *Catastrophe,* was pub-
            lished in 1983 (*The New Yorker*). Citations are from
            CSPL.

1986   *Stirrings Still.* A short prose text, Beckett's last major
            work was published in 1988 (Blue Moon and Calder).
            Beckett's French translation, *Soubresauts,* was published
            in 1989 (Minuit).

INDEX

Abbott, H. Porter, 5n, 164, 171, 172n
Adorno, Theodor, 44–46, 116–117, 132, 139; dispute with Lukács, 128–130
Aestheticism: Beckett's, 57–62
All Strange Away, 61, 133, 134, 141–142, 146, 147n, 165
All that Fall (*Tous ceux qui tombent*), 29, 38, 42, 43, 82, 96
Antin, David, 52
Anzieu, Didier, 1n
Aristotle, 6, 125
Arnold, Matthew, 34
Artaud, Antonin, 63, 118
Ashbery, John, 52
"Assumption," 149
Astier, Pierre, 170, 174n
Augustine, 60n, 94, 101; *Confessions*, 2, 6, 13, 18, 19, 22, 32
Authorship, 41–42, 47–49, 100–101, 118–126, 140, 145
Autobiographical dare, the: in Beckett, 162; in Proust, 160–161
Autobiography, 1–2, 3n, 18, 20–21, 22; and Beckett criticism, 1; and biography, 2, 20; and *Eleutheria*, 69; and *Krapp's Last Tape*, 65; in *Ohio Impromptu*, 174. *See also* Autobiographical dare; Autography
Autography: defined, 2; the Beckettian subset distinguished from autobiography, 2–22; and generic difference (drama/fiction), 110, 119–126, 174–175; in *Krapp's Last Tape*, 66, 81–86; as music, 62, 81–86, 104–108; and narrative teleology, 2–22, 87, 145–147; and political art, 127–148; in Proust, 179–180; and the reader/audience, 165–183; and reflexivity, 140–148
Avant-garde, 25n, 26

Bair, Deirdre, 2, 18–19, 19n, 128n
Bakhtin, Mikhail, 45
Balzac, Honoré de: *Père Goriot*, 167
Barker, Stephen, 24, 53
Barthes, Roland, 5n, 63, 84n
Baudelaire, Charles, 32
Baudrillard, Jean, 168n
Beckerman, Bernard, 166n
Beckett, May (Beckett's mother), 149, 162
Beer, Ann, 1n, 19n, 39n, 164n
Begam, Richard, 1n, 24, 54n
Bellamy, Edward: *Looking Backward*, 132, 134, 135
Benjamin, Walter, 46
Benveniste, Emile, 5n
Ben-Zvi, Linda, 50n, 153n, 176
Bernold, André, 85
Bible, 99; Genesis, 12, 14, 102–103
Biography. *See* Autobiography
Bion, Dr. Wilfred, 1n
Bishop, Jonathan, 7
Blau, Herbert, 24
Blin, Roger, 81n, 169
Bloom, Harold, 29n
Brater, Enoch, 1–2n, 20, 36n, 48, 124n, 125n, 151n
Brecht, Bertold, 130, 172n
Brewer, Mária, 118n
Brienza, Susan, 64n, 106n
Brooks, Peter, 84n
Browning, Robert, 34
Bruck, Jan, 139n
Bruns, Gerald L., 30n
Bruss, Elizabeth, 4
Bulwer-Lytton, Edward: *The Coming Race*, 132, 135
. . . *but the clouds* . . . , 158, 165–166